TRADING
ON VOLUME

TRADING
ON VOLUME

DONALD CASSIDY

McGraw-Hill

New York   Chicago   San Francisco   Lisbon   London   Madrid
Mexico City   Milan   New Delhi   San Juan   Seoul
Singapore   Sydney   Toronto

Library of Congress Cataloging-in-Publication Data

Cassidy, Don.
    Trading on volume : the key to identifying and profiting from stock price reversals / by
Donald Cassidy.
        p.   cm.
    ISBN 0-07-137604-6
    1. Stock exchanges.   2. Stock exchanges—United States.   3. Stocks—Prices.   4.
Stocks—Prices—United States.   5. Stock price forecasting.   I. Title.

HG4551.C325   2001
332.63'2042—dc21   2001031691

McGraw-Hill

*A Division of The **McGraw·Hill** Companies*

1 2 3 4 5 6 7 8 9 0 DOC/DOC 0 9 8 7 6 5 4 3 2 1

ISBN 0-07-137604-6

Printed and bound by R. R. Donnelley & Sons Company.

McGraw-Hill books are available at special discounts to use as premiums and sales pro-
motions, or for use in corporate training programs. For more information, please write to
the Director of Special Sales, Professional Publishing, McGraw-Hill, Two Penn Plaza,
New York, NY 10121-2298. Or contact your local bookstore.

This book is printed on recycled, acid-free paper containing a
minimum of 50% recycled de-inked paper.

To members of the
Market Technicians Association
and of
The American Association of Individual Investors

CONTENTS

ACKNOWLEDGMENTS

Many individuals have been helpful along the way as I shaped the thinking and conducted the research that made this work possible. One always hesitates to name some for fear of inadvertently slighting others.

Stephen Isaacs of McGraw-Hill was instrumental in carrying the torch for this concept after others had earlier considered it too radical and perhaps of narrow interest.

Donna Whittington and Denis Payne were of great help in introducing me to the Market Technicians Association community and to its resources. I owe special thanks to Shelley Lebeck, the MTAís librarian, for allowing me access to their trove of old and recent publications on technical-analysis subjects.

Chris Bouffard of American Century Investment Management, a long-time friend and former colleague at Lipper Inc., was a patient listener and a valued sounding board as these ideas formed and coalesced. Jeff Walker, an excellent trader and webmaster of www.lowrisk.com and of www.investormap.com, has been a ready supplier of ideas and data sources and valuable insights.

Joe Kenrich, now retired from the New York Stock Exchange, and Ann Price, who assumed the role of Archivist there, were most gracious in sharing trading-volume data. Chief statistician Pete Frien of Dow Jones, likewise, was very helpful in saving me many hours of laborious data acquisition by supplying detailed historical volume information via spreadsheet.

Current and former Lipper colleagues who were patient with my heavy use of vacation days as I wrote on deadline; they cheerfully picked up part of my time-sensitive load in helping with media inquiries. They are Ed Rosenbaum, Tom Roseen, Traci Gardner, and Joe Thurston. Jamie Wasserman provided me with crucial insights on the use of MetaStock and a helpful introduction to its Equivolume charting feature.

Members and program chairs of various investor groups in Colorado, Arizona, Michigan, North Carolina, Florida, Alabama, Ohio, and metro Washington DC provided highly engaged audiences for my early talks on this subject and in the process raised challenging questions and useful refining insights. Special thanks go to my long-time friend Wayne Baxmann of Texas for his ongoing support.

Last but certainly not least, my wife Belita Calvert has again been unreasonably patient with my gobbling up nights and weekends I know she would rather have spent sitting together in talking and reading—or even, perish the thought, getting away on a real vacation. Her understanding of my passion for this work has been a great comfort and help, as in my earlier book-writing immersions.

I thank you all and hope you will find the work as it has emerged herein to be worthy of your contributions.

Donald Cassidy

TRADING
ON VOLUME

PART ONE

Central Concepts

Theory and Action

CHAPTER 1

Volume Is the Cause, Price Is the Effect

Incredibly, trading volume is a hugely rich body of useful information about stocks that is widely ignored. To overlook the highly informative stories that volume tells about an individual stock's—or the broad market's—current condition and its future price prospects is deliberately to forgo half the free technical analysis information that the market offers you every day. No one should keep such blinders on. To do so would be financial folly.

In forecasting the weather, what meteorologist would note temperature and humidity but ignore wind and barometric pressure? None who expects to remain employed. In making a buy or sell decision, would a fundamental analyst study a public company's industry, management, competition, products, and financial statements and then ignore the price per share at which that firm's stock was trading? Of course not! That fundamentalist needs to know both parts of the equation, value *and* price, to make a fully informed decision. In an exactly parallel way, however, an extremely large majority of technicians study everything about price (change, volatility, correlation, trend, acceleration, divergence, momentum change, highs and lows, breakouts) but inexplicably have a huge, self-created blind spot: They pay no attention to trading volume.

The volume now in your hands (pardon the pun!) aims to provide you with a whole set of additional tools for analyzing stocks—intellectual weapons that investors and traders with whom you compete literally do not think about and therefore have no chance to use. Every day, and indeed every minute or hour that the stock market is open for business, two types of technical analysis information are being generated: data on price *and* data on trading volume. You are about to cease ignoring half the facts and will now embark on an eye-opening mental journey: You will find out what trading volume tells an astute observer about a stock. Having performed my own personal and family portfolio management using the added information dimension that volume brings, I can predict that you will be pleased to have invested the hours ahead in adding this entirely new aspect of technical analysis to your array of tools for making decisions.

Let us begin. We must start by looking briefly at what technically minded traders actually do, and why. Then we will use the balance of this first chapter to illuminate what trading volume means and how you can use it to deepen your understanding of stock price potentials. I should tell you, right from this early page, where I come from in terms of investment philosophy. I became fascinated with the stock market in the late 1950s as a young teenager. A math teacher created a classroom investment contest; the fact that I nearly won added excitement to the intellectual joy I had immediately found in playing the game. From that time my career goal was to participate professionally in the investment world, and definitely on the research rather than the sales side. All the years since my high school graduation have blessed me with the opportunity to earn a living doing something I love—a wonderful situation I imagine only a small minority of adults enjoy. After taking a degree in finance from The Wharton School, I have spent over 30 years studying the stock market from every angle I could. Here is what I have learned and believe:

- Investing in stocks is potentially hugely profitable. Consistent success comes not from luck but from ongoing hard work. Wild times like 1998 to early 2000 are rare exceptions and not the rule.

- In the long run, fundamentals (corporate performance in context of economic variables such as inflation and interest rates) determine the *values* of securities.

- Every day between now and "the long run," investor psychology drives people to buy and sell, and the results of those human actions are the *prices* of securities, which seldom equal their values.

- Individual investors have a choice to buy and hold passively, which predictably produces average results *if* they never panic or become overconfident and change their behavior.

- Those who work hard at investing successfully should expect to outperform the "averages." Such performance is possible either by knowing what companies will remain winners for a lifetime (unlikely) or by buying below value and selling above it. Translation: Winning requires timing.

- Timing well is definitely not easy. Neither is it impossible. The market is usually not efficient, though most academics wish it were. Prices definitely are not random, as random-walk academic convention traditionally has held. (If the market were efficient, all fundamental analysis would be in vain because no one could beat the others, as everyone would have the same, complete information). The efficient-market, random-walk proponents have constructed a view of the investment world that consistently fails to study price in *the context of volume.* More will be said about these points in Chapter 2.) In reality, successful timing, while not possible every moment, every day, or every month, is possible *on average* for those using a full array of intellectual tools.

- If you believe markets are efficient and prices are random, then you should save your time and energy and learning expenses; just buy index funds. However, if you are willing to probe more deeply, you will have an opportunity to achieve above-average returns.

- You can improve your chances of achieving above-average returns by studying both fundamental and technical factors. Neither alone will suffice. (If forced to choose one, I would opt for technical analysis—this advice coming from a person who was employed for some years as a sell-side fundamental analyst.)

- Technical analysis works *because* it studies the results of buying and selling decisions by human participants in the marketplace. Human emotions and behavior can be understood; crowd behavior is reasonably predictable and readily measurable. Crowd behavior creates temporary price extremes that differ considerably from both fundamental value and emotional-equilibrium prices. Getting that part of the picture right is what pays you above-average money as either an investor or trader.

- Trading volume is a measure of the crowd's size and emotional temperature. Without a analysis of this factor, technical analysis is only half informed. Buying and selling are reflected in trading volume, and they are the cause of price change. *Price is the effect,* and its cause is trading activity. Therefore, study volume carefully.

You might not agree with all of the statements above. But if you are willing to investigate them, you will find the next couple of hundred pages stimulating and, I believe, profitable. If you believe in market efficiency and price randomness and grant the alternative possibilities a fair hearing, perhaps you will discover some valid challenges to your assumptions by continuing ahead.

PRICE: THE WRONG FOCUS FOR STUDY

Virtually the entire investment and trading world, willingly supported by the central subject concentration of the financial media, is focused on price. This fixation is quite understandable, but highly unfortunate. Price, of course, is a proxy for scorekeeping. We measure our net financial worth (at a metaphysical level, I would prefer to say *wealth*) by adding up what we own and subtracting what we owe. As an important component of that overall valuation process, we keep score of how we are faring in the investment arena by tallying up the securities we own. Much of what we own overall is measured only imprecisely. Even an appraiser could not accurately guarantee what your antiques and art would bring if sold. Blue-book pricing on your motor vehicles is approximate. It would be pointless to pay for frequent appraisals of your realty, and even those would be only expert estimates at best. But our stocks and bonds and mutual funds? Ah—here we have a wonderful and mathematically precise way of keeping score: Their prices are printed in newspapers daily and are available electronically at the beck of a mouse or a few keystrokes.

Watching the stock market has become nearly a national pastime and for perhaps too many a passion in recent years. Those who are in the market and those who are still thinking about it alike are fascinated by the constant movement of prices. As with the temperature and humidity, the racing form, and the latest sports scores and team standings, stock prices change every time we look. "The Dow Jones Industrial Average [or NASDAQ Composite Index] Jumped [or Dove] by 300 Points Today!" the TV reporters and newspaper headlines scream. Microsoft rose or fell $3.25, IBM changed by almost $8, and Genentech moved by over $5. That hot IPO soared by 37 points in the first hour! We mentally multiply our holdings by the changes—and fret or celebrate.

Price tells the story since the price change multiplied by the shares owned equals the gain or loss. Price change is exciting. No change is a condition that is perhaps comforting to a wealthy retiree, but it is boring to most others. Price and price change get the headlines. When is the last time your local daily newspaper's banner headline shouted "Market Unchanged"? We love watching the prices go up and down, like the rapid action of a close basketball game where the lead keeps changing hands. It's exciting, and if the numbers move the way we want them to turn out, we get richer *while* being entertained.

Volume? It's a footnote to the story on most days. Occasionally it's mentioned in the subheadline when the market has a historically wild session. It's just a fact mentioned in the text's fine print when an individual stock makes a violent move because millions of shares have changed hands on big news. Or it's a few digits in the stock tables tucked between the dividend and the real interesting stuff: the closing price quote and the day's or week's net change.

Here's a bulletin, just in: Price is not set by the stock exchange or by some hidden controlling cabal of super-rich market professionals. Price literally does not change at all if there is no trading. In fact, a stock not traded is omitted from the newspaper listings! Price is set by the balance or imbalance of buying and selling orders. Orders to buy and sell are the results of individual and professional investors' deciding to do something. If there are no perceived reasons to act, there will be no trading. If trading volume is zero, price is in suspension. *Trading causes all price changes.* Trading, which can be mathematically measured as the volume of shares that change hands, is the cause that sets the price. Price and its change are effects.

A novice sports fan or concert attendee enjoys the rewarding net result of the players' efforts. The horn concerto is beautiful and rich and moving; a baseball player makes a spectacular fielding play; a halfback speeds downfield for the winning touchdown. A sophisticated fan of performance relishes the replays even more: He or she learns how and why the musician achieved the tone we loved hearing; that the outfielder knew the batter's tendencies and shaded a few steps to one side of normal position; that a pulling guard made a key block that sprang the runner; that a swimming champion implemented a new training regimen and gained strength. The difference is all in the details. The first-level observer sees the results and either enjoys them or does not. Those with second-level perception appreciate *why* success or failure occurred.

The people who study price behavior in a vacuum are overlooking the all-important details that predict future price action. Those who vow to look behind the exciting result (price change) and study the cause (the amount of trading volume) have a deeper and more rewarding understanding. Understand the cause(s) intimately and you have a much better chance of predicting the effect.

Wall Street lore has it that Joseph Kennedy, father of the late president, got out of the stock market in the early months of 1929 and thereby preserved much of the family's wealth because of an astute observation. While making his daily and nightly rounds in New York's financial community and social circles, he noted that every average office and blue-collar worker, even including the cabbies and bootblacks who served him, was in the market and had ready advice to offer others. Thus he concluded that there was no one left who had not already put their money into stocks; the rise therefore could not go on since all the available fuel had already been heaped on the fire. Unknowingly, Mr. Kennedy had discovered basic information that we now would call part of the added wisdom that behavioral finance brings to the study of market prices. He figured out that if the crowd has already done all it can or will do, prices are ready to move in the opposite direction because they literally can no longer maintain their recent trend. That golden nugget underlies the study of trading volume, which is why it should be an integral element of technical analysis.

Figure out what the majority is doing and you can discern in which direction price will move. Note accurately when the majority becomes an unruly crowd or mob, and you have pinpointed the time at which the effect of its more urgent activity (predominantly buying *or* selling) has reached maximum. Price movement is the net effect of changing balances between supply and demand. Trading is quantified and therefore measurable. Changes in trading volume imply changes in price direction.

SOME HISTORY OF VOLUME

Many market observers can recite the Ibbotson data—exhaustive historical documentation of actual average annual returns of stocks since 1926—and they can recall when major market tops and bottoms occurred and when the Dow Jones Industrial Average first scaled a certain level. Who remembers anything about volume? Virtually no one keeps track of its history. For the record, and as context for today's tumultuous daily trading activity, Figure 1–1 provides a summary of volume levels on the New York Stock Exchange (NYSE).

Several points are worth observing from the data in Figure 1–1. First, trading has increased enormously. In January 2001, the NYSE recorded its first 2.3-billion share day on the news that the Federal Open Market Committee, the FOMC, had reversed course and reduced interest rates. That day's trade exceeded the average *weekly* volume in 1997, and nearly equaled the total volume of 1979! And, while the numbers shown are for the NYSE, NASDAQ reported trading has recently been running at about 150 to 200 percent of the Big Board trading volume most days. Beyond that, we know that considerable institutional trading in listed stocks takes place on the Instinet system and other venues. That fact—the diversion of orders from the NYSE floor—plus the rise in individuals' participation during the roaring bull market of 1998 to 1999, accounts for

FIGURE 1-1

Volume Levels on the New York Stock Exchange

Year	Avg. Volume, Millions/Session	Percentage in Block Transactions*
1965	1.6	3.1
1975	4.7	16.6
1980	11.3	29.2
1985	109.2	51.7
1990	157.4	49.6
1991	179.8	49.6
1992	204.0	50.7
1993	265.7	53.7
1994	291.4	55.5
1995	364.3	57.0
1996	415.4	55.9
1997	528.8	50.9
1998	673.5	48.7
1999	808.6	50.2
2000	1,041.6	51.7

*Defined as trades of 10,000 shares or more.

the observed post-1995 decline in block-trading percentages.

As an astute market observer, you may have already noted an objection: At least some of the Exchange's rise in overall share volume is accounted for by a growing number of listed stocks and by stock splits. Therefore, one must be careful in making comparisons that delve too far into the past. When looking at individual stocks' volumes, you will notice that electronic databases and online charting systems adjust volume as well as price when splits take place. So, fortunately, comparisons for single stocks over time are valid. That is important because we will be doing a great many comparisons: from day to day, of active days versus prior peaks, of current versus average volume, of current activity versus that of a previous news-driven high.

ON A PERSONAL LEVEL

We could dwell on the billions of shares changing hands daily, but it will be much more relevant to bring the implications of changes in volume down to a personal level. Did you ever notice that whenever you get up the courage to buy a high-flying stock, it always seems to start going south almost immediately afterward? Or that when you finally sell a stock that has been causing deep pain, it seems to rebound sharply within days, almost as if delivering a personal insult? Well, for what comfort it might bring, you are not alone. Thousands of investors buy and sell late at the same time, for psychological reasons, which are explored in more detail in Chapter 2. When an unusually large number of people decide at the same time to buy or to sell, their combined action has two impacts: Obviously, their trading activity when summed up appears as very high relative total volume; since so many are trying to do the same thing at once (get in or get out), they affect price sharply. We will spend a good deal of time thinking together about the implications and impacts of crowd behavior.

Trading volume is a measure of the size of the crowd (not literally the *number of people* but rather the *quantity of shares* they caused to be bought or sold). Crowds have a strong tendency to be wrong when they surge to take extreme action. Once the crowd has begun to shrink in size, its potential pressure on price has already decreased, and as a result price direction must reverse. This is one of the most significant effects that changes in volume have on price: *They mark reversals*. For those who want to do better than average by not holding passively for the long term, this knowledge forms a major and powerful tool in forecasting, deciding, and taking action.

If you have any doubt about the role of volume in the advance or decline of stocks, examine Figure 1–2, a 3-month graph of volume and price action for Tricon Global Restaurants. As will be developed in the following chapters, the patterns of trading volume themselves actually change a stock's supply/demand balance, *and* the volume patterns on a chart clearly signal what is going on.

Casual observation shows five instances over a course of about 11 weeks when volume either peaked or spiked at over 1.5 million shares in a day. Also, there was a crescendo of volume reaching 1.2 million in the first few sessions of 2001. Four of these six high points in trading volume marked price reversals, and the other two (late October and mid-November) represented upside breakouts from trendlines or supply levels. In addition, we see two clear instances of volume fadeouts as prices progressed, a classic sign that a trend is near completion. These came in the middle 10 trading sessions of October, as selling ran out of steam, and through the latter half of November, as the stock advanced from 33 to 37. Yet another key volume warning was flashed on the fourth-to-last trading day in November, when 1.0 million shares traded just under 36—considerably lower volume than at the heights of previ-

FIGURE 1-2

Tricon Global Restaurants: Volume Changes Signal Price Reversals

Source: BigCharts.com; used by permission.

ous price upthrusts. The buyers were tiring. Thus, in just 13 weeks, there were nine major volume events, none of which failed to have significant price-predictive value.

Figure 1–2 has been included to whet your appetite for what follows; it represents only part of the breadth of implications of trading-volume patterns. In the upcoming chapters, a few of the major systems of volume/price analysis in current use are reviewed and their strengths and occasional weaknesses are examined. Our main thrust, however, will be to introduce some patterns of trading volume that have recurring and strongly predictive implications for stock price direction. If you are correct on the direction in which prices will move, you will reap unusual profits because understanding what volume is saying about upcoming price direction possibilities can vastly raise your ability to predict price. The following are significant and oft-repeated volume patterns that are discussed throughout the book:

- Predominance of price changes associated with rising, versus falling, volume days
- Extreme coincident buying or selling by institutions
- Multiple-day buildups or crescendos in volume
- Upside and downside gaps or short-lived runaways in price accompanied by event-driven spikes in volume to many times the

normal daily levels

- Decreasing volume as price trends become longer lived
- Decreasing volume at successive waves of price extremes
- Volume's meaning in persistently lower and dull market phases
- The December/January price-reversal phenomenon, which is actually a volume effect

Before we examine these many fascinating aspects of volume behavior, let's look at some of them, and document their frequency, in some of the more widely known Dow Jones Industrial stocks. An analysis of 30 stocks for just a 24-month time window comprising calendar years 1999–2000 produces the following key highlights of their volume action:

- 18 of the 30 suffered volume spikes on downside price gaps, for a total of 22 occurrences.
- 17 of the 30 enjoyed upside spikes, for a total of 21 occurrences.
- 16 of the 30 components displayed a total of 26 meaningful volume crescendos.
- 12 showed the disturbing pattern of lower volume at subsequent price tops.
- 16 showed 23 instances of clearly fading volume during price advances.
- All but one of the components displayed at least two such important volume events in 24 months.

Space does not permit printing all 30 graphs, but let's examine just two, as examples of the power of volume analysis. We have chosen two of the longer-time components, and certainly two of the stocks that are by nature least prone to highly emotional situations or major corporate surprises: International Paper (IP) and United Technologies (UTX). As events would have it, IP spent the years 1999 and 2000 going almost nowhere on a net basis, up for the first year and down the next. By contrast, UTX spent the first 14 months declining and the last 10 in a spirited advance.

International Paper displays six volume peaks at over 6 million shares a day (see Figure 1–3). Reversals were involved in all six (price highs at April 1999, early January 2000, early to mid-July, and late October, as well as price bottoms in late June and mid-October 2000). Sometimes stocks can change direction without an extreme and thus telltale volume event (the bottom in early October 1999, which coincided with an overall market reversal). However, as will be seen repeatedly throughout ensuing chapters, seldom do volume climaxes or spikes fail to coincide with price reversals

FIGURE 1-3

International Paper: Volume Peaks at Price Reversals

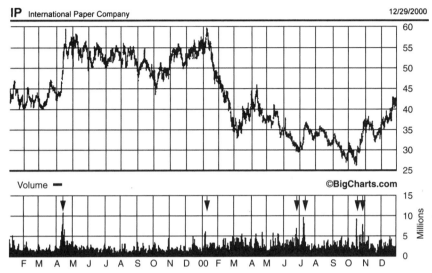

Source: BigCharts.com; used by permission.

by more than a day or at most a few. The conservative, long-term buy-and-hold investor could have let his or her capital lie unproductive in IP for two years, while other market participants who were more willing to exit and re-enter could have achieved significantly better results, either on the long side alone or even more so by using the short side as well.

The 5 to 6 million share area in daily volume stood as a level indicating important price junctures in 1999–2000 for United Technologies (see Figure 1–4). A week-plus crescendo of volume in April 1999 created a failing price run to almost $75, followed twice in the next two weeks by lower volume when the stock barely made new price highs above that level—signs of buyers' loss of interest or resources.

Spikes in mid-September 2000 marked, in rapid progression, both an exhaustion price high above $67 and a selling climax at about $59. By far the most dramatic explosion in volume (over 17 million in a day) during these two years came after mid-October 2000 as a brief but considerable decline reversed at $60 and a rally, unusually powerful in this type of heavy-industrial company, created a 33 percent gain in the next 10 weeks. But large peaks were not the only trading-volume features to mark the two years under study for UTX shares. Twice, although over quite differing time frames, a decline in the level of volume signaled that

FIGURE 1-4

United Technologies: Prices Peak at Price Reversal Points

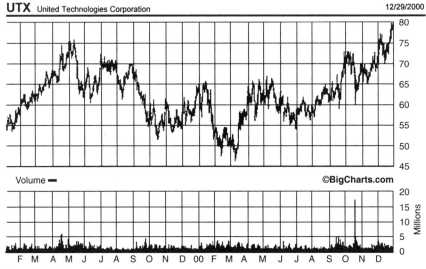

Source: BigCharts.com; used by permission.

an advance was about to end. The 3-month rally beginning at mid-October 1999 and carrying UTX from $52 to fractionally over $65 was marked by a persistently lower average daily volume. The actual high several days into January was accompanied by notably low volume—a deadly sign. The much shorter episode of fading volume came from mid-September 2000's price low at $59 to a rally high above $72; here volume trailed off even more sharply in percentage terms. Once again, a stiff price collapse followed when it became clear the bulls had run out of ammunition or interest.

You might be thinking that, very often, bursts in volume that we are calling *spikes* or *crescendos* are caused by news (a fundamental factor) and therefore should not be interpreted as technical analysis events. Two points of rebuttal to that thinking are in order. First, while it is true that very often some news (from product or legal or earnings information to as little as an analyst's opinion change) triggers the process, it is the *reaction of investors*, driven in large numbers to trade well above the normal amount of shares in a short period, that is the important technical event. There actually *are* some instances when news does not drive significant price or volume volatility. Whatever the stimulus that does cause unusually strong and widespread emotional response leading to very high trading volume—it can be company news or Federal Reserve monetary action, or election results, or maybe even sunspots—the mere fact that a huge number of people have made decisions and acted in similar simultaneous ways created a watershed in terms of altering the future supply/demand balance for the shares.

Our second, and quite telling, point to remember is this: High-volume events in most cases mark times when unusually large numbers of investors and traders react in the direction of news (good or bad, marking price gain or loss, respectively)—*and then the price move ends!* This phenomenon undoubtedly repeatedly confounds and frustrates investors and traders. "But the news was obviously so good," we can hear them saying, "and everyone knew it. How could the stock possibly *not* keep going right on up?" Therein lies a kernel of market wisdom, if you look at it for a while at a deeper level. Put aside the fundamental importance of the favorable news. Focus instead on the behavior of people, because it is the actions of people that make stock prices move. If indeed virtually everyone who was interested in the stock simultaneously took note of the favorable incoming news and bought, that fact alone would mean that for some time period into the future the buying has maximized and exhausted itself. Improved fundamental prospects alone do not keep a stock price up. Buyers are required. And when the heavy buying is done, the price is finished on the upside as well—not forever, of course, but for a long enough time and with enough downside correction in the immediate offing that selling is the only sensible course. Thus, we see that when unusually large volume culminates an existing price movement, it will often be caused by a capping favorable piece of information. The proper action is to avoid joining the crowd and, if anything, to act in the opposite manner.

Technical analysis works because it records the actions of buyers and sellers, who are the actual operative instruments in moving stock prices. *News does not change prices* (although sometimes it may indeed reveal a shifting of true future *value*). Only the action-causing decisions of a multitude of investors to buy or sell change price. But we are now getting a bit ahead of ourselves, for we have moved over into discussing investor behavior, which forms the subject of Chapter 2. Investor behavior is what moves prices. Crowd action extent and intensity can be literally measured as one charts trading volume. That is why volume analysis is the key to understanding price change. That is why we began these pages by stating that technical analysis that looks at price alone is suffering from a huge blind spot. Volume analysis, in conjunction with price analysis, constitutes a much-enriched technical approach to the market. Price is the effect; trading volume is the cause.

CHAPTER 2

Reality: Random Walk or Behavioral Finance?

Two major schools of thought on the nature of investment markets vie for your adherence. One is the random-walk theory of stock price movements, which is a major expression of the efficient-market hypothesis. Its alternative is a recently developed body of observation and theory referred to as *behavioral finance*. It is important for you, as an investor, to consider each theory. Following are brief, perhaps overly simplified views of the world of Wall Street according to these sharply opposed belief systems.

RANDOM-WALK THEORY VERSUS BEHAVIORAL SCIENCE THEORY

In the world of efficient markets and random walks, all the market's creatures—big and small—have equal access to and equal knowledge of all the information that could possibly affect the trend and level of stock prices. There is no information or insight that anyone could have that would improve his or her odds of success. Because everyone who cares deeply will know all he or she needs to, the markets that price securities are extremely efficient. There are no surprises, and what little changes in price that do occur take place in small, orderly, and basically random steps, just as flipping a coin might result in occasional runs of heads or tails. Everyone involved in the process is cool, logical, restrained, and civil. Basically everything can be explained entirely by scientific, mathematical, and statistical principles. All else is called "noise."

In the world of behavioral finance, human beings seem to have tromped across the manicured university lawns and have littered the perfectly swept streets of lower Manhattan. Through a variety of devices, from extraordinarily good research to strong professional networking, to spending 70 hours a week digging for answers and insights, to speaking with management, to watching the pattern of trading as it occurs (and, yes, to occasionally learning and using inside information illegally), some individuals (names like Lynch and Buffett among others come to mind) consistently seem to have more and better information than others, and they seem to have it sooner. Partly because of increasingly strict federal regulation of corporate disclosure, even analysts are often surprised (although one wonders what data they were independently studying that somehow earlier brought so many of them to the same exact earnings forecast!). Buy recommendations are sometimes related to corporate-finance client relationships; occasionally there are nasty insinuations that portfolio managers get research conclusions before Joe and Mary Sixpack. Human emotion seems to play about as great a part as logic, and occasionally more, in setting stock prices. People called "technical analysts" claim they have discovered some predictive patterns in stock price behavior, which they say work because chart patterns reflect human psychology and behavior. That behavior, not as cool and calculating and efficient as some might wish, occasionally reflects such raw human tendencies as fear and greed. Prices are pushed up violently by manias and then down at equal or greater speed by panics. Sometimes a stock will open down or up 30 percent from its prior day's closing level—hardly seeming very efficient or fair. Rather than small and apparently random, price changes are increasingly violent as huge crowds of participants, many of them quite inexperienced and underinformed, rush from one idea to another and from pole to pole emotionally.

My hints of what would come, in Chapter 1, may have already biased your answer, but I really must ask you: Which world do you see as real, and which is idealized and theoretical? Whether we might prefer it or not, the rough-and-tumble behavioral world of Wall Street does strike me clearly as more real than the University of Utopia version described first. We will review that efficient-market, random-walk world in a bit more detail shortly. But I will forewarn you: The rest of this book assumes that there are recurring patterns in the market and that they reflect human actions and reactions and crowds forming and dispersing. If it were not so, trading-volume data would not have any practical use and I would not have been able to use it for investment success for a number of years. But first, let us examine the random-walk theory, which implies that there is nothing you can do but buy an index fund and hold on to it until you need your money to spend in old age.

Although he does not claim to have originated the whole idea, Princeton's Professor Burton G. Malkiel is the most recognizable name when one thinks of efficient markets. His *A Random Walk Down Wall Street* is now in its sixth edition* since debuting in 1973. Changes and updating have brought this seminal work current, and it is worth contemplating. Earlier versions had staked out hard ground in favor of efficient markets and random walks, but the latest edition offers some softening and hints of concessions on a few difficult points.

Interestingly, like testimony carefully parsed in successive interrogations, random-walk theory has shifted ground since its first release a generation ago. Its original, now called "strong," version was

> that absolutely nothing that is known or even knowable about a company will benefit the fundamental analyst.... All the news that is public...[or] possible to know...has already been reflected in the price of the stock.... Not even "inside information" can help the investor. (6th ed., 1996, p. 189)

Then came this qualified version:

> No *published* information will help the analyst to select undervalued securities.... Professional analyses of these data will be useless...[since] the structure of market prices already takes...such into account. (p. 189)

But even that revised standard version required further softening:

> The history of stock price movements contains no useful information that will enable an investor consistently to outperform a buy-and-hold strategy in managing a portfolio.

What a massive shift of ground these revisions represent—no mention whatsoever of fundamental information! Let us put aside questions of what the professor must have been thinking while serving on the boards of directors of several actively managed mutual funds, which do not practice buy-and-hold religion as staunchly as they preach it. For whatever reasons, we are offered yet a fourth form of the random-walk construct of the world on pages 191 to 192:

> Fundamental analysis cannot produce investment recommendations that will enable an investor consistently to outperform a buy-and-hold strategy in managing a portfolio. (p. 144)

I would note the insertion of a key "waffle word" in the last two versions: "consistently." One could accurately say that professional meteorologists or heart surgeons cannot *consistently* perform their tasks without

---

*W. W. Norton, New York, 1996 in paperback.

error. But that does not make those practitioners worthless by any stretch of logic.

In fairness, Professor Malkiel has come a long way from his 1970s stance. He now concedes, "I am not saying that technical strategies never make money. They very often do make profits.… A simple 'buy-and-hold' strategy…typically makes as much or more money" (page 144). *There* is a concession that virtually amounts to a repudiation. Not only are followers of technical strategies not voodoo charlatans who have no hope of profiting, but indeed they *very often* do make money! But wait: At least a "simple 'buy-and-hold' strategy…typically makes as much or more money." That is about as clear as those furniture store ads trumpeting savings of "up to 70 percent and more." In other words, some people actually, apparently, *do* do better than the buy-and-holders! Must be so, because he says the buy-and-holders make "as much" as the technical analysis practitioners.

One of the major reasons efficient-market adherents have long been able to claim better or at least equal success for "buy-and-hold" against alternative approaches has been the cost of trading. These costs were principally commissions but have also included the bid-ask spread and the effect a large buyer or seller has in moving the price to his or her own disadvantage. It has taken 30-odd years for the random-walkers to waffle from their original moral high ground. Maybe in another generation they will notice that commissions have declined from multiple hundreds per 100- or 200-share transaction, to $5 and $8. They still fall back, though, on the defense that "the market is so efficient—prices move so quickly when new information does arise—that no one can consistently [that word again!] buy or sell quickly enough to benefit" (6th ed., 1996, page 191).

I must interpret that statement, complete with its qualifying waffle, as retreating all the way to the narrow world of *fundamental* information. Undeniably, blockbuster corporate news gives no room to buy-and-hold victims to bail out in time to be spared grievous financial body blows. But the professor seems now to have forgotten technical information—which develops over time and which allows an observant practitioner to take loss-preventive or profit-proactive actions, which I will explain later in this book.

The professor has come a long way toward the fuller information we technicians avail ourselves of. His preface (page 14) says, "While reports of the death of the efficient-market theory are vastly exaggerated, there do seem to be some techniques of stock selection that may tilt the odds of success in favor of the individual investor." While he still takes a few snipes along the way (references to monkeys throwing darts survived from earlier editions) and admits he is biased (page 139), he does admit "that it is impossible to rule out the existence of behavioral or psychological influences on stock-market pricing" (page 217). In so doing, it seems to me, he has all but repudiated the predictable, cool, calculating, efficient market he once sought to prove. Perhaps his latest version should bear a new title such as "A Nonrandom Walk Back Up Wall Street, Where We Discover New Truths." Making reference to an old story of a professor whose student thinks he sees a $10 bill lying on the ground, Professor Malkiel has come to the real world as of 1996. No longer does he quote the other academic who assures the student that the $10 must be an apparition because a real $10 bill would already have been scooped up, our random-walk advocate says on his penultimate page that "there may be some $10 bills around at times and I'll certainly interrupt my random walk to purposefully stoop and pick them up" (page 458). No doubt he has done well professionally and financially. One wonders what greater profit might have accrued if, rather than interrupting his random walk, he had reversed it in search of a different view of the investment universe.

What is it that the brilliant academic (and practitioner) random-walkers and the efficient-market proponents have missed? John Maynard Keynes referred, in apparent frustration, to certain "animal spirits" as reasons that economic *Homo sapiens* not infrequently does what seemingly makes no rational sense. Malkiel himself quotes Gustave Le Bon's 1895 work, *The Crowd, A Study of the Popular Mind,* with this pithy sentence: "In crowds it is stupidity and not mother-wit that is accumulated." The philosopher Nietzsche observed that "madness is the exception in individuals, but the rule in groups." Charles Mackay's chronicle of Holland's tulip-bulb craze, said it all in his book's title alone: *Extraordinary Popular Delusions and the Madness of Crowds.* We cannot phrase it any better. One seldom will see and document that which he or she does not intend to see. Those of a scientific and academic bent seek to define the world in scientific, mathematical, mechanistic terms. Conveniently and quite understandably, it serves one's discipline and professional standing well if one can amass mathematical and statistical formulas that explain the world at least reasonably well in terms of one's own discipline. Economists see people as economic actors, while sociologists see them as social animals, and criminologists focus on their propensity to behave violently and aberrantly. If you are a finance professor, you are surrounded with massive databases of prices of securities. It is natural to study those prices. The rigors of acquiring advanced degrees and publishing in academic journals require demonstrations of deftness with Greek symbols in handling reams of data. Data are exact and discrete and can be analyzed. If you are a financial academic, what you know and can handle and explain are financial facts. My major was in finance, and I love it. But I have learned from practical experience that there is more to the behavior of stock prices than can be discerned or predicted or proven from financial theory and price data alone. Those in isolation form a base too narrow for fully productive study.

I believe the crucial shortcoming of efficient-market theory is that it seeks to analyze markets in a sterile, mechanistic way that overlooks a central fact: Markets are the interactions of *human beings making decisions*. Those who see humans as automatons ruled entirely by pure logic and fact, I would propose, run a high risk of reaching imperfect conclusions because they have proceeded from an incomplete, if not heavily mistaken, starting point. Inside our heads are not just facts and logic machines but also drives and emotions. Our economic and financial behaviors therefore must be studied with that context included rather than excluded.

Behavioral finance, that exciting cross-disciplinary intersection of "psychology," sociology, finance, and economics, studies how "psychology" in the broadest vernacular sense affects the way that people behave when they make financial decisions. The insights of this relatively new way of looking at the world of investing have arisen *because* bright minds have decided to stretch their normal ranges of thinking and to embrace the possibilities of truths discovered by those from other perspectives. In this book, all that we will do is based on a perspective that regards the stock market as an interplay of people making decisions. We view people not as logic-machine robots armed with 100 percent of the available facts and insights but rather as often-conflicted combinations of intellect and emotion. We find that this goes a long way toward explaining how people actually do act, rather than how they theoretically should act. People in fact act less than rationally a good deal of the time, rather than rationally and efficiently in the academic sense.

It is often said, when referring to the embarrassing failings and misdeeds of some in business or politics, that "money does funny things to people." Indeed it does. It is not my intent to provide a lengthy treatise on what others have called "money madness." However, in the next few pages I will name and discuss some of the emotional and psychological influences that strongly affect financial decisions and actions. To provide a unifying context for that discussion, we will consider crowd psychology, or mob madness as a central concept. People in isolation can and do make some predictable and bizarre investment and trading moves. In the privacy and quiet of their dens, they may feel as though they are lone actors. The reality is otherwise. The milieu in which they as investors and traders live and operate is far from one of isolation. In fact, a great deal of the input they receive consists of the opinions, decisions, thoughts, and price-moving actions of a mass of other actors on the same financial stage. Those who try to make logical sense of the stock market miss this mass dynamic.

Because money and emotions are intertwined, the collective action of the actors becomes like that of a crowd, sometimes a "mad" crowd. Why not, then, seek to monitor and measure the action of that crowd, which makes up what we politely call "the market"? Our approach is to measure the size, intensity, urgency, and fever of the crowd by watching the trading volume generated collectively by individual members. We are not bent on reform, hoping to perfect humankind. Rather, we seek to observe what is real in the investment world and use that reality for our financial benefit. What we will examine in the chapters ahead is legal "inside" information—the evidence of what is going on inside the heads of many thousands and occasionally millions of investors, individual and professional, at a given moment in market time.

Why does random walk not explain the market? Because it focuses on prices and is blind to the psychology of the actors who are changing those prices. When conventional technicians study prevailing price movements, they are closer to being able to predict future price movements. We propose that the missing link in their chain of facts and logic is trading volume. Price study is sterile outside the context of volume.

INVESTOR AND TRADER BEHAVIOR: PSYCHOLOGICAL AND EMOTIONAL FACTORS

Actually, what I somewhat loosely referred to as "psychological factors" encompasses some anthropological imprinting from humankind's earliest days. In cave-dwelling times, survival was a constant battle, and we learned adaptive behaviors out of necessity. We learned never to venture out into the darkness, lest the beasts we hoped to hunt might instead prey upon us. There were no emergency rooms and flight-for-life helicopters! We also learned to hunt and perform other work as members of a group rather than as individuals. This led to our deferring judgments to the group or to the tribal leader, perhaps a shaman or guru or medicine man as we would now describe them. We learned to respect the unmanageable power of nature and the seasons: Stay in the caves during winter lest we freeze to death, and dive for shelter during violent thunderstorms in late summer. In sum, our early experiences all taught us to avoid risk and avoid independent thought and action. Such a mindset was functional in that bygone era for creating a reasonably safe social and economic unit, physically, but it is not very helpful today as we pursue financial investment strategies. The primacy of safety and deference to authority would have us accept the advice of any apparent investment experts and would imply that all our money should stay in certificates of deposit. Fear of loss would overrule our willingness to assume necessary and potentially profitable risk.

Avoiding Pain

Advance the film a few eons to the present day. In our childhood we were exhorted to seek safety above all else. Parents and grandparents and babysitters and child-care workers and teachers all urged on us a cautious course: Don't run with scissors in hand, don't chase that ball into the street, stay in the back yard, and so on. This probably got us through child-hood relatively unscathed, but it underprepared us for the competitive challenges and daily risks of adult life. Thus, loss aversion takes first place over gain seeking for the vast majority of us.

For a host of complex and interacting reasons, we strongly prefer to avoid pain of all sorts—the psychic as well as the physical. A not-inconsid-erable source of pain is uncertainty, whether in our finances or in other parts of life—health, parents' and children's welfare, office politics, potential cor-porate takeover, and so on. Psychologists have demonstrated that when peo-ple are forced to function under heavy uncertainty and stress, they tend to revert to childlike and subrational behaviors, such as impulsiveness, escapism, and fighting. Apply this mindset to the financial markets arena: Other than working as a trauma surgeon or air traffic controller, we could not easily construct a more stressful occupation than that of an active par-ticipant in financial markets. Stories of floor traders in the commodity pits, age 30 and burned out, with ulcers, hypertension, substance-abuse prob-lems, and broken marriages are well known. Even if we do not earn salary or commissions on Wall Street, by becoming investors and especially by trading more than just occasionally, we expose ourselves to high drama and high stress. (Such discomfort, combined with feelings of inadequate exper-tise, probably explains why many casual investors are willing to opt out of the action and hold passively for the long term.)

Combine preference for pain avoidance with a tendency to act as group animals rather than as lone wolves, and you have a prescription for poor investment performance. An investor who cannot stand the heat in a declin-ing market and who cannot stand the loneliness of missing a soaring market (despite knowing intellectually that valuations are ridiculously high) is high-ly prone to selling low and buying high. Multiply that single investor by mil-lions, and you have a classic case of an unruly and violent crowd. Mob action in the markets causes manic highs (or *fads, bubbles,* or *manias*—choose your favorite descriptor) and panic lows. It is this rather predictable feature of human behavior that underlies our ability to analyze stock trends not in isolation but instead in the informative context of trading volume. Ever-changing volume, monitored over time, tells you about the trading crowd. Mass action moves prices, and when mass action starts to dissipate, the price move is over, and it will not continue in the same direction.

Psychology teaches us that certain situations and stimuli are quite likely to cause fairly predictable responses. The well-known experiments with Pavlov's dog demonstrated the behavioral results of conditioning and reinforcement. Subsequent experiments have shown that the likelihood and degree of response to a stimulus is highly correlated with the vividness of that stimulus. Thus in investment markets, we become convinced by existing trends that the future will look like the past, and we react strongly and in unplanned ways when striking (positive *or* negative) news confronts us. In the Internet age, we have gained the wonderful benefits of readily available and predominantly free information on demand, every hour of the day and night. If we avail ourselves of those benefits too much, however, we become like an exposed raw nerve ending and find ourselves overstimulated and worn thin mentally. In that depleted mental condition, we are likely to make poor decisions. So, psychology strongly shapes our behavior, and of course our behavior determines the results. In *The Mind of the Market,* author F. J. Chu quotes Chinese military scholar Sun Tzu as advising leaders and warriors to "control your emotions, or they will control you." Eight words worth remembering!

Key Factors That Drive Behavior

Let us consider some of the key psychological and emotional forces and factors that shape and often drive the behaviors of investors. As the title of a currently popular book by Hersh Shefrin aptly puts it, the catalog of issues goes way *Beyond Greed and Fear.**

Ego

In western society, our feelings of self-worth are closely tied to our knowledge and perception of our financial net worth. This has huge implications for how we act and react in the stock market. When things go well, our heads tend to swell irrespective of whether we have been smart or merely lucky to be onboard the train. When things go badly, we tend to blame others rather than accept personal responsibility (merely one of several expressions of denial in our market behavior). When things go very badly, the blow to our narcissistic self-concept becomes unbearable. In extreme

---

*Harvard Business School Publishing, Boston, 1999.

cases this leads to suicides, but in vastly more instances it leads to either total denial and retreat or to capitulation, both of which serve to relieve the pain. Capitulation is most commonly thought of as occurring near or at market bottoms, when panic selling occurs. But it applies as well, although seldom in as concentrated a time frame, in manias and bubbles: At some point all but the most staunch value investors give up resistance to losing by remaining outside the game. When they buy, they capitulate to the pressure and to the crowd's noise. When large numbers of investors or traders capitulate simultaneously, we record this phenomenon as a major increase in trading volume; it marks an unsustainable amount of price pressure in the recent direction, implying imminent termination of that price trend.

Overconfidence

Commonly thought of as a product of an overly well fed ego, overconfidence in investing and trading actually represents a more complex mindset in psychological and operational terms. Professors Odean and Barber of the University of California at Davis have produced from extensive discount-brokerage-house records some detailed studies indicating that males tend to trade more frequently than females, who tend less toward overconfidence. Likewise, younger investors trade more heavily than older ones. The studies by these professors correlate greater activity with lowered financial returns.* That is one aspect of the damage overconfidence can cause. Another, however, is a dangerously unwarranted sense of grandiosity. Roman myth tells of Daedalus, who mistakenly thought he could fly closer to the sun than was safe. Some teenagers believe they are invincible, until their fearless behaviors end in tragedy.

The better an investor's experience, the thinner the air becomes in the upper altitudes and therefore the more easily confused the thinking. We witnessed the results of that false sense of effortless soaring as the great Internet bubble, or mania, topped out in early 2000 and technology stocks then fell and suffered what, as of this writing, has become a 65 percent decline. Overconfidence is not a problem in the depths of a bear market or in the early and middle stages of a price advance. It operates late in long rallies, and it ensnares a great proportion of participants in the final stages of the price blowoff. Fortunately, those of us who look at the market in emotionally defined terms and watch volume as our key indicator can detect the growing extent of such overconfident folly by watching the trading totals.

---

*Brad M. Barker and Terrance Odean, "Trading Is Hazardous to Your Health: The Common Stock Investment Performance of Individual Investors," in *The Journal of Finance*, vol. 55, no. 2, April 2000.

Loneliness

As discussed earlier, most humans tend to be group animals rather than loners. This tendency has been both subtly and deliberately conditioned into us, in our anthropological imprinting and in our childhood socialization. Therefore, we have a difficult time standing alone, marching to that different drummer's beat. This loneliness is what makes contrarian investing so difficult. You can be 100 percent convinced that your fundamental analysis is correct, but being what feels like the only adherent of your position becomes increasingly difficult as the workout time lengthens.

One means to escape loneliness is of course joining a crowd. The perceived pressure to do so is small at first, but it builds cumulatively over time, and almost exponentially as stock price moves become larger and more powerful. When this is also happening to you, it is also happening to others in large numbers at the same time. That is what causes both bursts of buying and avalanches of selling. People simply reach a point beyond which they can no longer endure the pain of holding an unpopular or self-isolating opinion and the stock-holding status (being out in a bull market, or staying in through a decline) that goes with it. Capitulation occurs. When it does so in many people virtually at the same time, we have extremely large trading volume that *defines the end* of a price move. Once again, volume tells the tale.

Anchoring or Framing

Studies by psychology researchers have shown that we have a strong tendency to evaluate new information in the context of recently received or previously familiar information. We also estimate quantities under the influence of seemingly meaningless outside factors. In one famous and remarkable experiment, a group of psychology students stationed themselves near the large wheel of luck in a casino—the wheel guests can spin once for a major payoff. Various numbers appear on the wheel. After each spin, the students asked nonstudent guests standing near them for their personal estimate of the number of member countries in the United Nations. Consistently, the responses tended to be biased toward the most recent number spun on the wheel—a totally irrelevant but very handy number. If we can subconsciously suffer such biases in our estimating abilities, it is easy to see how the world of numbers and opinions and forecasts that we call "Wall Street" can get inside our heads and prompt us to do some amazing things.

One of the clearest implications of such anchoring or framing in the context of recent information is our subconscious but strong tendency to expect recent trends or patterns to continue. On a very short term basis, that

makes us believe that a rally of 7 consecutive days' length is quite likely to
continue, whereas both statistically and in actual experience such phenomena occur only about once each 2 years. Likewise, when the market—or,
even more importantly, our own particular stock—loses ground for several
days running, we have a difficult time believing that the bloodletting will
ever end. Such thinking tends to encourage our bailing out near bottoms
rather than cashing in our chips more happily near tops.

On a longer-term basis, this framing tendency of our minds helps lull
us into complacency after a long string of quarterly earnings gains by a
company or a run-up of several years by the general market. Whether you
see it as conditioning, reinforcement, or framing, the result is that we
become strongly predisposed to believing that the recent trend is "bound
to continue." Reality says that business expansions do get interrupted by
recessions and that stock prices do not rise straight to the sky without correction, if for no other reason than that P/E ratios cannot rise forever. The
strange stuff going on inside our heads confounds our thinking so that we
willingly believe otherwise, with resulting damage to our portfolio values.

Cognitive Dissonance

This is a concept in psychology that deals with the great difficulty we have
in accepting new information that is strikingly contradictory to our past
beliefs. When we confront such shocks, we tend to reel into uncontrolled
emotion and irrational action, or we retreat into a cocoon of denial and
inaction. It takes a long time for us to be able to recover and to accept the
new information, and all the more so when it is negative. Examples are
the loving and perhaps naive spouse confronted with undeniable evidence
of an unfaithful partner's philandering; our shock when a youth leader or
clergy member is revealed as a perverted pedophile; and our shock when
a long-trusted neighbor turns out to be a counterfeit money printer, money
launderer for the syndicate, or international spy. In investment terms,
we have what analysts and the media politely call "negative surprises."
These range from earnings shortfalls and dividend cuts to much more serious breaches of trust: Directors or officers resign without explanation,
recent financial statements must be restated by the auditors, who themselves have been bamboozled, or analysts find they have been cleverly
misled by management and its financial public relations spinners.

The more sinister and shocking the revelations, the deeper the immediate stock price collapse and the longer the period of recovery will be—
assuming the company is viable and does endure beyond its newly revealed
difficulties. For the investor, the facts of the revealed debacle are only part
of the deeply troubling problem. We believed the company was reputable

and the earnings were real. Not only must we deal with the shocking new information that that belief was false, but the stock price that we believed was reasonable has been destroyed. We had been accustomed to XYZ trading at $20, but virtually or literally overnight it has gone to $3. These shocks are not easy to take. For some, panic and immediate exit are the response. For others, the pain is so profound they fall into paralyzed shock and can do nothing. Such an experience with one of our stocks is of course impossible to isolate. As a result, an investor may become easily emotionally shell-shocked, paranoid, and thus unable to deal rationally with other unaffected stocks. Our overall market behavior is degraded.

Denial

A convenient way of escaping unbearable pain and the stress brought by cognitive dissonance is to pull up the mental covers over our faces and hide in bed while the world goes on without us. This can result in deepening financial loss. The widely cited "cockroach theory" of bad news holds that once you see one, there will likely be more. Indeed, earnings disappointments most frequently last longer than one quarter. If a company's affairs are to go from bad to somewhat worse, hindsight will tell us that the first loss was the best loss to take. However, that advice is often easier to give than it is to receive. Taking a loss is a direct body blow to the ego (not to mention the pocketbook)—it shatters our confidence in our judgment abilities; it requires overcoming the psychic shocks of cognitive dissonance; and it just plain hurts. We are lonely because we do not want to share or admit what we are going through. None of this is helpful when we must deal with the cold immediate facts of a declining stock price. When the bad news is not shocking or of deeply ill portent but simply disappointing, we tend to be forgiving of our stock (because that helps us to forgive our own frailty and misjudgment). Denial will later lead to regret, but refusing to take action at present still allows us the hope of recovery. In contrast, overcoming denial will harvest a clear and undeniable loss today, and real pain now hurts more than possible pain in the future.

Vividness

The bigger and more sudden the noise, the more we flinch. The opposite also hold true—the more exciting a promising story (as practiced scam artists have known for centuries) and the more sharp the rise in a stock's price, the more irresistible will be our impulse to act and act immediately. Doing so will by definition mean we are joining a crowd—those thousands of other people who are all scrambling to buy that stock at the same time (or to sell it, if the news happens to be bad). Again I must point to the

age of Internet news, on-screen babble, and flashing, vivid-color quotations, and stock prices screaming up or down their charts. All of this stuff
makes us more likely than in the past to react immediately and impulsive-
ly. What is wonderful about analyzing the world of stock market action in
terms of crowd or mob response is that we can see such folly before our
eyes literally while it happens, and we can trace its size and intensity (and
its predictably imminent unwinding) simply by watching the trading-volume bars on our charts. If we understand the emotional dynamic that is
pushing the crowd to its foolish concentrated action, we can resist participating and can take advantage of the temporary madness of the market by
selling if we own and, further, by shorting if we are so inclined. Volume
tells the tale and gives the signal.

In the past few pages, we have described seven major psychological
or emotional factors that strongly drive behaviors, or in stock market
terms, that prompt buying and selling actions. There are others, of varying
and perhaps lesser urgency and strength. This book is not intended as an
all-inclusive catalog of behavioral finance explanations of the market.
Others provide that benefit and that delightful learning, and more are
undoubtedly still to come in the future as this discipline grows and deep-
ens. Before we conclude our present chapter, however, we offer a sort of
timeline of emotions as a stock or whole market proceeds through a cycle
from bottom to top and back down again to the depths.

A TIMELINE OF EMOTIONS THROUGHOUT A STOCK MARKET CYCLE

In the following discussion we will omit any references to exact time frames
and to percentages or to levels in major market indicators so there will be
no implication of precision in estimating the scale of price moves and time
windows. What is important to derive here is the sequence and poignancy
of the emotional experiences that attach to the market's movement. Market
pundits and apologists are fond of remarking that "it's different this time,"
but that is true only at the inconsequential level of specific details. Human
nature does not change. Each market cycle will always be different is size,
but nearly all will display parallel underlying psychological content.

The Bottom and the First Rally

Let us suppose that the market in general, or some individual stock of
interest, has recently undergone a deep and somewhat lengthy decline. We
of course do not have a time machine that will allow us to peer back to

today and thereby know for certain what date and price in fact will be seen by market historians as the bottom. But let us now look at a price chart generated thereafter, on which we can indeed identify that bottom. The first rally from the bottom will be greeted with considerable doubt. The preceding decline has been long and painful and frustrating. There have been several rallies that failed along the way, many bottoms that did not hold. Why should we believe that this latest apparent bargain level is any more durable than those? At some point the number of courageous buyers who were willing to step in and risk their cash at or near the bottom will become exhausted. At that point, what will later be seen as a temporary rally top will be formed. The doubters of the new bull market's first rally will start to feel that they have been vindicated in their dour expectations. "Here we go again, down once more and who knows how far," they will be muttering. The struggle between courageous early buyers and experience-fortified doubters plays out in almost every major new bull market's early phase. That, I believe, is why so few bottoms are shaped like the letter V and so many look more like a W—although the two lowest points are seldom on exactly a level plane.

The Next Rally

For whatever combination of reasons, the decline that follows that first bull market rally does not take hold to the degree that it smashes to new lows. Prices hold. Trading is lighter than in the final crash, whether the price stops falling slightly above or slightly below the old bottom. Many observers will attribute the success of this price test to some piece of good news or perhaps to a decrease in bad news. We of a technical analysis bent who base our judgments on human behavior are more inclined to believe the second bottom holds because the first was so violent and so damaging that it has already shaken out nearly all holders who are shakable; therefore, there is not any more fear during this test than has already been felt and expressed in panic selling.

The First Major Leg Upward

Once a growing number of market participants (many of whom are now still heavily in cash because they sold near the old bottom) see that the secondary or testing decline has indeed held, they individually come around over time. More and more of them conclude that the bear market has probably seen its end and that the bargains they have been watching are worth owning before they get away. However, because the recent bear market has done such painful damage and is not at all a distant memory as yet, there is no major scramble to get out of cash and into stocks all at once. Some people take longer than others to become convinced and to take action, moving cautiously and gradually at first. Sometimes the move above the highs of the first rally does evoke a temporary buyers' panic, but it is short lived. There are, after all, still doubters out there who are not prepared to bury the dead bear as yet. They will not join any rush to buy, and if they have some stocks they wish they had not held all the way to the bottom, those may now be thrown overboard to the "fools" who are in a hurry to buy all of a sudden. Thus such a rush is brief if indeed it does occur. The faster prices might rise, the more people perceive that the bargains they'd been savoring have suddenly disappeared or at least faded badly. Their freshly earned bear market education reminds them not to be too confident or they will get burned. So any early and fast rally tends to be self-limiting. As the major upward leg continues, however, larger numbers of people are coaxed off the sidelines. Each correction that does not turn into a downside rout draws in a few more cautious but now convinced-on-balance bulls. Time passes and confidence seems to have returned. If the recent bear market was associated with a business recession, some signs start appearing that things are no longer getting worse, and perhaps some concrete events demonstrate that expansion has returned. Certainly the Federal Reserve will have been working hard to make that happen for quite some time, by now.

A Correction

Stocks, of course, cannot go up without interruption forever. With or without an apparent trigger in news events, the major leg ends in a correction. But by this time the distance up from the old scary lows has become far enough, and the economy is palpably improving enough so that few, except the diehard nay-sayers, predict the end of the bull and the start of a new bear that will claw its way to lower lows. We simply must live through this little correction. Relax and remember you're a long-term investor. Let the market do its digesting, and all will be well quite soon. Doubt has largely been banished in favor of cautious confidence that all is well in the world of Wall Street once again. Sure, there have to be bear markets every once in a while, and we've just been through one of them, and everyone knows that the market goes up about 7 years in 10, so it is not time to expect another collapse. Hang in there and your faith will be vindicated—that is the prevalent thinking and the mood reflected in newspaper and Internet and magazine commentaries.

Another Major Upward Leg

Doubt has been banished to the memory heap. Faith has been vindicated. We're certainly not acting as crazy as people did (note the third person) at the top of that ridiculously high old bull market. There are good stocks to be bought and owned, and great companies on whose fortunes to ride. Doubt has been put aside. We are now into the phase of general conviction that all is well in the world and long-term buy-and-hold investors are indeed the smart ones. How dumb it was of some people to panic and sell in this greatest of all countries! The majority is now on board for the new bull market's ride. Those who have let the train go by are fairly few, and they are feeling lonely and left out—passed by due to their own overcautious natures. The next correction will give them a chance to buy at slightly better prices and thus feel safer than they would by jumping right in today after this latest rally.

Another Correction and Then More New Highs

As the time and price distance from the bottom keep growing, conviction turns to confidence. Any decline is a buying opportunity. After all, remember the 1990s? Long before we ever got to that silly blow-off stage, we all learned that you buy the dips and you'll be right every time. Here or there a magazine cover celebrates the market's prosperity: Perhaps a bull is prancing upward, or maybe the year's hero portfolio managers are enshrined in some hall of financial fame. Confidence begins to slide over into nearly full-time celebration. Talk at social events turns to one's market exploits. You really mean you're *not* in that one or that group yet? Wow! Everyone else I know is. Celebration starts to bubble everywhere. You see cartoons in nonfinancial media about people getting rich quick, and the plots of TV sitcoms and movies sometimes center on how nicely people are getting wealthy in the market. It has been a long time since anyone has seen a cartoon with someone standing on the ledge contemplating a leap of despair. What's to despair about?

Rotation of Leadership

At some point whatever group or concept or technology was pulling the train will take a pause. But this is, after all, a bull market, so another type of stock will immediately assert leadership in its place. The natural process of leadership rotation. Every group will have its time. Fortunately, modern computer technology enables all of us to quickly identify the new momentum leaders and move our money, so our recently pleasant rate of return will not be interrupted. Some would call that overconfidence, an attitude that winning is virtually inevitable. After all, whom do you know that is not in the market and not making it right now? See what I mean? This is a whole new ballgame. The rules are different this time. Didn't you read that new study by those professors that justified today's P/E ratios based on the changes in accounting and greater technological productiv-. ity? At this point, some people who made good money in the previously leading groups will borrow on margin or on their home equity because they don't see any reason to miss an even faster and more profitable ride in this new sector that is just starting to take off. Why not ride in first class? You call that a little greedy? Nah, it's just plain being realistic. This market still has a lot of legs left.

The Top, But of Course No One Knows It Yet

Whatever the reason—in fundamentals, in news from overseas, in the monetary policy, or just in the running out of people's bullish psychology being matched with new money to fuel the fires—at some point the actual top will be seen. The averages will look a little tired, but there will be one or two groups that are still streaking ahead even while the advance/decline breadth is cooling off. People will still be in a greedy mood (they will call it "natural and well-founded optimism," of course). They will have become so conditioned to the market's rising for a long time and a great percentage distance that they will have no doubt the present phase is just another temporary correction. They will be anchored in their recent past experience, projecting it ever forward to the future they (want and) expect.

The First Meaningful Decline

Well, look at what happened: We've actually had a correction here. The newspapers duly remind us that an "official" correction in market lore is about 10 percent on some major average, while it takes a full 20 percent before the phrase "bear market" dares be dusted off. So, not to worry. We've started back up again and that little haircut on prices was a healthy cooling off. The market can't keep going unless there's some "wall of worry" to climb. So let the silly doubters worry about the drop that's already over now. There's nothing wrong with the economy or with this market. Everything is fine. This is denial, but because no one yet knows that it is false confidence, it is not yet able to be labeled as such. So, we have gone from celebration to greed to anchoring in the recent past and are now actually in denial that a bear market has started (which we cannot yet know because that time machine still does not work).

A Lower High and a Lower Low

I simply can't believe it: That last rally actually did not carry up to a new high. But look, such-and-such is still running away, and the X group is still going gangbusters. There is no evidence of a recession or a bear market. I'm holding on, and if it goes any lower, I will buy more (if I don't get a margin call). I simply do not believe what happened to such-and-such a company, or that that go-go hedge fund busted, or that that little bank made those stupid loans. How can a few people be so dumb as to find a way to lose money when there's prosperity all around us? The speaker of such sentiments has now gone beyond denial and is suffering from cognitive dissonance because, in fact, things have deteriorated, and there has been a fairly shocking bankruptcy or other nasty event that should not have taken place if the boom were still on.

Another Leg Down, and a Little Steeper Now

This is starting to feel not at all nice. In fact, I heard that my neighbor's boss got this massive margin call and couldn't meet it. They sold him out! It has been a period of some months now since the highs, and no longer is there hardly any contingent of faithful bulls who tell us the present discomfort is just a correction that will support an even stronger next rally. I don't hear anyone talking about their stocks and funds at the club anymore. I actually know of a few people who've gotten burned. Not me, of course. I'm a long-term investor and I can take the heat. But it *is* getting pretty hot here now. You know, this last week has been a little scary. But I see some real bargains, so we must be close to the end by now.

Gravity in Command

Yikes! I thought I'd already gotten out of anything that still had some hot air in its price, but that reaction to the disappointing earnings in XYZ sure was a stunner. Down 42 percent overnight. This is getting ridiculous. Stocks have come down so far they really are good bargains, and yet where are the people who should be buying them? At some point a dark day arrives when one or more of the major averages is hit with a dive measured in the middle single digits in percent terms. Trading volume hits either its highest in this decline or its highest ever. There is talk of mutual fund investors cashing out and forcing the portfolio managers to sell to meet redemptions. Three or four days in a row the newspapers carry stories about how many margin calls were sent out by the major online and full-service brokerages. A couple of major newspapers or magazines show front-page pictures of floor brokers, their ties askew, in full facial and body sweat and tickets strewn all over the exchange floor. People who have stoically held on so far are now dropping like flies. Even if they don't have margin calls to worry about, they start calculating how much they will have left for retirement if they get out now and just put it all in a money market fund. One morning the bottom literally melts away and there seem to be no buyers in sight. In spite of all best intentions, many stockholders can no longer take the stress. The pain is un*bear*able! My losses are so big, that even though I will hate myself for being so stupid, I just have to get out so it can't hurt me even more. That last self-preservation impulse, felt by many at once causes an absolute panic wave of selling that lasts a matter of hours. It is over. But of course almost nobody believes it. What if there are more margin calls tomorrow? Look at that volume! What if some brokerage firm goes belly up? It has been so vivid and so long and so painful, that it's impossible to have any confidence it will not continue. (These last sentiments indicate that total capitulation has occurred. It is intellectually there to be noted and acted upon. But doing so is very, very scary.) Thinking in volume terms, panic and selling have reached an absolute fever pitch. In a matter of some weeks we will look back and realize that this was the frightening point of maximum disbelief. And then, somehow, the selling dried up. We of course do not have a time machine that will allow us to peer back to this moment and thereby know for certain that today's date and price in fact will be seen by market historians as the bottom. The cycle is complete. Another bull market will begin on this day, and like the bear that is now expiring, it will ride on wings of emotion that will vastly outrun the extent of the fundamental change on which it is allegedly based. Value determines price in the very long term, but emotion sets price all the time between now and then.

Now, did that feel like a random walk to you, or much more like some sort of an emotional roller-coaster?

CONCLUSION AND SUMMARY

In this chapter it has been our purpose to set out the intellectual basis on which our volume-analysis approach to stock-price prediction rests. It is important that you understand where this is all coming from so that what follows in the balance of the book will form into a sensible and internally consistent body of information and advice. That is why we have taken time to explore some basic psychological ideas. We see these as truly governing stock price action in other than the long term (where fundamentals will rule) because these emotional forces and factors first drive human beings' responses to their stimuli in the form of placing buy and sell orders. Price does not change in response to news; price changes in response to people's reactions to news. If no one reacted to new information on a given day, there would be no trading and therefore price would remain unchanged. Thus we elevate trading volume as the subject of high-value study if one wishes to understand and predict price movements.

Certainly, there is no single perfect and complete formula for predicting market prices. We adamantly reject, however, the underlying assumption of the efficient-market theorists that if there is no perfect answer, there can be no answer at all except chaos and randomness. In the long run the prices of stocks are undeniably driven by their fundamentals. Benjamin Graham said that in the long run the market is a weighing machine but in the short term it is a voting machine. Those votes are opinions rather than meticulously accurate assessments of value. So we see that emotions drive up prices from panicky depressed levels that are well below value, to manic levels totally divorced from any realistic concept of valuation and therefore wildly above reasonable value—and all the way back down again.

Sun Tzu's admonition that we must control our emotions lest they become our masters is a central rule for achieving investment and trading success. You live and operate in a stock market strongly driven by emotions, whether of the moment or of the week, a great boom or a scary recession. It is necessary to become highly equipped to control your emotions in order to succeed in such an environment. But functioning well in such emotionally charged surroundings is virtually impossible *unless* you understand the emotions of the market, the group, the crowd, the mob. We must start by understanding our environment so that we can guard ourselves in it. How great is the range of mispricing (which is either a danger or an opportunity depending on your level of preparation and understanding)? In the 1990s, common stocks on the New York Stock Exchange (excluding issues under $5 and closed-end funds) experienced a remarkably strong average (albeit not smooth) annual growth rate in earnings of about 11 percent a year. Those same stocks fluctuated over an average *annual* range of 65 percent. Those who counsel passive buying and holding apparently are willing to give up the vast majority fraction of the potential for profit. They do so in the fear that they will fare badly in the attempt and therefore might lose. I find a 65 percent range—which contains on average several cycles adding to well over 100 percent in many years—highly appealing as an intellectual and financial challenge when contrasted with 11 percent. For those who are willing to participate on the short as well as long side of the market, the possibilities are literally doubly as great. There are no guarantees, of course, but the potential is high in contrast to 11 percent for the passive strategy.

We will analyze volume of trading as the key additional source of illumination brought to the task of sorting out the market and attempting to predict price. Our thesis is that the crowd forms and reaches mob size and intensity, and then retreats after having done its work. We can measure that crowd by the depth of its footprints, by the amount of trading it is doing. Once the crowd ceases to grow, its price impact has been maximized. Price must then move in the opposite direction. Knowing this may indeed prove a major expansion of your perspective on how prices come to be set and come to change. Knowledge is power, *but only in the hands of those who will use it.* For that reason, Chapter 3 will briefly detour into the necessity of freeing the mind for taking action. As will be developed, it is clear that markets move faster and with greater volatility than in the past. To be successful as more than that 11 percent-destined buy-and-hold investment passivist, you must be ready to act rather than contemplate when the crowd gives its telltale signs of immediately pending price change through volume traded.

CHAPTER 3

Don't Contemplate. Act!

It is not my intention or wish to make my readers into short-term traders. Virtually nothing in this volume on volume deals with day trading. That said, we must be realistic about the stock-trading world in which we find ourselves as the new millennium has dawned. Market volatility has increased considerably over just the past decade. Pressure for short-term performance has driven many if not most institutional investors to exhibit herdlike behavior in their buying and selling (Chapter 8 discusses that matter in considerable detail). Their tendency to move large blocks of stock ever more frequently means that trading volume is greater, and as a result prices are being driven to more frequent and sharper reversals. Rather as the good drives out the bad in the model of Gresham's law, the present reality of high volatility virtually forces those who would be successful to join rather than ignore the activity.

The bottom-line message is this: As you learn about a number of different ways to observe and measure the effects of volume on stock price behavior, taking advantage of your newly learned insights and skills will absolutely require your acting promptly rather than contemplating at leisure. Volume analysis will signal in the large majority of situations a crowd's immediate formation and, quickly thereafter, its dispersal. When the volume changes in the ways we will describe in subsequent chapters, price change will follow directly. In a few cases it will be the same or the following trading day. In most of the volume-dynamics scenarios you will learn to watch for and recognize, the crowd leaves its unmistakable footprints in the form of trading volume over a stretch of several days. When that mass-action pattern has played out, price must and will reverse without delay. It will do you

little if any good to observe and categorize these patterns as you see them—
only to wait before taking appropriate action. If and as you wait, the price
advantage that the accurately perceived trading-volume pattern will have created for you will rapidly dissipate and disappear. Fundamental developments
in the life of a company (changes in revenues, profits, cash flows, book values, and dividends) and in the overall economy (interest rates, tax laws,
demographic shifts) certainly drive the *values* of stocks over the long run.
Between now and the ever-moving long-run future, that is, in the near term,
stock prices are just as surely driven by the psychological perceptions and
the emotions of people—individual and professional investors—who decide
in varying numbers at different times to buy or to sell. As you will see in
later chapters, the rising and falling of trading volume enables you to measure the crowd; in combination with directional change in price, volume of
trading forecasts future changes in price direction. When volume—literally
the driving force of the whole action—changes, price will change as a
result. If you want to take advantage of this cause-and-effect phenomenon,
you must act.

THE PATHOLOGY OF INDECISION

This chapter will focus on improving your ability to take action. In particular, we will seek to help with the much more difficult of the two ends of a
stock transaction: selling. It is very clear that investors and traders have
immensely more difficulty acting to sell than acting to buy—although neither activity seems easy. All financial decisions carry with them some level
of discomfort, which I believe is based on two major factors. First, our standard education and training for life does not include any instruction in carrying out research and decisions in the investment world. That creates an
accurately based sense of inadequacy. When people feel inadequate to a
task, most naturally seek to avoid having to perform it. The second problem
surrounding buying and selling is the absolute uncertainty of future events.
By nature, many more people are risk avoiders than risk seekers. Our egos
would like to win, but we know that losing will hurt. Our pride has us wishing to be proven correct rather than wrong, wise rather than foolish. Because
we have never seen the future in any detail, we know absolutely that when
we buy or sell, we do not know which way price will move next. If we have
unknowingly acted in the past as part of a crowd, we have an experience-
based sense that seemingly whatever we do, the gods of investment fate
more often than not frown on us. At least in the very near term our action
is proven mistaken. That negative feedback at worst, and at the least our
sure knowledge that we are dealing in an unknown outcome, will also

act to impede our taking action. Self-perceived inadequacy and external uncertainty are a powerful combination.

With uncertainty equally surrounding both kinds of acts, why is it, then, that buying seemingly is so much less a problem than selling? I see a combination of external and internal factors at work here. First, of course, buying is done in a spirit of optimism, and most people prefer that mindset to one that is neutral or negative. Second, the machinery of Wall Street is set up to promote our purchasing rather than disposing of securities. On balance, new issuance of securities far exceeds the amounts repurchased by corporations. Securities salespeople are trained to *gather* client assets and to put those assets to work. Consequently, they are generating ideas about what the owners of capital should buy, not what they should sell. Besides, advising you and me to buy seems the properly optimistic, and the almost patriotic, thing to do. What salesperson wants to be associated with "negative thinking"?

A recently released (1999) study by the staff of the U.S. Securities and Exchange Commission gathered what were thought to be "all" the buy and sell recommendations issued by domestic brokerage firms over a 10-year period. When the two piles of reports were tallied up, recommendations to buy outnumbered those to sell by the nearly incredible ratio of 46 to 1. So clearly the investing public gets a great deal less help in selling than in buying, to say the least. One of the major reasons underlying that fact is an internal conflict of interests between the corporate finance departments of broker-dealers and their research departments. While the research analyst in his or her proper function should wish to ferret out all the available and relevant facts and thereby come to a well-founded conclusion regarding whether to buy or sell, the investment banking side of the firm has another interest. Those members of the brokerage family want to be on ever-constructive terms with corporate managements so they can put together financings, takeovers, and spin-offs—all of which involve considerable fees. For this reason, most brokerage firms strongly discourage (read: prohibit) their research analysts from using the four-letter "s" word. A variety of other terms are substituted, most commonly "hold" and "long-term buy" and "accumulate." The uninitiated individual investor, especially seeing an advice to "hold," simply does not understand the unwritten code: That word paradoxically means to sell. Only "strong buy" or equivalent words actually mean to buy or literally to hold. Thus, the act of selling a stock systematically gets almost no support from the brokerage community. When an individual broker verbally advises selling, all too often it seems to be for one of two reasons: First, the sale will free up money for a purchase suggestion about to be made; or second, things have gone so badly with the old position that neither the customer nor the broker can endure the pain of watching the price decline further. In such a construct, an investor *at least subconsciously* comes to associate the act of selling with negative results.

A great deal of psychological baggage attaches to the act of selling a stock. And all that weight naturally acts to inhibit our ability to "pull the sell trigger." Over the next few pages we will name the problems selling causes us. Doing so may not erase those weights, but at least it will help you to identify the nature of your psychological enemy so you can spot it and thereby more effectively battle it.

At an almost trivial and quickly apparent level, there is a huge difference between how we feel when we buy and when we sell. Buying, of course, is *always* done in optimism, whereas only sometimes do we get a financially positive result when selling. And even when we do happily record a monetary profit that will show up on Schedule D, the immediate act of selling carries with it a sense of foreboding that we are probably making a suboptimal decision. Probably never in one's investing lifetime does as individual investor sell out at the all-time high. Therefore, we just know in our bones that when we sell, we will commit an imperfect act. Will our former holding rally a point by the end of the day or a few points before we open up Sunday's financial section? Worse yet, will the apparent turkey we unload today somehow rise from corporate obscurity to become the soaring eagle of the next decade? Neither is a pretty prospect in our ego's eye.

What this amounts to is a matter of open-endedness versus closure. Putting aside the infrequent act of covering a short sale, buying is not only done in optimism but it also creates an open-ended set of possibilities: Our stock or our chosen mutual fund seems to have all the promise of a newborn infant. We literally can only imagine how far it might go, how high it might fly. The possibilities are seemingly unbounded, and at the very minimum are uncertain, unquantifiable. But we do presume the future's outcome to be positive, or else we would not be buying at all. So the act of buying rides across our mental stage like a charging white horse. Not only does buying initiate possibilities but it opens a situation in which we have full power and freedom to control. Ownership of a stock continues to offer us positive potentials (whether for recovery or for further paper gains) until and unless we decide to close off those ongoing opportunities. One of the reasons people find it easier to buy than to sell is that they give themselves some degree of permission to make imperfectly priced and timed purchases. They can allow themselves such freedom because once a buy has been made, the result of the decision is unresolved: If the stock goes down a few points, that is not a disaster since your holding period is open-ended and totally within your control. Therefore, an imperfection in one's buying execution can be repaired with time and market movement. Even if our purchase almost immediately shows itself to be unfortunately timed and priced, we can immediately comfort our egos with reliance on the presumed fundamental strengths of the company (in fact, it has become an even more compelling bargain!) and with the absolute control we have over allowing our position time to work out. This is like a delightful but imaginary basketball or football game without a clock—one in which we can end the game at will once our side is ahead. We can therefore be relaxed about early setbacks, which we consider to be only temporary.

Selling (again except going short) evokes quite an opposite set of feelings. At the very least, selling is not a beginning but an end. Deep inside our emotional memories, "ends" conjure up old friends we regret having lost contact with after our ways diverged; divorces that officially recognized a failure or mistake; and funerals. Not exactly the sorts of stuff we seek or cherish. Selling is a closure that we can cause—or can postpone. If we opt for closure, we know it brings at least one of two somewhat distasteful consequences: Either we quantify the size of a mistake when we actually take a loss, or we incur an income tax liability when closing out a gain. And in either case, we face that gnawing suspicion that our act will be proven imperfect. Probably at some time the stock we gave up on will trade at a higher price than we garnered. Selling carries none of the comforting open-endedness of buying. Once we sell, we have set the final score forever, subconsciously putting the result into that "permanent record" we so greatly feared while in school. The final score is either a win or a loss. And even if it is a win, it is tainted with an undeniable knowledge that we may well soon find that we could have done better, and that while we had some success our skills and judgment have clearly been shown to be less than ideal. Because we know the negatives that a closed-out position carries, we strongly resist taking the one action we have at our command: rather than sell we hold and thereby push away needing to deal with all the stuff that will immediately arise when or if we do finally sell. Buying keeps our options open, and selling forever forecloses them. As freedom-loving individuals, we strongly prefer having the power of unused options.

In reality, of course, absolutely nothing keeps us from reopening our ownership in a given stock, even immediately after we sell. (The wash-sale rule does not invalidate that assertion. It does not make repurchase within 30 days illegal but merely imposes some slightly complex record-keeping and may postpone our taking a tax loss into a future year. If a stock should be bought, it should be bought by us as well as anyone else!) But unfortunately, we have set up some internal bars to the liberating possibility of rebuying what we've sold. If we buy a stock at 30 and sell at 40, only to learn of some new reasons to expect that stock to go even higher, we have two significant hurdles to overcome. First, we strongly resist paying more than 40 to re-enter because that makes us feel dumb and we have clearly lost some money (even aside from commissions). Having once been able to buy this stock at 30, we now subconsciously set up 30 as a reasonable standard of what a fair or desired (or even personally *deserved*) entry price should be. That old price of 30 was based on facts as the market knew them some time ago and probably has no real relevance as a standard now, except that it tugs irrationally at our greedy subconscious. If the stock's price happily trades below 40, we are at least potentially able to give ourselves permission to re-enter. For each point the stock recedes below 40, we feel increasingly wise for having sold it at that higher level. Unfortunately, this ability to stroke our own ego becomes an increasingly important game of self-satisfaction. Should the stock decline to 34 before rallying, if we do not buy it there, we have set up yet another inhibiting condition for our reentry: We will now feel badly that we did not get back in that low, as the stock rallies back to 36 or 37. As you can see, the existence of a closed-out position in a stock sets up in the mind of its former owner a whole galaxy of problems and hang-ups that other investors or traders do not suffer. You must put out of your mind that former position and its details and approach this stock afresh, as you would any other opportunity. That may not be easy, but it is necessary.

Selling a stock requires that we confront and conquer what psychologists refer to as *cognitive dissonance.* In laypersons' terms, that means a sudden disconnection or reversal. And it is a reversal we must ourselves create. Through and including yesterday, the stock you were holding represented an up-and-coming firm with growth prospects, good management, and attractive products and strategy. And all of that was presently being priced by the market at what we considered no worse than a fair price and probably a bargain (or else we should not continue holding it!). Today, in order to sell, we must conclude that at least some part(s) of our owner's scenario were flawed. Maybe a competitor after all is starting to eat our company's lunch. Maybe management was not as smart as we thought. Or, most to the point, we must conclude that the stock's price is no longer attractive. (And of course we must make that last judgment in an arena of uncertainty in which we absolutely know there is no way to ascertain the truth in advance.) Yesterday it was smart to hold the stock; today that must now be false in our minds in order for us to part with it. Wow.

Selling a stock can occur in any of three price zones: We can take a profit, or sell it at roughly what we originally paid, or admit a mistake and suffer a loss. Each of those zones brings its own kinds of emotional misery when we try to sell there.

Many more people are able to accept losses at the end of the tax year, when "at least I will get part of it back from Uncle Sam," than during the course of the other 11 months or so. We can see this very clearly in the significant rises of trading volume on declining stocks' charts in a year's final few weeks, as discussed in some detail in Chapter 15. The tax benefit of taking a loss is equally available at all times, but somehow its nearby availability in December or its required postponement for another full year helps us to take the paper loss we have otherwise refused to admit and close out. The tax benefit is somewhat of a face saver and a pain assuager. Otherwise, we would have a very difficult time accepting the fact of our own human imperfection: We misjudged an unknown future and have, at least for the present time, been proven wrong. Our entire cultural experience has been shaped by attempts at being perfect, best, right. Our parents constantly asked that our playful early child always "be good." Older siblings would report our transgressions when we stepped out of line. Our parents and teachers urged us to seek all A's so we could get into the best school at the next level, so we could get the best jobs and own the most adult toys and the highest possible social status. Any shortcoming, we were told, would blotch our "permanent record"—a mysterious but life-altering scorecard that apparently was kept locked away at least for a time in the principal's office. On the athletic field nothing less than a win in the championship game was considered acceptable. At work, 110 percent effort was the minimum expected, and sometimes even that would not suffice, as we felt a single visible mistake could have us shown the door on a moment's notice. In our private lives, our wardrobes, vehicles, and vacations needed to be only the best. Summing it all up, we accepted and self-administered a great deal of perfectionist expectations, despite being fallible human beings. Now carry all that baggage into the investing or trading arena, where we tend to hear of only the successes of our neighbors and colleagues. Add the further pressure that for all too many of us, money is a primary scorekeeper of success. Wealth, salary, and profit measure the man (perhaps a bit more so than the woman, but that is a gender gap that *does* seem to be closing). Here we are, faced by what to do with a stock position on which we have a loss. Denial often works well, at least for a while. Hope springs eternal that some dot-com IPO we bought late and have seen decline 95 percent will somehow regain its earlier price levels.

No matter what the odds, we see holding on as offering at least some possibility of vindication for our intellect and judgment. Selling at a loss would mean abandoning all such hope and admitting a mistake, a failure. Thus selling at a loss is very difficult. If we were less governed by our own emotional drivers and more calculatingly rational in our actions (as traditional academics assume all investors are!), we could let go a stock at 18 that we bought at 20 when we saw the chance to gain 50 or 100 percent on a better opportunity. But getting even in our present stock all too often rules the day. Perfectionism is the enemy.

Selling a stock that is roughly unchanged from our buying price is the least difficult zone in which to take action, but it is not entirely free of its hindrances. Settling for a tie is not anywhere near as bad as taking a loss, but still it is short of the coveted win we seek. We are subconsciously bothered by our inability to show the required degree of patience, a virtue our parents frequently reminded us we lacked. So we lean toward being well-behaved investor-citizens and holding on—after all we don't want to become known (to ourselves) as short-term traders, and besides, we know that every transaction costs money. We have been constantly educated (or propagandized) to be a well-behaved buy-and-hold investor. So selling some stock before we've truly given it a full and fair chance to work out tends to run against what we've been told is good behavior. Besides, that one we sold in boredom and frustration 3 years ago turned out to be a hot acquisition story less than a month later, and it really hurts that we left 60 percent on the table.

Selling a stock at a gain also presents its problems. This is quite interesting in that repeated brokerage and academic studies indicate that many investors tend to sell their gains early (for unduly small profits) and let their losses run. It appears that once a narrow area of fairly small gains in a short time period has been surpassed, investors and traders have a great deal more trouble selling stocks at gains. A considerable amount is going on inside our heads in this area. For starters, we have an ingrained dislike for paying taxes. The greater the gain, the more dollars we will need to render unto Caesar. [There exist only three antidotes for this mental illness: giving the asset (and the tax problem) away; waiting until it goes back down so low we no longer have taxes to pay; and dying.] On a deeper psychological level, however, there are reasons we have big problems parting with our winners. First, they have treated us well. They stroke us every time we look up their prices. How can we walk away from what for us personally has become "a proven winner"? We know this company and its paper-profit-proven (assumed) virtues. We were right in our judgment to buy and were also correct when we resisted those periodic temptations to sell during market adversity. And besides, the stock would not be doing so nicely right now if all were not on the up and up at corporate. Why rock the boat that is sailing so well? If we do sell this known winner, even though it has given us occasional sleepless nights, we must find something better—and that means better after taxes. The future is unknown, but we have a certain amount of familiarity with this adopted family member—sort of a case of the devil we know versus some other.

When and at what price to sell a winner is a constant and disturbing conundrum. Since August 1982, with fairly brief exceptions the market has gone up over time, so we feel the odds against us if we sell. That is a large number of years of almost perfectly consistent conditioning. We just know that if we sell, it *will* go higher, as if in a personal rebuke to our daring to part with it. If it is making all-time highs, apparently the whole world has acquired our earlier wisdom that this is the one to own. And if the price gains are coming in heavy trading volume, so much stronger is the immediate proof: "Everyone" wants it, so who are we to differ? If our stock has recently traded at higher prices than it now carries, we suffer nonsellers' regret. We revise actual history and somehow recall that we "knew we should have sold it then," but on some retrospectively constructed excuse did not do so. Somehow, any past high price that this stock once enjoyed was deserved, thereby rendering a lesser current quotation a temporary mistake of the market that will be corrected if only we exercise patience. To sell now would be a mistake whose degree we can literally measure in points and percentages, right down to the decimal! If our patience in waiting for a return to (or above) former glorious heights proves ill founded, the whole psychology of taking losses increasingly rules our mental space. What we bought at 20 and once was 60 but now would bring us only 30 is a loss of 30 points, much more prominently than it represents a gain of 50 percent, in our minds. And taking a loss represents failure.

Incredible as it may seem, not only the fear of failure but a fear of success can misguide our investing and trading behavior. Deep in our subconscious, when we have a huge percentage gain honestly earned over time by good research thinking (put aside the occasional broker's gift of a hot IPO that jumps way out of proportion to its true merit), we fear that taking that huge gain will set a bar so high that our future performance may never again equal it. We will be on the decline, having seen our best long ago. Gains and wealth are indeed a powerful scorekeeping device we use in measuring self-worth. Too bad. Not only do we as humans have much else of great real or potential worth, but in very practical terms such fear of success can keep us from accepting a profit that now is at risk because a stock is too high—or which trading-volume patterns show is about to decline.

SEVEN POWERFUL ANTIDOTES

Lest you begin wallowing in a sea of despair that winning must be virtually impossible as we carry around such heavy collections of emotional baggage, let us now move on to some solutions to these problems. The seven antidotes to the inherent problems surrounding selling consist of two attitudes to keep in mind and five prescriptions for positive action.

The most important single antidote to selling aversion is simple, although some may not find it easy to carry out. Taking this action is necessary if you are to succeed in investing. So I list it first because failure here will render moot the various other suggestions for improved selling success. Here it is: **You must give up on being perfect.** Perfectionism, no matter how deep a problem for you or what its specific cause(s) in your life experience, will predictably make you fail in investing. The perfectionist investor (or trader) has unreasonably high expectations of his or her potential in the market. This can manifest itself in near-paralyzing indecision even at the point of buying. But considerably heavier weight is brought to bear at the point of selling because of those closure-versus-freedom issues described earlier. Trying to execute a perfect exit from a stock, meaning at both its highest price to date *and* at a price it will never again reach, is an impossible standard. If you allow yourself to demand such perfection, you will die owning each of your present holdings. And even if you overcome your irrational need to be perfect in real time, your perfectionist tendencies will probably rear their ugly heads in the form of second-guessing after the fact. Any rise to a further price high literally measures the size of your mistake when you subtract the actual price you received on sale. And if you are spending mental energy punishing and questioning yourself, you are robbing yourself of full mental presence in making future decisions. The market is a difficult enough game without your trying to win it with some of your intellectual arsenal diverted to other (futile) pursuits. *You absolutely must let go.* Do the best you can in both buying and especially selling each stock or mutual fund, and walk away. I know that this flies in the face of all your training and culturally imposed expectations in other parts of life. But if you fail to do it, you will remain tied in mental knots and be unable to act skillfully at best, or perhaps not at all at worst. Think of an athlete who did not perform as he or she hoped at a prior crucial moment: If the athlete dwells on that past shortfall, his or her career is over. Instead, the athlete must put it away and move on, focusing fully on the next big moment and each smaller moment in between. There is no simple prescription for how to accomplish this, except to exert

sheer mental will and not allow yourself that irrational, unreasonable, perfectionist luxury. If you cannot do that, you cannot manage your own investments and must turn the process over to others.

Closely related to the above-described issue of perfectionism, but
applicable to all investors and traders even if they have conquered that
irrational primary profit killer, is our memory of our cost price in a stock.
Difficult as it may be, you need to put that number out of your mind. We
improperly anchor to that piece of historical data, in part because it is
vivid to us. Certainly, it has some importance. It defines the line in the
sand between profit and loss. However, in the large majority of cases that
price is irrelevant to the rest of the market's participants. Exceptions are
purchases in initial public offerings (where a large crowd of others keeps
that price prominently in mind); purchases at upside breakout points
(where a large number of technicians became aware of your stock's attraction); and instances in which your cost price coincides with a price area in
which heavy volume (distribution) was traded. (The special significance
of this third item is discussed in more detail in Chapter 7.)

Stock price action probably will be influenced by the proximity of
your cost price in the three cases cited because heavy trading took place
at or around such price levels. This is because a large crowd of other
investors or traders is (irrationally but undeniably) relating their opinions
about the stock to their own cost prices. In such cases the fact that many
others see as significant what coincidentally is also your personal cost
price means that it is likely that price reversals will occur when that price
is closely approached in the future. Crowds, which of course we measure
in terms of volume of stock traded, do exert a considerable influence on
future stock prices when they become excited by any fact or perception.
Putting aside those three specific exceptions, your cost price is irrelevant
to all other market participants. If you bought 500 or 1,000 shares and
the total trading that day was in the hundreds of thousands or millions,
and total trading since your purchase date has been in the multiple millions of shares, the fact of your purchase is as important to the market as
a single grain of sand on a beach. Unfortunately, because we as humans
anchor our behaviors around the events that have dotted our existence,
you have a normal but badly serving tendency to focus on your cost price.
Please, try to forget it. You measure profit or loss, and all the ego implications that attend those results, from your buy price. The rest of the market has no such memory of your trade. You will be prone to insisting on
getting even if and when your stock drops below your cost. That will
serve you badly. New fundamental and technical facts about that stock,

including how much volume has changed hands at various other price levels, are much more important. Our overly strong tendency to want to get our money back in a losing stock before allowing ourselves to consider other uses for that capital will have you focusing with misplaced zeal on waiting for your stock to return to breakeven. All I can say is, get over it! That price is a false goal you have set up and can do you no good. (And the older your position is, the less relevant it conceivably might be to the market.) Much more relevant are such factors as new fundamental news, overall trends in interest rates, and P/E levels *now,* and other prices on the chart that represent significant technical changes in status—not the least of which are historical or future trading volume increases or decreases. These will be covered in upcoming chapters. For now it simply must be taken on faith that you need to *forget your cost price.* Remembering it will adversely bias your future decisions.

Next we come to the first of two attitudes that I find essential to one's ability to outperform the market. First, this: Things change. If you insist on holding, by being unable to sell, please start to understand that at this moment, *your investing fate is out of your hands.* I will repeat my frank disclosure from an earlier chapter: I reject the notion that stock price movements are random as well as the inevitable implication thereof—namely, that one cannot outperform the market averages. The majority fails, but a minority does win. Those, in my experience, are investors and traders who understand the degree to which investor psychology (collectively, crowd irrationality) is the primary cause of price action. They watch for the footsteps they can predict, which so often can be measured by trading volume, and *they act when they see the signs.* I will categorically state that you must be able to sell as readily as you buy, in order to succeed at investing—let alone at trading! Unless you can sell, and sell reasonably well, your success depends on the permanent validity of your initial stock selections and on the good or bad timing (and therefore pricing) of your entry points. If you happened to succeed at buying during times of widespread market distress, you have a chance of outperforming the major averages. However, that assumes that the companies you chose to invest in will turn out to be among the rare few that survive for your investment lifetime and continue to produce sustained exemplary fundamental results. The latter is no more than a long-shot bet, especially as the competitive business world becomes more international and as technology changes at an accelerating pace.

Things change. AT&T directors were forced to cut dividends by over 80 percent in late 2000. This was the first reduction in dividends ever by that firm, and in this case "ever" includes through the Great Depression of the 1930s. Nothing is sacred. Look back to the list of Nifty Fifty stocks favored by institutional investors in the early 1970s. You will be shocked by the drastically changed fates of many. Consider that Woolworth, Bethlehem Steel, International Harvester, International Nickel, and assorted other once-dominant firms have long since exited the Dow Jones Industrial Average as has-beens. Remember the bankruptcies of Penn Central, TWA, Pan Am, Western Union, Massey Ferguson, and many more erstwhile leaders in their fields. W.T. Grant and, as of early 2001, Montgomery Ward are once-huge national names in retailing that are no more. Would you actually chose a portfolio of investments for a child or grandchild, and legally or otherwise lock yourself into an inability ever to sell? Most people laugh heartily at such a preposterous suggestion. However, many investors commit such a crime against their own capital after the fact. Somehow, of the many thousands of stocks and mutual funds that were available for purchase at various times in the past, those few actually chosen magically become sacrosanct and untouchable. The accident of present ownership can all too easily drive you to erect a mental prison in which you can make the mistake of trapping your money and your opportunity to grow your wealth for the long-term future—if you cannot sell. I always strongly hesitate to make any analogies between stock market investing and various forms of organized gambling. However, one comparison does seem appropriate here: Continuing to hold a stock for no more significant reason than that you once bought it is like religiously betting on the same horse every time it comes to the pole, regardless of its well-established record. If you cannot sell, your fate is out of your hands. And the picture actually darkens beyond that prospect: If you virtually cannot sell, you are doomed to selling poorly. If you are unable to pull the trigger to take a profit or to limit a loss, eventually you will arrive at a point of panic or intolerable pain and will sell a stock at a major loss. Fear and avoidance of pain are powerful drivers. If you cannot sell a stock reasonably well, I predict that at some point you will succumb to selling it unreasonably badly. Being able to sell well requires being able to sell readily.

A second point to remember about long-term holding: It implies that eventually your returns will become average, or as statisticians would say, regress to the mean. This is not a byproduct of alleged price-action randomness. It is a fact of business life. Companies and industries and technologies go through four major life stages: embryonic or developmental, growth, maturing, and decay. Not every company you might now own will survive over the long term. If you have chosen well, some will perhaps be great long-term winners for you. Others will crumble at worst or stagnate at best. A few might remain at length in the great mediocre middle, although survival and evolution theory suggest the opposite. If you buy and hold, the good will be offset by the bad, and your return over time will tend toward average. That sort of outcome should be unacceptable to you if you are working hard at your investment life—if you are reading serious investment books and applying other efforts toward outrunning the masses. Tom Bailey, an enduring major player at Stilwell Financial, the managers of the Janus Funds, was quoted by *The Wall Street Journal* as saying that "good long-term performance is good short-term performance[s] put together.* "If you are stuck as a helpless and passive holder, you are unable to nail down good short-term performance when you get it, and you also are doomed to suffering through periodic disastrous bear markets. All of that is a penalty of your own choosing if you cannot sell. And, as noted above, there is the very real chance that if you never sell well, you might actually sell badly when the emotional discomfort becomes unbearable.

Back now to some prescriptions for concrete action to ensure that you are able to sell when circumstances signal it is appropriate. *Cut your commissions costs to a minimum!* No, not by refusing to make and implement decisions as the reflexive antitrading academics would prescribe, but by moving your assets to deep-discount brokerage firms. Obviously, a commission dollar saved is an increased dollar in profit earned. But the importance of minimizing commissions per trade goes well beyond that. Two of the most frequently cited rationalizations millions of investors use for being "unable" to sell are commissions and taxes. These are convenient means of shifting the blame for inability to sell off oneself. How come you were somehow able to *buy* that stock, despite having to pay a commission? In decades of listening to investors and over a hundred speeches to investor groups, I have never once heard anyone say they cannot or could not or did not buy a stock because of the commission. Discomfort with selling, which runs deep for reasons explored in the preceding several pages, is easily covered up if you have a ready scapegoat. So get rid of that excuse. Open any financial newspaper or financial magazine, or surf to a major stock market Web page, and you will find dozens of brokerage firms offering trades for $10 and less. Use one or two of them (the suggestion of more than one will answer your possible convenient objection that the one firm you choose may suffer a Web site crash at an inopportune time).

As long as we have treated one major rationalization for people's professed reluctance to sell, let us dispose of the other. While ultimately

---

*December 29, 2000, p. C-19.

you cannot do anything about taxes except retain all your present holdings until you die, you ought to put that rationalization for inaction out of your repertoire too. Did you buy that stock before 1913 when the federal income tax was enacted? No? Well, then the existence of taxes is not a new rule surprisingly put into the book since halftime. You knew about taxes when you bought. I'll assume you did not become an investor out of a masochistic desire to lose money and thereby cleverly reduce tax collections. So how can you use the existence of taxes *now*, when it is time to sell, as a reason to hold a position that, on its merits, needs to go?

The following tool will help you know what to do and help you actually do it *because* you will know the action is correct. (While clearly we will never know future price action in advance, this tool provides some degree of certainty and thereby helps enable us to take action under conditions of uncertainty.) Risk aversion was a proper and indeed vital mechanism for human survival in cave-dwelling times. We learned to defer to the tribal leader and to the will of the group. We learned not to take risk by going forth on our own. There was strength in numbers and a high probability of death in individualism. Well, all of that serves us very badly in financial matters these many millennia later. We must take risk, and we must routinely part company with the group in order to make profits. One of the major virtues of using trading volume as a signaling system for making decisions on when to sell (and buy) and when to refrain is that volume by its nature both points out and measures the size of the crowd. And the crowd gains its unusual and unhealthy size only when a large number of people act at the same time, predictably but irrationally, in response to stimuli. Risk aversion, or comfort seeking, is primary on the list of drivers that consistently serve investors badly. The matrix in Figure 3–1 succinctly captures four classic comfort-seeking (or discomfort-avoiding) behaviors. Acting in the ways listed in the matrix literally amounts to a plan to buy high and sell low! It is also a recipe for avoiding bargains and for holding onto stocks that are overdue for price correction. *Avoid comfort-zone behavior in your investment decisions,* and you will routinely move opposite the crowd, which is driven by base animal instincts. This is a very hard thing to do, until you get into the practice and find how consistently it works. If you have ever been so excited about buying a stock that you could not wait for the market to open, and simply had to buy at market rather than miss being onboard, you were exhibiting comfort-zone behavior. If you have ever sold a perfectly good stock because the overall market was careening lower and you were scared out of your wits, you were diving for cash to avoid the discomfort of being in stocks. When the momentary set of circumstances becomes so intense that you feel overwhelmingly forced to take action, you will make a mistake that will soon be

FIGURE 3-1

Four Classic Comfort-Seeking Behaviors

		When a stock, or the market, is...	
A n d		**UP**	**DOWN**
a n i n v e s t o r i s	IN	Hold what is too hot because it makes our ego feel so good.	Bail out low, because we can no longer take the emotional (ego) pain.
	OUT	Jump in late so as to end estrangement from the group who have been enjoying huge, rapid gains. Stop missing the boat.	Avoid buying because things look really scary. Wait until prices have risen so you can feel more safe in buying.

evident. The reason is that your level of discomfort from failing to take action is being replicated in tens of thousands of other investors or traders at the very same time.

Together, those who take action in the direction that seems so unavoidable and necessary will form a large crowd whose decisions collectively create unusually large trading volume. Being part of the crowd is the natural and comfortable thing to do. It is also the unprofitable action at the time. It will seem very strange—indeed, uncomfortable!—but the next time you are panicked, do some buying. It will make you reach for the antacids, but in a day or two it will have you in a profitable position. After you have done this a number of times, despite the fact that at the time it seems intuitively backward, you will develop a serenity while all around you are losing theirs. You will sell into the huge volume of panic buying, and you will buy at bargain-basement prices when the crowd is selling in huge droves from panic. Arriving at those times when, in an individual stock or the whole market, volume is at frenzied levels will tell you when to do what others would tell you is foolish. They are doing what makes them in huge numbers feel comfortable; you will be doing the opposite, and it will make you more wealthy. You can regularly be on the correct side of transactions by noting when a crowd has formed (large volume of trading, with price moving sharply) and then by giving the wrong-headed mob what it wants. If it urgently wants cash (is panicking to sell), give it some of yours for some of its good stocks. If the crowd cannot stand to hold cash and insists in huge numbers on having more stocks, sell them some of your stocks that they most desperately want and take their unwanted cash. In short, move towards *dis*comfort!

My seventh suggestion, again a direct call for clear action, will aid you greatly in escaping the seemingly impossible tug of war between holding and selling. Clearly, we cannot actually know the future in detail, and, as discussed earlier in this chapter, we absolutely will not make perfectly correct choices all the time. We must act on our best *judgment* (not our instincts, as in the comfort-seeking paradigm above) and then move on. I have found countless times that a very good way of ending the debate about hold versus sell is to simply ask myself this: *Would I buy it right now at today's price?* Strangely ironic as it may seem, by thinking about buying, we can get good answers about selling. First, realize this: Holding is by its nature passive buying. When you hold, you are recommitting your capital for a future starting now, to exactly where it was up until this minute. With no commissions or taxes to pay and no conversation with a broker, when you hold you have sold and instantly repurchased the same stocks. Whether you do it by decision or by default is irrelevant. At any moment you could be 100 percent in cash if you so decided. Staying in the stocks you now own is the same as taking a cash position and buying exactly those stocks. Actively or passively, you have decided to put (keep) your capital there. Once you have defined holding as back-door buying, your hold-or-sell question becomes rephrased as, "Do I want to buy this, right now, at the current price?" Would you buy it if you had the cash available and such a move would not violate your intended asset-allocation balance? If you hold it, that is exactly what you will be doing—buying it for another day, or for whatever amount of time transpires before you next look at your portfolio.

Part of your decision about whether you'd presently be a buyer will of course be based on fundamentals—Is the P/E or the yield acceptable? Part will be based on technical action—How has the stock acted lately, and would that drive you to be a buyer or not? Importantly, the comfort-zone construct discussed above will be of help to you again here: If you find that the reasons you would be a buyer actually amount to seeking comfort or fleeing discomfort, the proper answer is that you should not buy now; therefore, you cannot logically hold. So you must sell.

AN ADMONITION: PUT CREDENCE IN VOLUME'S MESSAGE

We have explored seven suggestions that should help enable you to take action—especially when selling a stock is the question of the hour—more readily than you previously could. Woven through them on several occasions you have heard a recurring theme: Volume of trading tells an important story about what the irrational crowd is doing. Volume tells tales about the market and about the condition of individual stocks almost all the time, not merely when huge bursts of trading occur. We have only begun our exploration of what volume has to say and why it provides valid guidance for those who will listen and heed. I cannot emphasize too strongly that the way to achieve above-average returns is to take advantage of the unusual opportunities the market periodically provides, much as Benjamin Graham described taking psychological advantage of his manic-depressive business partner, Mr. Market. Market volatility and dominance by price-moving institutional giants makes it imperative and urgent as never before that you be able to act promptly. You must free yourself of vainly hoping never to make any mistakes, of never having an occasional stock-market regret. When you see signs that say it is time to act, you cannot profitably take the matter under lengthy advisement. Prices change a great deal in little time. Therefore, when you receive signals that action is called for, you must act rather than contemplate.

The signals that trading volume provides, which you will discover and explore and learn in the upcoming chapters, are useful exactly because they are based on a realistic assessment of the psychological factors that have prompted large numbers of other investors to act, or refrain from acting, in the same way at the same time. When triggers are very intense in a concentrated time period, they prompt irrational action by the crowd. You will always know why the crowd believes what it does: The news will be readily available on any stock market Web site or in any financial newspaper or magazine. Sometimes the very size of the trading volume in a given stock or market sector will tend to push you to believe that "everyone clearly knows something since they are obviously staking their money on it." That thought in itself is a volume signal. As we will explore (particularly in Chapters 9 and 10), when the crowd has finished acting on its passion of the moment, there cannot be enough investors or traders left to force price to continue to move in that same direction any longer. When the crowd is done, the price move is done. So believe what the volume data tell you.

PART TWO

TRADITIONAL VIEWS ON VOLUME

CHAPTER 4

Tick Volume and Daily Net Volume

One of the earliest-invented and most basic ways of tracking the patterns of trading volume is referred to as *tick volume,* or *net tick volume.* Some technical analysts also refer to this approach as tracking *on-balance volume* (OBV). A number of popular online technical analysis programs include an option of charting OBV, so it is easy to use without a major expenditure of personal tracking time. Our detailed explanation in this chapter of tick-volume analysis and daily net volume analysis will give you a well-structured context in which to understand the meaning of transaction volume. There actually is meaning in the details, so we must note and analyze them if we are to capture intellectual benefit from them. There is much more to the market's movements than price alone: Volume is an extremely valuable second dimension that actually gives price change increased and richer meaning.

ON-BALANCE, OR TICK, VOLUME

The premise underlying tick-volume analysis is that the volume associated with each individual trade indicates the amount of supply and demand for the stock at a particular price at a particular moment. Thus the change in price from one trade to the next indicates the source of greater pressure or urgency, whether from sellers or buyers, that drove the latest transaction. The latter point may be made more practical and specific by saying this:

> Trades on an uptick are assumed to be caused by more-urgent buyers, while trades on a downtick are assumed to be caused by more-urgent sellers.

> An *uptick* is defined as a trade that takes place at a higher price than the most recent prior trade that occurred at a different price. A *downtick* is a trade at a price lower than the most recent different price.

So, in a sequence of trades at 200, 201, 202, 201, 201, and finally 200, the first trade at 201 and the one made at 202 are upticks, while the second trade at 201 and the last one are downticks. The second consecutive trade at 201 is referred to as a *zero-minus tick,* or a *zero-downtick,* because it was at the same price (thus, zero change) as the prior trade, while that prior trade itself was a downtick.

Not only does the direction of each successive trade indicate that the present net pressure is stronger from among the buyers (uptick) or from among the sellers (downtick), the size of the trade matters as well. Thus, tick-volume students record the size of each sequential trade and keep a running plus-and-minus total of volume for the day (or over a longer, cumulative, time span). Their assumption is that a trade of 1,000 shares is more meaningful than a trade of 300 shares since the former represents a larger, more powerful and dedicated participant in the market.

Note the details of the sequence of trades listed in Figure 4–1 and the resulting tick-volume interpretation (for simplicity, we use a high-priced stock and pretend it trades only on round dollar prices).

Here we see a stock that tick-volume students would say is under accumulation during the minutes or hours covered by this 10-trade sequence. A total of 1,500 shares has changed hands from sellers to buyers, but it appears that the buyers are more urgent or exist in larger num-

F I G U R E   4 – 1

A Theoretical Sequence of Trades

Trade No.	Volume	Price	Net Tick Volume
1	100	$300	0 (prior price not known)
2	100	301	+100
3	200	302	+300
4	100	301	+200
5	200	302	+400
6	100	301	+300
7	300	302	+600
8	100	302	+600
9	200	303	+800
10	100	301	+700

bers than do the sellers. How can we draw that conclusion? Starting with trade 3, each of the trades that pushes the price higher is one of at least 200 shares, while each of the trades that results in a lower price is a smaller one, in this case of just 100 shares. So we can see that from the time of trade 2 to the consummation of trade 10, the price of the stock is unchanged on a net basis, while the volume tells us a richer story via tick-volume analysis: There has apparently been net accumulation by buyers who are more numerous, more powerful, and/or more urgent. [I have used the word "buyers" in the plural form, although it is possible that perhaps only one buyer (or seller) exists who is trying to accumulate (or dispose of) a larger overall position in small pieces—perhaps to camouflage from the rest of the market the size of his or her total interest.]

In the sequence of transactions just analyzed, trade 8 merits special discussion. This 100-share transaction took place on a zero tick, in that its price was equal to that in trade 7. Tick-volume students attach two differing interpretations, and resulting tallies of net tick volume, to such a trade.

In the list of trades presented, I have assigned no net volume value to trade 8, with the result that the cumulative net tick volume in the final column is unchanged. The alternative interpretation is that such a trade was made at a higher price than the most recent transaction at some other price and therefore should be counted as a net-plus tick. That school of thought might reason that trades 7 and 8 could have represented the same buyer (taking 100 shares each from two sellers a few minutes apart) and therefore it would be arbitrary to assign no net tick volume to the later trade (8). If the buyer had been satisfied in a single transaction that brought him or her 200 shares at once, the full 200 would have been counted as net positive tick volume.

The other way of looking at it, which is reflected in the mathematics I adopted in the listing, sees trade 8 in a different light. It assumes that one cannot know for sure whether trades 7 and 8 represented the same buyer, and therefore we must assume they did not. Trade 8, then, represents a different buyer than the prior trade. This buyer was able to find a seller at $302, not needing to bid higher to find a willing seller. Therefore, trade 8 is interpreted as representing an equilibrium moment in the market for this stock, when both a buyer and a seller appeared, each equally willing to transact business at $302, which was the latest prior price. This interpretation says that trade 8 represented neither a more-urgent buyer nor a more-urgent seller but instead a meeting of equally motivated parties on the two sides of the trade. For that reason, the trade should not be counted as a net accumulation event, and certainly it is not one in which a seller pushed the price lower either; thus it has zero tick-volume value.

Both interpretations arguably have merit. You can choose whichever makes intuitive sense; for proper tick-volume interpretations over time, all that is required is consistent application of the same rule to all zero-change trades. The one potential weakness of the zero-value interpretation occurs in the case in which, for example, the 8 trade might have been for 2,500 shares—considerably more than the typical trade in the overall sequence. The zero-value approach for no-price-change transactions would ignore (by zeroing out) the largest and potentially most significant trade of the day, merely and arbitrarily because it occurred after rather than before the 100-share trade 7.

At this point, it is worthwhile to step back and analyze why a collection of trades involving differing sizes at changing prices has significance. The simplest interpretation is that, clearly, buyers are seeking more shares in general than urgent sellers are trying to unload. This is true. But another and more sophisticated line of reasoning also applies; it has to do with the total sizes of the amounts of stock bid for and offered at various prices away from the immediate market price level. Here we must define the usual way of quoting a stock. The simplest quotation one can ask for (via broker conversation or via electronic inquiry) is the last sale price, or "last" for short. That is already "history," so to speak. If you were told that the last price was 57 and that the current spread (closest bid and ask prices) is 57 to 58, you could see that there is at least one willing buyer at 57 and no apparent sellers before the price would rise to 58. You might guess, probably correctly, that the trend of the price is upward and that the next trade is more likely to be made at above rather than below 57. But there is even more information available, beyond the quote or spread. This richer data trove—have you guessed?—consists of not only price but also *the amount of stock* that is being bid for and offered at the prices quoted.

Again, to limit the mental strain created by following the example, we will use round numbers, or full-dollar quotations. Except in very thinly traded securities, this would not be the actual pattern. Prior to decimalization, the reality surrounding a stock in the $50+ range might have been that it traded in eighths or even sixteenths. After decimalization, it may trade in dime or nickel or even penny price increments. Continuing the above-cited hypothetical example, suppose that you ask for a "quote and size" rather than for a simple "quote." You would be told not "57 to 58" but now "57 to 58, 10 by 15" or some such numbers. In sequence, these figures would tell you that

the best (highest) current bid price is $57 per share;

the best (lowest) current asking price is $58 per share;

and (the size) equals the following: There are 10 (100-share) blocks being bid for at 57 (thus a total of 1,000 shares wanted), while there are 15 (100-share) blocks being offered at $58 (a total of 1,500 shares for sale).

You know a bit more than earlier. Depending on whether this stock trades lightly or heavily, a difference of just 500 shares between sizes at the quoted bid and offer prices might or might not be significant. The heavier the usual trading volume, the less significant a difference of just 500 shares would be. There could be 10,000 shares bid at $56 and only 2,000 offered at $59, the prices next further away. Unfortunately, the specialist on the exchange floor is required to disclose only the nearest bid-and-ask prices and the sizes of total interest only at those prices. Therefore, electronic quotation systems carry no more than that information, so you would not see the very large bids standing at $56 unless all the bids for 1,000 shares at $57 were first satisfied with sellers willing to take market price to get out. Only then would the current quote and size reveal the 10,000 shares wanted at $56.

We began by supposing that the quote and size was "57 to 58, 10 by 15," and we discussed whether the difference of 500 shares between the two sides of the market might be significant. Suppose, however, that the quote and size were reported as "57 to 58, 10 by 150." Wow! From such a quote you would deduce that it will take only a little more than 1,000 shares of selling "at market" to push the stock down below 57 (the bid price) while it is going to take a much larger amount of buying to push the price above $58. That is because the "by 150" part of the quote and size answer means that there are 150 blocks of 100 shares (totaling 15,000 shares) being offered at $58. Therefore, to move the stock past 58 is going to require more than 15,000 shares in at-market orders, or that those sellers decide to cancel those orders at 58. The sizes of the bid-and-ask quote represent potential trading volume. Those buyers and sellers will have their orders "hit" (i.e., filled) only if and when enough at-market orders arrive to eat into the standing orders at specified prices (57 or 58). But by being told "10 by 150," you would have the knowledge that potentially a large volume of stock is being offered at 58, and therefore you would conclude that upward price movement in the near term is going to be more difficult to achieve than downward price movement. This knowledge of pending future trading volume might well influence whether you decide to place an order immediately, and if so, what kind of order (market versus limit) and at what specific price. Volume information (in this case, an indication of the size of probable *future* volume) has greatly enriched your

perception of the market's status and near-term outlook. Volume information indeed introduces a whole additional and very valuable further
dimension to your mental picture of the stock.

Having absorbed the meaning and significance of quote and size data,
you are now in a position to better understand what was probably happening as the sequence of 10 trades occurred in our mythical $300 stock.
Assuming that matching at-market buy and sell orders were not almost
magically arriving at the exchange at the same instants in time, you now
see that it was very likely that trades 2 through 10 were eating into the
price-limited orders previously placed for the stock. Specifically, starting
after trade 2 occurred, and continuing through the completion of trade 8,
the quote was probably "301 to 302." Trade 3 was probably an at-market
buy order for 200 shares, and it was apparently satisfied out of some
unknown supply of offers at $302. At least 200 shares must have been
offered at that level, or the buyer's order would have been filled as 100 at
$302 and the remaining 100 at an even higher price. Then comes trade 4.
This appears to be an at-market sell order of 100 shares. No one is bidding
$302, even though that was the last actual traded price, so the seller is filled
at the best standing bid, which is $301. So the stock ticks down a dollar to
$301, on just 100 shares.

Trades 5 and 6 precisely repeat the sequence and the description of
the apparent market circumstances as prevailed for 3 and 4. Both of the
later trades were presumably market orders, and each of the new market
participants was satisfied by using up part of the standing orders and volume at the bid-and-ask prices. So we can reasonably assume that there
were at least 400 shares offered at $302 (enough to satisfy buyers at trades
3 and 5). And we know that the size of the bid at $301 was at least 200
shares since that price prevailed when the sellers causing trades 4 and 6
were satisfied. Now comes trade 7, a buy of 300 shares. It is also satisfied
at an uptick to $302, meaning that apparently there had originally been at
least 700 shares offered there (or else the price would have needed to go
higher to find sellers of 700 in total). So we can see from our tick-volume
analysis that during the recent sequence of trades there has been a preponderance of buying pressure (those uptick trades occurring on volumes
of 200 or more while the at-market sell orders were each for only 100
shares). Net tick volume is telling its observers that even though the price
is fluctuating between $301 and $302, there appears to be more pressure
from buyers than from sellers.

Now comes that very interesting trade 8. It is subject to various interpretations, as discussed earlier. One possibility is that someone who
owned the stock saw it all the way up at $302 and decided to sell at mar-

ket, at the very same time another trader saw the stock acting well and decided to buy at market. These orders would be matched at or near the last price, which was $302 at the time. That possibility argues for a zero tick score for trade 8 since it represents an even standoff between new buying and selling pressure. Clearly we did not have an at-market seller alone, for that would have dropped the stock to $301 again, so obviously the 100 shares here cannot reasonably be counted in the selling-pressure column. Another interpretation is that we were observing in trade 8 an at-market buyer being satisfied by the overhanging pool of sellers willing to take $302. That view sees 8 as continued net buying pressure, implying that 8 should be scored as a net plus in the tick-volume tally. We cannot be positive.

Trade 9 gives us some new information. Since it moved the price up to a new level of $303, we can reason that, first, it clearly represents buying pressure (count a plus 200 shares in the tick-volume cumulative total) and, second, apparently the existing overhanging supply of shares at $302 has been exhausted by trade 8. Because no more stock was available to satisfy new at-market buyers at $302, the new net buying pressure forced the price up in order to find a willing seller. Third, we can now (but only after the fact) deduce that a total of 800 or 900 shares had been offered at $302 (depending on the interpretation of transaction 8)—and those shares were taken by our at-market buyers at trades 3, 5, 7, and possibly 8. (This of course assumes for simplicity that no new limit offers at $302 came in at the back of the line and that no old offers at that price were pulled while we were watching the sequence of trades unfold.)

Trade 10—100 shares on a $2 downtick to $301—clearly counts in the sellers' column as we tote up net on-balance tick volume. It also tells us that, at least temporarily, there have been no more buyers willing to pay $302, even though the stock has last traded at $303. Maybe the buyer or buyers that caused the earlier upticks have been satisfied, or maybe they have stepped away so as not to drive the market higher before they bid for more shares. In any event, we do see that apparently there are still buyers at $301, although we have no idea how many. Right after trade 10 occurs, it would be a very good time to ask for a new quote and size, to see how large the buyer pool at $301 still is.

To recap, then, we have seen that between trades 2 and 10, apparently a net buying pressure of about +700 (some would say, +800) shares has been observed to be satisfied. The tick-volume follower would conclude that while price has not changed on balance (starting and finishing at $301), the situation is healthy in that there has been more buying than selling pressure, evidenced by the volume of the individual trades. A positive tick-volume story would encourage potential buyers, and perhaps also existing holders, to remain technically bullish about the stock in the very short term.

Tick-volume students would plot a line representing cumulative net volume, below the graph of prices. In the case of the example discussed here, the price would be unchanged on a net basis while the tick-volume or on-balance line would have risen by a net of 700 (or 800) shares. The interpretation of this picture would be that there is slight positive divergence in that the volume line is stronger (rising) than the price line (net, flat). Therefore, one would say that there has been less net selling pressure than buying pressure, so the stock was technically healthy over the near term.

It is important to note that tick-volume or on-balance volume studies will not at every moment or even every day give a meaningful reading. A parallel reading does not yield much useful information when the plot is running in the same direction as the price change. Divergence, however, is supposed to be of predictive value. In the extremely brief sequence of trades in our sample, the divergence was positive in terms of volume pressure, implying accumulation of the stock by buyers we deemed to be more powerful, numerous, or urgent than the sellers. If the net tick volume had been negative against a flat price trend, the tick-volume interpretation would have been that the stock was under distribution—a negative portent of the future.

It clearly is possible to plot a cumulative net tick-volume line from trade to trade throughout the day. This type of plotting could become extremely large in the horizontal dimension over a period of many market days. For this reason, many tick-volume or on-balance volume followers will choose instead to plot a daily graph showing the stock's opening, high, low, and closing prices as a vertical bar with tick marks, and they will plot the entire day's net tick volume or OBV as a single upward or downward plot on the volume scale. This type of graph is economical in terms of space and yet still contains the richness of the day's net volume information. Over a period of three or more days, a net tick-volume trend might emerge from the successive individual plottings, telling a story about accumulation versus distribution, or buying versus selling urgency or pressure. Again, it will be the *difference* in the direction of OBV over time, if any, as compared with price direction, that tells a predictive story about price. Price alone might say little, but the addition of trading-volume information enriches the overall picture of what is happening in the market.

Some followers of the OBV technique will apply it to the overall market by plotting totaled net tick volume of all or selected stocks (perhaps the Dow 30) against the net price movement of the market indicator.

At times this will prove of some value. However, in today's institutionally dominated market (see Chapter 8 for much more on that subject), it is possible that concentrated, huge-volume selling or buying pressure in a single stock in response to news may skew the mathematical result. For example, suppose that AT&T is downgraded by a prominent analyst, and as a result, its trading volume for the day is 25 million shares with a net tick volume of minus 6 million. Suppose that each of the other 29 Dow stocks experiences a fairly trendless day but quietly shows accumulation of 100,000 shares on a tick-volume basis. In this example, the net tick volume of the Dow components would be computed as minus 3.1 million shares for the day (plus 2,900,000 shares for the other 29 components, minus 6,000,000 shares for AT&T). In that instance, would you say the market evidenced true net selling pressure, such that you would interpret the day negatively? Probably not. One stock's extreme behavior happened to overbalance and mask the action shown by 29 others that all moved in the opposite direction. Therefore, I would advise caution in applying the OBV technique to groups of stocks. Further, by doing so one is literally illustrating the dangers of the proverbial mixing of "apples and oranges." For example, a positive tick volume of a million shares in a $50 stock means there was apparently $50 million of net buying power exerted. A negative tick volume of 2 million shares in some other $20 stock means $40 million of net selling pressure there. Together, we see a net inflow of $10 million of money, which should be interpreted as a positive for the "overall market"—and yet the net tick volume of the two stocks combined reads as a negative 1 million shares. The latter "net" reading is not meaningful because it represents the admixture of some $20 shares with other, $50, dissimilar shares.

DAILY NET VOLUME

As compared with the rather detailed and intuitively logical tick-by-tick volume-tracking approach just described, daily net volume is a simple approach that has some rough edges. It was developed for use many decades ago, in the precomputerization age when daily newspapers formed the primary source of information on stock transactions for the public investor not able to follow the market on a full-time, real-time basis. It has its significant limitations because of the way it handles data. The major theoretical objection to the use of daily net volume in a cumulative sum-and-difference approach as described above is that the daily net volume approach arbitrarily assigns all of the day's volume to the net price change direction of the day. As we saw in the preceding example, there can be differences between the net price change and the true tick-by-tick volume total. Let us consider the example again to explore that aspect.

Suppose we add to the trades listed in Figure 4–1 a few more trades before the day's trading comes to a close, as shown in Figure 4–2. Suppose further that trade 1 is the morning's opening transaction, which was in fact unchanged from the prior trading date's closing price of $300 per share. Therefore, since today's closing price is $299 (the price of trade 16), we say that for the day our stock closed "down 1." And yet our tick-volume analysis indicates that the net volume for the day was a positive 600 shares. Perhaps the price decline late in the session reflected general market weakness caused by some news unrelated to this company; this appears plausible since the stock fell off from $303 to $299 mainly on small trades and with net negative tick volume of only 200 shares (from trade 9 to 16 at the close). So, we conclude, there was hardly any urgency to the afternoon selling here. The day's final trade, apparently a 300-share buy order since it created an uptick, might even have been the morning's persistent 200- or 300-share buyer coming back to scoop up a little more stock at a relative bargain; maybe that buyer will be in action again tomorrow morning.

Every observation one might make about the stock on this day thus seems positive—with the single exception being that it closed "down $1" for the day. Yet, the *daily* net volume approach views this day as a negative one because the closing price for the session was lower than that on the prior day. Total volume for the day was 2,400 shares, and the daily net volume approach will have its follower assigning a negative sign to that number since the stock closed down. In effect, the daily net volume view of the stock ignores all the details of all the trades until the closing bell. It then compares today's close with yesterday's close and assigns a direc-

FIGURE 4–2

Continuation of the Theoretical Sequence of
Trades Given in Figure 4–1

Trade No.	Volume	Price	Net Tick Volume
11	100	$302	+800
12	100	301	+700
13	200	300	+500
14	100	299	+400
15	100	298	+300
16	300	299 close	+600

Source: BigCharts.com; used by permission.

tional sign accordingly, in this case negative. It then attaches the entire day's activity (in this case, some 2,400 shares) to that directional sign. You can see that at least on occasion the daily net volume method might misclassify a whole day's activity as to direction. It will not necessarily do this regularly, as it can well be argued that on most days the net price change may be in the same direction as the net volume change. Thus the day's activity would be posted in the proper way: positive or negative.

There are further possible scenarios in which the daily net volume approach may create a misimpression of a stock's internal strength. For example, suppose on Monday the stock is up 2 points on a total volume of 15,000 shares. Further suppose that on Tuesday the stock is sharply higher in the morning, trading up as much as 5 points, but then the afternoon sees a retreat wipe out all but 1 point of that gain. Suppose the morning volume (mainly on the upside) was 12,000 shares and the afternoon volume (mainly on the downside) was 13,000 shares. Because the stock still managed to close higher for the day overall, despite having wiped out nearly all of its early gain, the daily net volume approach assigns a plus sign for the day, and it counts the day's total volume of 25,000 shares as positive volume in its cumulative historical total. Thus this approach says Tuesday (which many would consider a bearish high-volume reversal day) is counted as even more bullish than Monday, when the stock finished up twice as much on lower volume. As you can see, there is a great deal behind the mathematics in a system like this, and one must pry open the lid and look inside before giving it simple and cheery acceptance. Again, the major questionable aspect of the daily net volume method is that it ignores all trades during the session as to their individual characteristics and assigns a net volume direction to the stock as if the closing trading price were the only tick of the day and carried all the session's volume with it. Quite a mathematical fiction!

WEAKNESS OF BLIND RELIANCE ON MATHEMATICAL FORMULAS

To be fair, however, one should note that the two examples given are possible exceptions to the general expectation that "up days" in price terms will generally be accomplished on positive tick volume and "down days" on negative tick volume. Therefore, it can reasonably be argued, most days the daily net volume approach should produce appropriate rather than misleading signals. Thus, it would be argued by supporters, most of the time this method is valid. It is quite true that no technical analysis method based on rigid mathematical rules can be expected to produce perfect results all the time, and therefore exceptions must be tolerated.

Even the net OBV approach described earlier can be criticized on the basis that sometimes the price direction on consecutive trades is caused by a sweeping move in the overall market rather than by specific supply-and-demand changes for the stock under study. For example, if the Federal Open Market Committee (FOMC) issues a pronouncement on its view of interest rate trends that spooks the stock market, a rapid decline of a few percent in major market averages might occur within an hour or two. During that period, buyers in the stock we are watching for tick volume may simply stand aside and wait for the general market to find support. Therefore, that particular stock might well fall as if through a vacuum of buyers on several consecutive trades, officially recording negative tick volume in the process. Does that action reflect directly on the stock itself? Hardly. It was caused by the market. At the most extreme, perhaps the few sellers that caused the downticks were getting margin calls on other stocks and chose to sell our issue to meet them. In no way do their sell orders represent any urgency to sell *our* stock specifically. And yet, their trades count as negative tick volume in the overall scheme. No system is perfect.

SUMMARY OBSERVATION

For all the exceptions and caveats, however, systems of tracking volume associated with price change have value because they reflect an underlying truth: Stock prices rise because there are more and more urgent buyers than sellers, and declines occur when there are more and more urgent buyers taking action. Therefore, if you count the volume and watch the direction in which price moves when volume is heavier, most of the time you will be seeing a valid indication of the net strength of supply and demand for the stock in question. Ultimately, the relative size of the pool of buyers versus that of sellers must drive the net price direction. In the next chapter, we will assume that most of the time the volume and the price change are not being artificially influenced or skewed and that therefore one can indeed use day-to-day volume patterns over time to judge a stock's technical strength.

CHAPTER 5

Daily Up or Down Price-and-Volume Combinations

As we developed in Chapter 4, a key concept to bear in mind is that *the amount of trading volume within a given trading period for a stock is important and useful information.* While popular Internet-available charting programs allow the users to display data in intervals from 1 minute up to 1 month, it appears that the most commonly tracked and probably the most intuitively meaningful time unit is the day. This seems logical or sensible since our lives are organized into day-and-night combinations. We sleep, arise, bathe, and work (or play) in daily units or cycles. A child's early patterns are formed around daily routines—first the comings and goings of the parents (in *their* daily pursuits) and the routines of darkness and light marking proper times for sleeping and resuming activity; then soon a rhythm of packing off to daycare and then school—and returning later on—all exactly once per day. The concept of daily repetition is so strongly absorbed that sometimes children have difficulty with our adult shift from weekdays to weekends. Try explaining to a 3-year-old why he or she cannot go to spend this day in fun with their daycare friends simply because it is Saturday!

Thus, we see that the rhythm and routine of days is important in our civilization. As adults, we absorb and create patterns centered around the 24-hour clock. Beyond the basics of sleep and waking, we take a standard number of meals (one each of three differing kinds) per day; we commute to work once daily; we read a given newspaper each day; and we gather added news of the world—including the financial sphere—in personal habit-formed ways: a certain radio news program while driving home, perhaps a certain TV network's evening news hour, and maybe the 11 o'clock news as a routine preface to retiring to bed.

THE TRADING DAY AS A MEANINGFUL UNIT

In recent years, increasing numbers of us consult favorite Internet sources for news daily, and in many cases at the same time(s) of day—all as part of our daily routine. The news media report happenings in the investment world in daily slices, reflecting the historical practice of trading exchanges to open and close daily at set hours: trading sessions. It has been well documented that the predictably largest average price changes occur overnight—between the closing bell one day and the opening of trading the next. A good deal of additional information, especially including developments overseas, accumulates overnight but in addition, investors or traders sometimes formulate a revised outlook and approach since the previous day's close. A significant part of that revised mindset is based on reports we have digested about what happened in the market itself in the prior day's trading session. In both our broader personal existences and our investing lives, multiple days tend to blend together. While we turn the calendar page once monthly and note the coming of a new calendar year on cue, our major perceived unit of time is a day's worth. Therefore, much of our study of the stock market's movements—as contrasted with our study of companies' fundamental progress and value—is based on the day unit. So we will spend the greatest amount of our study of trading volume focused on the trading day as a meaningful unit.

Because of the strong influence our daily rhythm, we naturally perceive and react to movements in the stock market when measured in per-session or daily units. While the electronic media, highly equipped with access to historical databases, *could* report stocks' movements in differing or lesser time units, they tend not to. Occasionally we see references to year-to-date price movements and to 52-week high and low price ranges. But almost never will we be shown price (or volume statistics) on a basis other than the end of a calendar day. For example, a report of a stock's price change from noon yesterday to noon today would seem to us striking or strange for its uniqueness. The full trading day is our standard unit of reference. Except for those who are professional (and especially intraday) traders, we judge how stocks have performed on a net basis from one day's closing moment to the next day's close. Therefore, the study of volume on a daily basis is potentially equally as important as the much more widely practiced watching of net daily price change. This chapter focuses on the meaning and importance of combinations of rising and falling prices and trading volumes measured per full daily session.

MINIMUM INCREMENTS OF PRICE AND VOLUME CHANGES

On any given trading day, a particular stock can finish the session above, at, or below its final price of the prior trading session. Common parlance is "up," "unchanged," and "down." Historically, the minimum increment of price change in the U.S. market for all but the lowest-priced stocks was $1/_8$ point, worth $0.125. Years ago, I read somewhere that this derived from "pieces of eight" and Spanish dubloons. In the 1990s, trading in intervals of $1/_{16}$ ($0.0625) per share was mandated and then became more commonplace. The introduction of *decimalization,* or trading in one-penny price intervals, begun in summer 2000 and accomplished fully in 2001, raises an interesting question: How small a net price change for the day, after hundreds of transactions have taken place, is meaningful? Is a one-cent net gain or loss in price (following a price range of perhaps $1.50 per share) actually significantly different from no change at all—the status that traditionally has been labeled "unchanged"? For practical purposes, we must still deal with the concept of "unchanged" because it exists. (Some market technicians try to interpret the meaning of an unchanged price by looking at the stock's direction late in the day, or by noting—as in candlestick charting—whether the last price was above or below the morning's opening level; others choose simply to ignore days of unchanged prices.) However, by far the most common condition for a stock's price is to be up or down on a net basis for the trading day. Given that general observation, one can characterize each stock's performance for a given trading day not only in one dimension (price change) but, more meaningfully, in two dimensions: *price as well as trading volume.* Thus, we have the matrix shown in Figure 5–1 for identifying a stock's behavior for each trading session: On any given day, excluding days of zero net price change and the extremely rare occurrence of daily volume exactly equal from one day to the next, one can record a stock as falling into any one of the four boxes.

One could certainly argue that trading volume in individual stocks should be viewed in the context of relative activity in the overall market. For example, with activity extremely slow on the Friday after Thanksgiving, it could well be argued that a stock whose own Friday volume was down 5 percent from its Wednesday level was "more active" on Friday if trading on the NYSE as a whole was down by 40 percent or more.

FIGURE 5-1

A Matrix for Identifying a
Stock's Behavior

Especially in the absence of corporate news, which tends to stimulate trading activity, such reasoning seems fairly compelling. In your own tracking and interpretation of individual stocks' price *and volume* movements, you may indeed wish to make such mental adjustments to the reported raw numbers. (Similarly, many market observers credit a stock that closes the session unchanged with an "up day" if the overall market was markedly lower.) Such mental adjustments may in fact enable you to classify all daily price and volume movements as legitimately fitting into one of the four boxes in our matrix.

Interpreting the matrix is quite straightforward on an intuitive basis. As discussed in Chapter 1, a change in the volume of trading in a stock from day to day (or, for that matter, from hour to hour and so on) indicates a change in the amount and intensity of interest in buying and/or selling that security. When trading volume doubles, it is safe to assume that shareholders representing twice as many shares decided today to buy and sell, as had been the case yesterday. Price changes become all the more richly meaningful when one overlays the volume dynamics involved. Thus, we can deduce intuitively and logically that a price movement accomplished on heavier trading volume carried more information than an equal price change accomplished in lighter trading. In effect, the tally of trading volume counts the size of the crowd: More shares were urgently bought on an up day accompanied by rising volume, or more shares were urgently sold when price declined in heavier trading. If price change measured in the arbitrary time unit from one day's closing bell to the next is worth observing, then change in volume during that span is equally notable.

INTERPRETING COMBINED CHANGES IN PRICE AND VOLUME

Because we know that the size of the crowd interested enough to trade in a given stock is a meaningful piece of information, it is important to record changes in the size of the crowd. (For purists, we admit to defining the size of the crowd in terms of its economic clout—that is, by how many shares it represents, rather than the number of decision makers behind those buying and selling decisions. Economic markets are not organized on a one-person/one-vote principle.) In the illuminating world of volume dynamics, change in volume is every bit as important as change in price; the two together are more than twice as meaningful as either alone.

We now arrive at crucial interpretations of the combined changes in volume and price: *What happens on greater volume is more indicative of trends than what happens on lighter volume:*

> Price up accompanied by greater volume is bullish.

> Price down accompanied by greater volume is bearish.

Rather than ignoring what happens on days when volume is lighter than on prior or following days, we can reasonably interpret action on lighter-volume days as being a resting or countertrend phenomenon. No matter how wonderful a stock's fundamental story, experience clearly reminds us that its price does not and cannot rise every day. There are days when profit takers become anxious to cash in some of their paper gains, and there are days when an overall negative mood in the market keeps otherwise bullish investors sitting on their hands and postponing intended buying. On such days, price is likely to recede from its prior level, in which case one can interpret the combination (price and volume both lower) as not being bearish. Conversely, if a stock (or the overall market) has been declining in fairly active trading, on a day in which selling abates, or some bargain hunters appear, or in which some buyers react to favorable background news and thus raise prices—but with lower trading volume—the change can really not be interpreted bullishly. Thus, price up on lower volume is bearish. Therefore, we conclude that the interpretations in Figure 5–2 of the four boxes in our matrix are valid.

FIGURE 5-2

A Matrix for Identifying a
Stock's Behavior

	Volume	
	Higher	**Lower**
PRICE		
Up	Bullish	Bearish
Down	Bearish	Bullish

One should not slavishly buy or sell stocks immediately upon noting a day demonstrating bullish or bearish characteristics, respectively. What is more meaningful than a single day's indications is a stock's tendency—perhaps the predominance of its collected signals—over time. Figure 5–3 gives an example of 15 days' volume and price readings for an imaginary stock. In this example, the net price movement is flat during the 3 weeks, but overall there have been more days when the volume and price combination has been bullish. Thus, the person looking at price alone would see the stock in a neutral light, while he or she who watches volume as well would have a richer picture and, in this case, a bullish interpretation—via volume dynamics—of the sideways *price* action.

Unfortunately, the investment markets do not always give perfect technical signals based on the same length of observation windows. (The "market" is the sum of the actions of hundreds of thousands of individuals' decisions each day, and humans are not mathematically predictable, mechanical actors on the stage.) Therefore, it is impossible to say that the tracking of preponderantly bullish and bearish signals from our daily-basis volume and price matrix over some precise span of days (for example, 10 days, as above) will give perfect entry and exit points. Probably periods as short as 5 days are too short to be meaningful: Even strong bull markets occasionally take a week or longer to pause and digest their gains.

FIGURE 5-3

Fifteen Days' Theoretical Volume and Price Readings for an Imaginary Stock

Day	Price Close	Price Change	Volume	Volume Change	Signal	10-Day Percent Bullish
1	22		10,000			
2	22.25	+0.25	15,000	Heavier	Bullish	
3	22.50	+0.25	16,000	Heavier	Bullish	
4	22.75	+0.25	12,000	Lighter	Bearish	
5	22.25	−0.50	11,000	Lighter	Bullish	
6	22.00	−0.25	8,000	Lighter	Bullish	
7	22.25	+0.25	11,000	Heavier	Bullish	
8	22.50	+0.25	9,000	Lighter	Bearish	
9	22.75	+0.25	18,000	Heavier	Bullish	
10	22.50	−0.25	20,000	Heavier	Bearish	
11	22.25	−0.25	12,000	Lighter	Bullish	$\frac{7}{10} = 70\%$
12	22.00	−0.25	14,000	Heavier	Bearish	$\frac{6}{10} = 60\%$
13	22.50	+0.50	23,000	Heavier	Bullish	$\frac{6}{10} = 60\%$
14	22.25	−0.25	15,000	Lighter	Bullish	$\frac{7}{10} = 70\%$
15	22.00	−0.25	11,000	Lighter	Bullish	$\frac{7}{10} = 70\%$

Much longer periods such as 50 or 200 days, however, are likely to exhibit clear-majority signals only with some delay after price has already begin reversing. A change in the majority reading for a given stock over some shorter time period is usually useful, especially if that reading contrasts with the overall market's general direction. For example, if the general market is moving sideways or lower and a given stock starts showing combinations of predominantly bullish volume and price action, something notable is happening in that stock that is bullishly out of line with the overall average trend.

CONSIDERING THE CONTEXT OF PRICE AND VOLUME CHANGES

It is important to note that the analysis above is confined to a single stock; it does not compare volume in one stock to that in another, nor does it try to relate the individual issue's volume to the total on its exchange. That having been said, it is worth noting that occasionally one might consider the broader context and therefore mentally adjust the signals provided by the raw data. As an example, consider the Friday immediately after Thanksgiving in the U.S. market, virtually an unofficial holiday, a day when trading volume is usually extremely light. Suppose that on that day an individual stock you are watching for its volume and price action combinations should display only slightly lower volume than on the pre-holiday Wednesday—without any published news trigger. You could reason that in relative terms your scrutinized stock had *higher* volume on Friday—that the overall trading dropped by maybe 50 percent while your stock's activity was only 10 percent slower. On that basis you might justifiably consider the volume on that Friday to be up rather than down, and you could record it as such, perhaps with a footnote. On an everyday basis, however, I would not recommend the effort of calculating relative volume change (stock versus overall market) since investors that track daily volume and price dynamics are not doing so and therefore you would be giving yourself a false signal. Virtually all traders who are watching a stock's volume as a clue to its possible future price direction most certainly watch actual (not adjusted) volume!

Another important qualifier must be added to our views on the virtues of following daily price and volume trends. These can be used nearly all of the time, but with three important exceptions. One is when the timing is immediately prior to the quarterly earnings-per-share (EPS) release date for the company you're watching. In that case, clearly the imminent injection of major fundamental news into the information mix means that all technical bets are off. The news will dominate the next price move: The stock will be unchanged or slightly higher if the news is good ("good" meaning against consensus expectations); if the news is bad, the stock will decline quite sharply. It will prove foolhardy to follow technical signals such as volume and price dynamics immediately before predictably major fundamental news is about to be announced. A very fine Web site will prove quite useful in this regard and will save you the cost and time of phoning a company's investor relations office:

>   http:/biz.yahoo.com/research/earncal/

After reaching this page, merely enter the ticker symbol of the stock you are studying and hit "go." You will be shown the date on which the next EPS news is expected. Interestingly, and also importantly, the table displayed also indicates the date on which staff maintaining the database most recently verified the timing with corporate management. Another way of using this valuable Web site is to enter today's date or tomorrow's in order to see what stocks are due to report immediately. Better to be in the know than in the dark!

VOLUME CRESCENDOS AND SPIKES

Two other situations exist in which reliance on the usual signals given by our daily volume and price matrix must be suspended. These are in cases of volume crescendos and volume spikes. As Chapter 9 will explain, crescendos that persist for more than about 5 days are quite unusual, and they imply that at least on a short-term basis the stock's price move has been exhausted and is likely to reverse or correct. Therefore, if you have been watching the daily volume and price dynamics of a stock and are about to buy or sell (or short) it on that basis, be sure that the final 5 days or so in your window do not represent a crescendo of rising volume. This means that the crowd has already assembled and taken action on the stock, and you would be quite late to enter at that point.

Our final exception to the regular use of the daily volume and price combination matrix relates to volume spikes, as will be discussed in some detail in Chapter 10. A volume spike for a given stock is a day's trading that is many, many times the prior day's trading and is well above average for the past year. Often a spike is *the* highest-volume day in a year or two. Without having read and absorbed what Chapter 10 reveals, you might be highly impressed by the volume on the spike day and would be prone to taking buy or sell action in the same direction as the market moved on that day. That would be a big mistake. A spike in volume, virtually always occurring coincident with—and causing—a sharp gap in price, represents a major informational and psychological watershed in the stock and cannot be ignored. Routinely acting on your findings from our daily volume and price matrix would be like foolishly conducting business as usual right after a major scenario-changing event. To avoid spoiling the plot of Chapter 10, for now let us simply but strongly say not to follow the matrix's signal when or shortly after a volume or price spike has occurred.

ACCUMULATING VOLUME OVER A WEEKLY OR MONTHLY INTERVAL

A legitimate question might be, Can the technique explained here be adapted for more leisurely use, such as by accumulating volume over a weekly or monthly interval and observing the net price change over that time frame? I would advise against it. Not only have I never seen any recommendations of that technique nor observed any practicing technicians use it, but it makes little intuitive sense. In terms of today's rapidly moving investment markets, a week (let alone a month!) is a fairly long time window. A lot of news and a lot of technical signs occur during such time frames. People, especially those who look at the markets from trading and technical viewpoints, think in daily time units and operate on a daily rhythm. Over the course of a week, the combining or mixing of 5 days' volume and price information could very well conceal internal details of great value. Suppose, for example, that volume on Monday is quite heavy and the price rises a good deal in dollar or percentage terms. Suppose that the volume on the remaining days of the week is average to slightly subpar, but price drifts moderately lower. Daily signals might indicate a preponderance of bullish observations. Suppose that the stock actually closes Friday down on light volume due to a general market downdraft, but as a result, it is down slightly for the calendar week. In that case, the accumulated volume for the week will be high because of the high Monday activity (which was bullish) so the signal will say "volume up, price down = bearish." In a similar way, a whole month's data, when combined into a single net observation, can be dominated by one or two high-volume days (or large price-movement days driven by the general market direction). In that case, the reading would be meaningless. (Likewise, intraday traders would see full-day data as too slow and too cumulative and would prefer net volume and price change readings on an hourly or 30-minute basis for their purposes.) In my experience, daily is the most useful window length for this indicator.

SUMMARY

The daily volume-and-price matrix tracks ongoing, but routine, changes in buying and selling interest in a stock. Days of higher volume are days when the predominant direction of price pressure (from sellers or from buyers) is being revealed. Days of lower volume are resting or short-term correcting days. A predominance of bullish or bearish combinations of daily price and volume data, rather than a single day's signal, is what to seek and act on. But neither a very short nor very long time window works. Finally, be sure to observe the relatively infrequent but very strong exceptions mentioned just mentioned above, when it is wise to suspend use of the daily matrix.

CHAPTER 6

TRIN, or the Arms Index

One of the very earliest, if not the first, of the formalized ways of using trading-volume data came into acceptance in the late 1960s. This chapter summarizes and explains it, which is important since the original book disclosing and deeply exploring it is now out of print.* The so-called Arms Index, named after its inventor, is valuable in an operational sense primarily for short-term swing traders, although it also has considerable merit for longer-term traders for timing purchases and sales. TRIN, as The Arms Index is now most commonly known, is very important to understand as an analytical tool. Its basis in theory—namely that trading-volume behavior is a central body of knowledge for understanding where the market is headed—lines up almost perfectly with our thinking.

A BRIEF HISTORY OF TRIN

In 1964, neither the personal computer nor the electronic spreadsheet had yet been invented. Compiling data was a laborious, manual process unless one could afford computer power, and even then the data needed to be keypunched onto IBM cards and fed into the system. Programs that now run in seconds often took hours to complete. We who actively invest in the new millennium have an amazing array of information and tools available to us—largely free as well—as compared with what existed less than 40 years ago. Until 1965, the major stock exchanges did not, until after the close of trading, tally and publicly release volume statistics on stocks that

---

*Richard W. Arms, Jr.: *Profits in Volume*, Investors Intelligence, Larchmont, New York, 1971.

were up versus the volume of activity in stocks that were down. The intro-duction of this data made possible a whole new dimension in technical analysis *during* the market session. Prior to that time, if we wanted to compute what is now known as TRIN, we would need to add up by hand the individual volumes of all 1,500 or so stocks traded on the New York Stock Exchange. The data might be available to us if we lived in a city where late editions of the evening newspapers carried full NYSE tables and closing volumes. More likely, we would need to wait for the morning papers. The job would be mind numbing, and we would not finish before trading had already started on the new day.

In 1965, all of that changed for the better. The stock exchanges began releasing, during the trading session and with only a few minutes' delay, the counts of advancing and declining stocks and the totals of their trading volumes. The exchanges' huge mainframe computers made this new information available. Richard Arms, Jr., then a stockbroker with an old-name regional brokerage firm in Boston, quickly saw huge insight to be gained by tracking the newly available data. He reasoned that calculat-ing a fairly simple ratio would enable a market technician to discern whether the pressure, the urgency, or the heaviest action occurring on the exchange floor was more in the rising stocks or more in the decliners. That knowledge would tip off the technician to which way the "smart money" was moving and should be a reliable indicator of imminent shifts in price direction.

Underlying all of this is what we have been emphasizing in prior chapters: Price and price change are merely by-products of transactions between buyers and sellers. Those trades occur because buyers and sellers are sufficiently convinced (by whatever combination of factors) to take the action of placing an order. The relative (im)balance of buying and selling orders, measured in shares rather than in number of trades, determines the predominant direction of prices. If there are lots more shares demanded than present holders are willing to give up at the current price, supply-and-demand economic theory says that a higher equilibrium price will need to be set in order to find enough sellers to meet the demand. So we surmise that if the price rose, there must have been more urgency on the part of buyers than of sellers—and the reverse must have been true if the price fell. Of course, for any trade to occur, there must be both a seller and a buyer. So it is not enough to observe that "buyers equal sellers." What is more useful to note for purposes of market analysis is that the urgency or pressure apparently came from the buying (or selling) side *and also* that the relative size of the pool of interested traders was either large or small. For reasons discussed in earlier chapters, we understand that noting the size (and change in size) of the crowd is important. Therefore, we watch volume at least as carefully as we watch price since price is the by-product of the decisions and actions that trading volume is counting.

Dick Arms quickly realized that the newly available intraday statistics on trading allowed him to compute where the pressure was coming from, and when and how sharply it might be changing. He developed and back-tested his "Short-Term Trading Index," as he first named it, and soon shared it with an editor at Barron's, the Dow Jones publication, who was considerably impressed. Accordingly, during 1967 the world of investors and traders first learned the nature and details of "The Arms Index" in an article entitled "Jack be Nimble." The Arms calculation quickly lost its full four-word moniker in favor of the abbreviation TRIN, taken from the first letters of the words *trading* and *index*. A major brand of desktop quotation machines adopted TRIN in 1970, and it has been institutionalized ever since as a household name among technicians. Since the early 1990s, CNBC has printed the updated TRIN each minute during the trading day on its ticker display running across our TV screens.

THE FORMULA FOR TRIN

The TRIN formula is as follows:

$$\text{TRIN} = \frac{\dfrac{\text{number of advancers}}{\text{number of decliners}}}{\dfrac{\text{volume in advancers}}{\text{volume in decliners}}}$$

A value of 1.00 is considered neutral, while any value smaller than 1.00 is bullish, and any above 1.00 is bearish, *for purposes of end-of-day and intraday interpretation.* (Later in this chapter, we shall note that a very interestingly different interpretation obtains when TRIN is used for longer-term forecasting.) One can readily see that readings can never go below 0 and that therefore divergence from the neutral level can be biased on the upside, where readings are theoretically unlimited (but in actual practice very rarely much above 2.50 or so). Stating it another way, TRIN's range is from 0 to infinity, with 1.00 considered as neutral.

Understanding how the index works, and beginning to sense why the various possible readings are positive or negative in implications, will be aided with the help of a few examples. First, suppose we have these data during a market session or at its close: Advances and declines are each 1,500 in number; furthermore, trading volume in stocks that are up so far for the day is 600 million shares, and by unusual coincidence so is total

trading volume in stocks that are down for the day. The TRIN formula
would read thus:

$$\cfrac{\cfrac{\text{Number of advancers}}{\text{Number of decliners}}}{\cfrac{\text{Volume in advancers}}{\text{Volume in decliners}}} = \cfrac{\cfrac{1{,}500}{1{,}500}}{\cfrac{600{,}000{,}000}{600{,}000{,}000}} = \cfrac{1.00}{1.00} = 1.00$$

As noted earlier, this reading of 1.00 is considered neutral, indicating a
market in which the pressure or urgency from sellers equals that among
buyers. (Technically this might literally not be true since the formulation
captures each stock in terms of shares traded rather than their dollar value
traded. Thus, for example, a $10 stock with a million shares traded is
counted as providing the same evidence of buying or selling pressure as a
$75 stock that also has a million shares traded. But the data required to
compute the dollar pressure are not readily available all day on the fly, and
the original 1960s formulation has long been institutionalized.)

If you do the calculations, you can see that there are 1,500 stocks up
for the day, which show an average of 400,000 shares traded per stock.
Likewise, there are 1,500 stocks down for the day, and these show an average of 400,000 shares traded per stock. Perhaps looking at it this way, you
can get an easier sense of the equilibrium of buying and selling pressure
than by looking at the official formula itself: The average rising stock is no
more or less heavily traded than is the average declining stock. One cannot
say that the bulk of overall market action or activity has been in either stocks
people are demanding heavily or in stocks they urgently wish to dispose of;
it's been a standoff. We are really not focusing on the number of advancers
versus the number of decliners here. Our attention is on the *relative volumes*
in rising stocks, on average, versus the heaviness of activity in falling issues,
on average. If you remember your high school algebra, the formula can be
reformatted to read as the average volume per declining stock, divided by
the average volume per advancing stock. Dick Arms says that the fact that
TRIN readings of below 1.00 are "good" (bullish) rather than bearish is
strictly a statistical effect of the order in which he arranged the component
numbers when writing out the formula the first time. (Had he placed the volume figures in the upper part of the complex fraction, readings over 1.00
would have been bullish. The rest, as they say, is history.)

The data you need to calculate this TRIN index, in case you are not able
to find a Web site or quotation machine displaying it per se, are readily found
at this URL:

http://quote.yahoo.com/m0?u

That Yahoo! page will show you, among other statistics such as new 52-week highs and lows, the numbers of advances and declines as well as the volume in rising and falling issues, on each of four markets: the NYSE, AmEx, NASDAQ, and the Bulletin Board. Thus, you can compute a separate TRIN for each market, or even a single TRIN for the combined overall markets.

Now let us proceed to look at a set of market statistics that would represent a bullish reading for the TRIN:

$$\frac{\dfrac{\text{Number of advancers}}{\text{Number of decliners}}}{\dfrac{\text{Volume in advancers}}{\text{Volume in decliners}}} = \frac{\dfrac{1,500}{1,500}}{\dfrac{900,000,000}{600,000,000}} = \frac{1.00}{1.50} = 1.67$$

Here we have a trading day on which 1.5 billion shares have changed hands, excluding trading volume in stocks presently unchanged from their prior closing prices. (Remember, we look at only the gainers and losers and their respective volumes, omitting the data on the unchanged issues.) But you will now notice above that the volume in rising stocks is 900 million shares, or an average of 600,000 shares per advancing stock, while all the other relationships of data are the same as in our first, that is, neutral, example. Intuitively we would say that clearly the weight of the action on this trading day, at least so far, has been in the rising stocks. Stocks that are up are being traded, on average, 1.5 times as heavily as stocks that are down. Because of the nature of the formulation, the actual TRIN reading is the inverse of 1.5, or 0.67, which is interpreted as bullish in the short term. You might prefer to think of the number as saying that the volume per declining stock is only two thirds as heavy as volume per rising stock, so the bulls are in control.

Let us now look at a more bearish situation, again still holding the numbers of gainers and losers arbitrarily equal as we have so far:

$$\frac{\dfrac{\text{Number of advancers}}{\text{Number of decliners}}}{\dfrac{\text{Volume in advancers}}{\text{Volume in decliners}}} = \frac{\dfrac{1,500}{1,500}}{\dfrac{600,000,000}{750,000,000}} = \frac{1.00}{1.80} = 1.25$$

Here we see a day in which 1.35 billion shares have been traded, with gainers and losers equal by count but with more volume occurring in those stocks that are declining from yesterday's closes. Specifically, we can compute that the average declining stock has traded a half million shares (750,000,000 divided by 1,500) while the average stock that is up has had only 400,000 shares traded (that is, 600,000,000 divided by 1,500). Our immediate interpretation would be that there is a negative bias because the heaviest trading, on average or in the aggregate, is occurring in stocks that are falling rather than in those that are rising. Thus, the TRIN here is computed as 1.25, which is negative in short-term implications—the heavier action is coming in stocks that are moving lower.

Finally, let us look at a more normal sort of a day, in which the numbers of advances and declines are not somehow magically held equal:

$$\frac{\dfrac{\text{Number of advancers}}{\text{Number of decliners}}}{\dfrac{\text{Volume in advancers}}{\text{Volume in decliners}}} = \frac{\dfrac{1,900}{1,400}}{\dfrac{800,000,000}{650,000,000}} = \frac{1.3571}{1.2308} = 1.10$$

Here we are examining a day that market observers who look only at advance and decline statistics would think was a pretty solid win for the bulls. We who know the special value of watching trading-volume statistics, however, would differ in our interpretation. Yes, we see that advances outnumbered decliners by a good margin—a bit better than 4:3 as shown by the 1.36 ratio. But our concern is that volume of activity in the stocks that were up was not quite as enthusiastic or heavy on average as in the stocks that finished lower. By actual computation, the average volume in rising stocks was about 421,000 per issue while the activity in declining stocks averaged a bit over 464,000, or about 10 percent more per stock. Thus the TRIN reading for the day on this stock exchange is 1.10, or moderately bearish.

THE SHORT-TERM INTERPRETATION OF TRIN READINGS AND MOVEMENTS

In his 1971 book, Mr. Arms said that TRIN readings below 0.75 on an intraday or closing basis should be considered strong bullish signs for the very short term, while readings over 1.25 should be viewed as quite bearish. He also said that it is not only the level of the TRIN ratio itself but, even more importantly, the direction and the speed of change that should be observed. Thus, for example, if the current reading is 1.10 but it was 1.40 less than an hour ago, one would interpret even an above-neutral level as showing rapid intraday improvement—declining pretty sharply and therefore getting better fast, so to speak. Because those would be intraday movements seen only a short time apart, their importance would be mainly in their use by traders, who would be more willing to add long positions or who would likely want to cover any shorts. It is indeed very important, so we stress it again, that the individual day's end and intraday TRIN readings are of use primarily for very short term trading and entry and exit timing purposes. They typically serve no purpose at all in calling major market swings.

THE (SURPRISING) LONGER-TERM INTERPRETATION OF TRIN

Generally, as any analyst of a technical bent would agree, we should consider volume patterns to be significant evidence of the major trend of the market. When the volume is heavy, we are in most cases looking at a day whose trend is in conformance with the overall direction. On days of lower volume, the dominant participants in the market may have temporarily stepped away, and therefore the market's direction will probably turn out to be countertrend or corrective in nature. Stating the case from a bull's perspective, up on heavy volume and down on lower volume is positive since it indicates that the heavier pressure of determined activity is pushing prices higher rather than lower.

This interpretation works most of the time because much more of the market's existence is usually spent in upward trends or downward moves, rather than in the rarer formation of reversal areas. Thus, as the careful crowd watcher would put it, the majority will be right much of the time, but when the majority becomes extreme in its views and actions, and when there are almost no strong objectors to the current direction, a moblike situation exists and *those conditions* are unsustainable. They are realistically unlikely to obtain for long because extreme emotions are very strong in degree but short lived in the time dimension. They are also unsustainable because, when opinion reaches a near-unanimous state, it cannot move any more to one side than where it already is. In the vernacular, "When everyone has bought, where will any further buying come from?"

Bringing this back to the realm of TRIN readings, it is healthy to have the indicator either sitting moderately below 1.00 or declining in value most of the time. What is quite striking about the TRIN numbers in actual practice, however, is that too much of a good thing for too long turns out to be an unsustainable excess of bullish activity. Very low readings day after day for an extended period of time generally mark what hindsight will show to have been a meaningful price top. Conversely, a long series of days with very high (individually, bearish) TRIN numbers marks a run of excessive and therefore unsustainable pessimism, or a bottoming area over the medium to longer term. In effect, this means that the interpretation of TRIN becomes flipped 180 degrees when one moves from the short to the longer-term view. The majority can be right for a good while, but when it becomes an unruly mob of a single mindset, its time has run out.

You will recall that the TRIN indicator was first disclosed to the public in 1967. It created quite a stir among technicians, and a good deal of number crunching and back testing ensued. A number of analysts pointed out after some research that a 10-day moving average of the closing daily readings could be used as a way to identify not short-term or intraday changes in direction but instead more important *interim or sometimes long-term market turning points.* Experiments with 5-day, 7-day, and 8-day and 12- and 13-day averages showed these constructions to be less reliable than the long-popular 10-day moving average that so many technicians customarily use with price behavior. Windows shorter than 10 days produced too many whipsaws and false signals, while longer windows were not sensitive enough to catch some important turns.

After some study and consideration of this evidence and his own further developmental work on the TRIN concept, Dick Arms settled on this rule for 10-day interpretation:

> When the 10-day moving average of TRIN is under 0.60, sell;
> when the 10-day moving average of TRIN is over 1.50, buy.

If you think about what such readings represent in terms of market tone and dynamics, you will readily understand why such numbers make intuitive sense as useful signals of trend reversal. In market timekeeping terms, as seen by technical analysts, 10 days can be viewed as a fairly long (and therefore significant) period of activity when the action pretty consistently has skewed heavily to one side or the other psychologically. Focus for a moment on the TRIN numbers. A single day's TRIN of 1.50 means that for a full trading session, average volume of declining stocks was fully 50 percent greater than the average activity in stocks that were rising. And we are talking about probably 1,000 or more stocks in each group, so when we say 1.5 times as much, that is a high ratio to be in effect over such large numbers of individual stocks. For the very short term, then, 1.50 is a bearish TRIN.

But now think in terms of 10 days—two full calendar weeks or one calendar week plus parts of two others surrounding it. If you see a market that is strongly dominated by sellers, to the extent of generating an average TRIN of 1.50 for that long, you are very likely witnessing a fairly panicky selling spree that will not last much if any longer and that will mark a meaningful bottom. The converse could be said in cases in which the 10-day average of closing daily TRINs is at 0.60 or below. It is well documented in actual data that major market averages extremely seldom close up or down for 10 consecutive days—in fact, only about one such rise and one such decline occurs in every 10 years! Probably even in a couple of weeks of pretty nasty and persistent selling pressure, there might be one day when the blood-letting abates and some rebound is seen. In that scenario, such a day might likely produce a TRIN of under 1.00. And if that 1.00 must be included in a 10-day average that has to reach 1.50 to generate a major longer-term buy signal, the remaining 9 days would need to average a bit over 1.66 to generate the requisite average score. That is indeed a very extreme emotional condition on the downside—a volume-dominated spree of selling that will burn itself out once all the weaker-stomached players have sold out and stock has moved on balance to stronger hands.

Therefore, the two seemingly contradictory ways of reading TRIN are both logical. A high TRIN in the very short term is bearish *for the short term.* But sustained periods of very high TRIN readings, such that a 10-day moving average of the data can reach 1.50, mean that a major emotional washout has been taking place. That condition is unsustainable, and therefore a high *longer-term* TRIN reading represents a longer-term *buy* signal. That is why I noted this "TRIN irony" as being a conceptual parallel to the difference between gently positive net on-balance daily volume readings (up on higher-volume days, down in lower trading) and extremely high, concentrated, and sustained volume such as would characterize a buying panic and therefore a market top of some lasting significance. Summing it up, a mild preponderance of bullish (or bearish) sentiment as expressed in daily volume data implies sustainability of the established bullish (or bearish) trend. But an extremely lengthy period of overwhelming buying or selling pressure marks an emotional blow-off and therefore inevitably a point at which the price direction cannot continue and so must and will reverse. Thus, what seems to be a contradictory interpretation of extreme TRINs in the longer-term context actually makes sense. And it works in the real world (Figure 6–1). A TRIN of 0.60 is called a *major top.*

THOUGHTS AND OBSERVATIONS ABOUT TRIN

Just as no one fundamental yardstick or rule of thumb will work perfectly at all times or for all stocks, we should realistically also expect that no single

FIGURE 6−1

Ten-Day Moving Average Ratio of NASDAQ to NYSE TRIN,
January to April 2000

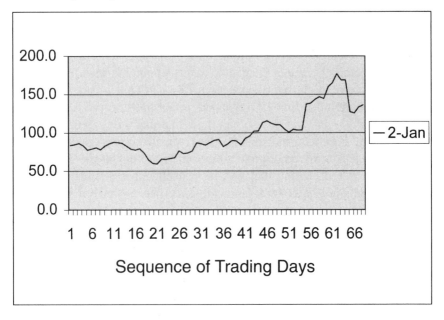

technical indicator will prove ideal in all situations. The TRIN concept and its application have some very strong points to recommend them and some areas of concern as well. Let us examine these briefly, in order to deepen our understanding.

First and foremost, I would say that the TRIN concept must be judged as valid in its essence. That is because the calculation and its application are based on the central importance of volume as describing what is truly going on in the market. The TRIN formula incorporates the number of total advances and total declines, and therefore it captures to a degree the concept of breadth, which is followed by many in the form of cumulative (and 10-day) net advance and decline lines. But the TRIN goes further in a very important dimension: It measures the balance of volume pressure behind the net advances and declines. As such, it adds a richness similar to the addition of color to a black-and-white photograph.

But there are a couple of rough edges that cannot go unmentioned. First, as noted briefly earlier in these pages, volume by its nature is tallied on the basis of shares and shares do not all have equal money value. Therefore, the TRIN calculation is subject to bias if there is a systematic difference occurring as between high-priced and low-priced stocks. For example, three rising $10 stocks each with a million shares traded count for more than one declining $50 stock with 1 million shares traded. The official TRIN calculation would see this kind of a market as neutral since the average volume of decliners would be equal, at 1 million shares, to the average volume of gainers. Flow of money, which more truly measures buying pressure, is negative in the example given. Similarly, a given single stock counts twice as much the day after a two-for-one stock split because on average its volume will be twice as much measured in shares. None of this probably matters a great deal of the time since in a large universe of stocks (perhaps about 3,000 with net non-zero changes on a given day on the NYSE) the biasing effects will tend to even out. That is true unless a significant shift in market leadership is in process. A change in favor of small-capitalization or low-priced stocks would not be captured by the TRIN. The heavy weight of share volumes in institutionally owned and typically higher priced stocks would drown out the subtle change occurring in terms of rising strength in their smaller cousins. But such shifts, admittedly, occur only occasionally, so this is hardly a fatal flaw.

Another theoretical imperfection of the TRIN formulation is that it counts the entirety of the day's cumulative volume in each stock as if it were all upside, or all downside, volume. In relatively thinly (inactively) traded stocks, this is not a grave problem as the indicator is calculated in a way that puts greatest weight on the most heavily traded issues. But sometimes such issues' being counted in the manner they are can lend an artificial and therefore perhaps misleading tilt to the TRIN calculation. Suppose, for example, that a very heavily traded stock makes a considerable gap move at the opening on very heavy volume. Let us imagine, for the sake of argument, that Hewlett-Packard exceeds the analysts' consensus guesstimate on quarterly earnings per share by a couple of cents and receives upgraded recommendations by two major brokerage houses such as, perhaps, Merrill Lynch and Goldman, Sachs. HWP opens up $2 a share at 41, and probably 15 million shares trade in the first hour of the session. Now let us suppose that some negative influence enters the market's collective thinking. Perhaps the latest jobs data or the retail sales figures are interpreted as implying that inflation and interest rates are going to be on the rise. A sense of unease sets in and grows as the day wears on. The advance and decline balance turns negative fairly early and gradually erodes for the remainder of trading hours. Even HWP, after its initial buying burst, starts to be weighed down by the negative overall mood.

Its early rise of $2 maxes out at $2.25 after about 90 minutes, but then its net price gain for the day gradually narrows for the following several hours. There are minor rallies once in a while, but the net trend from the midmorning price level is gradually lower. Volume, however, remains heavy. Some mutual funds are taking profits due to HWP's fortuitous rise, while other investors including some institutions are coming in to buy later in the day at prices less elevated than if they had joined the early buying frenzy. But the overall market mood, driven by those economic numbers, is exerting a downward price drag on balance. By midafternoon, HWP is now ahead by just $0.50 or $0.25 a share, and its volume is 35 million shares. Casual inspection would imply that net on-balance volume for the day is probably negative (upside volume early and downside volume ever since). But in the TRIN calculation a single stock that earlier was up over $2 on 15 million shares is now exerting an even stronger bullish influence than it was earlier, despite the fact that it is now up only a minor fraction but its volume is up to 35 million shares. The market keeps sliding, continuing gradually to wash out the early gain in HWP. At 3 p.m., with 39 million shares having changed hands, the stock goes to $39, net unchanged for the day. Those 39 million shares—accounting for perhaps 4 percent of total NYSE volume in one single stock, now fall out of the up-volume tally, and the TRIN calculation surges several basis points. The market keeps sliding, and finally HWP cannot hold at $39 despite the buying of bargain hunters who feel lucky and smart to have the bought the stock at yesterday's closing price *after* knowing the overnight good news. But now the tape says $38.90 and volume is 41 million shares, still about 4 percent of total Big Board turnover. HWP now becomes one of over 1,500 stocks in the "decliners" tally but most importantly, its 41 million shares jump from neutral into the down-volume total. The TRIN again takes an upward jolt. Perhaps some short-term traders note the two sudden recent accelerations of the TRIN to the upside (bearish) and sell their positions, driving more stocks down for the day. The details of one stock, heavily traded, have had an undue influence on the TRIN reading and on actual trading.

One additional corollary of the above scenario is that users must be cautious in their tendency to draw conclusions very early after the opening of trading, when only relatively few stocks have opened. That would be especially true in cases in which a number of normally heavily traded issues have not yet quite opened, either up or down. Rapid and jagged movements in the TRIN can be expected in the first half hour or so.

None of this cripples TRIN as a generally valid tool. But our vignette does illustrate how certain imperfections might exist around the edges. Again, of course, no perfect system or indicator exists. If one had been discovered, we would all be contentedly retired in comfort and would be multiplying our wealth on automatic pilot using that "secret" formula.

Let us now look at some realistic boundaries for the use of the TRIN. In its basic short-term formulation, the TRIN is designed for use during the market day so that its students can sense mood changes very early, before much price change has shown up. Therefore, to be of use, TRIN readings must be watched by someone who is devoting his or her entire attention for $6\frac{1}{2}$ hours per day to trading the market. In practical terms, that excludes the vast majority of traders and investors who work 8-hour day jobs and can only occasionally glance at the market.

The longer-term, moving-average application of the TRIN, however, seems to have considerable merit for calling more significant market turns. That in itself provides useful potential for a much larger number of investors, beyond the relative few who are tuned in all session and every moment. The elegance and essential virtue of TRIN in this context come from the fact that a 10-day moving average indeed will capture in unequivocal statistics the extreme (and therefore unsustainable) emotion-driven behavior of the crowd at exhaustion tops and bottoms.

That strong positive having been noted, we should also propose some logical limitations on the use of TRIN. First, because its mathematical nature gives disproportionate weight to the largest-capitalization and typically most heavily traded issues, decisions to buy or sell based on TRIN movements and levels should be applied only to such stock, or to indices and futures representing them. Logically, the TRIN should be a useful tool for someone buying and selling SPY, the S&P 500 Sector Spider. However, if you were seeking to make moves in micro-cap stocks, whether they were listed on the NYSE or elsewhere, TRIN might not tell a true or relevant story *for that area of the market.* It is entirely conceivable, for example, that a prolonged period of sidewise market movement as documented by the major market averages and confirmed by generally narrowly neutral daily TRIN readings could be masking either a concerted building of strength in small-cap stocks or, conversely, a deterioration in their support. By their very nature as small parts of the calculation, they can slip through essentially unnoticed.

SUMMARY: ONE TRIN, OR MORE?

I would advise those following the TRIN to strongly consider applying it separately to each of the three major U.S. equity marketplaces. Most commonly, TRIN readings are computed based on NYSE stocks alone. While they of course do not always tell the whole story, they do represent a great deal of the invested wealth of shareholders, and therefore an NYSE-based TRIN captures the essence of what they are doing and

feeling. The NASDAQ, while somewhat dominated by the huge indi-
vidual-issue volumes in such stocks as Intel, Apple, Dell, and Cisco,
generally does represent a marketplace for younger, higher-technology,
faster-growing and entrepreneurial companies. Watching a separate
TRIN computed from NASDAQ advance/decline and up/down volume
totals would therefore have considerable merit. Prior to the recently
established domination of American Stock Exchange trading by the
exchange-traded funds,* I would have said calculating an AmEx-based
TRIN would have given insight into small-cap, mining, and energy
stocks. I would not attach much analytical value to it now, however.

Whatever one or more TRIN statistics you may calculate, it does seem
sensible to be aware of this technical statistic on at least a daily basis.
Knowing what is going on under the simple surface of advances and
declines and major popular market averages and indices is important.
Because TRIN captures the absolutely necessary trading-volume element of
the tug of war between buyers and sellers, an investor (let alone a trader!)
should not be uninformed as to what it is saying.

---

*iShares, HOLDRs, QQQ, SPY, DIA, and the various S&P sector baskets normally occupy about
   six or more positions among the AmEx's 10 most actives and over 75 percent of total share
   trading.

CHAPTER 7

Equivolume and
Ease of Movement

In Chapter 6 we explored a major innovation in documenting buying versus selling pressure, now called TRIN, invented and developed by Richard W. Arms, Jr. He may not have as many patents as Thomas Edison, but Dick Arms also developed another extremely useful construct in technical analysis centered on trading volume. This chapter will explore that concept—the ease of price movement. The primary output of this analysis, which has become a major addition to the tools available for technical analysis, is the charting method Dick Arms named "Equivolume Charting." We will begin by explaining and discussing that important technique for focusing on volume's effects, and we will conclude this chapter by examining Arms's calculation of ease (or difficulty) of price movement, which is based on the same philosophy about volume as that which underlies Equivolume chart analysis. For those readers who wish to pursue these topics in greater detail and in the words of their founder and developer, the book *Volume Cycles in the Stock Market** is recommended.

As a crucial introduction to the concept of Equivolume chart construction and study, Arms succinctly stated a central observation, with which I agree and which stands as the *raison d'etre* of this volume: The market generates only two significant types of technical information, which are price *and volume*. Thus one ignores volume—half the available data—at his or her peril. Prior to the introduction of the Equivolume chart method in Arms's 1971 book, cited in Chapter 6, there were only two

---

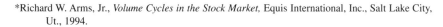

*Richard W. Arms, Jr., *Volume Cycles in the Stock Market,* Equis International, Inc., Salt Lake City, Ut., 1994.

major types of stock charts in use: vertical bar charts and point-and-figure
(P&F) charts (Japanese candlestick charting has only lately become a con-
tender for rising attention in the West). A number of books and courses on
the P&F technique (of which I am not a supporter) are available for those
wishing to explore it, so it will not be explained here. In my view, its
essential weakness is its total exclusion of volume as a factor in technical
analysis. The key elements of the three principal charting systems are
summarized in Figure 7–1.

Most students of the stock market, once they move on from fundamentals alone into the revealing world of technical analysis, begin by constructing and then examining and analyzing daily bar charts. In these, each
day's market activity is summarized visually in a few straight-line strokes.
A vertical bar is drawn from the lowest price of the day to the highest
price. All bar charts include a tick mark on the right side of the bar at the
closing price level. Most (and I believe the more informative) also include
a tick mark at the left side of the vertical bar, noting the opening price
level. At the bottom of the bar chart, using a separate scale, total volume
for the trading day is plotted as a vertical bar rising from the zero line.

Two major variants of vertical bar charts have come into use over the
years. First, some users have adopted the practice of charting price on a
semilog scale so that equal percentage moves occupy equal vertical distance. The original approach was to use standard, nonlog graph paper, and
it remains the choice of the majority of users. Some major Internet charting programs and nearly all advanced commercial technical analysis packages provide a choice of vertical scale type. Second, and more recently,
some users have begun plotting volume in color, with red representing
down (price) days and black, green, or blue indicating an up (price) day.
Again, some major Internet charting facilities offer the volume color feature as a user option. Such choices reflect the central importance of noting whether volume is heaviest when prices are rising or declining, as dis-

FIGURE 7–1

Key Differentiating Elements of Chart Types

Chart Type	Inclusion of Volume	Horizontal Axis: Basis
Point and figure	No (!)	Reversal counting
Vertical bar	Yes	Time counting
Equivolume	Yes	Volume (!)

cussed in some detail in Chapter 5. Color helps the brain to integrate the price-change and volume ideas, but it does only part of the required work.

DEVELOPMENT OF THE EQUIVOLUME CHART

Arms found that the eye movement and mental integration required to visually analyze traditional bar charts created an unnecessary strain. As you look at a chart, you must indeed glance up and down for each day in order to fully capture and understand that day's action, which of course includes not only the price movement but also the all-important volume information. Many casual stock chart users tend to skim over, or even entirely ignore, the crucial volume portion of the picture because of this required "work." That tendency to overlook or at least short-change the volume aspect is of course supported by our natural tendency to think primarily about price because price is what tells us how much money we are making or losing and how rapidly. But volume cannot be ignored.

To make the volume itself as visually accessible and important as price, Dick Arms created a new approach to stock charting called *Equivolume.* Whereas on a vertical bar chart the horizontal scale is set in equal increments by the passage of time in days (or, now widely available on the Internet and elsewhere electronically, in minutes, hours, weeks, months, or years), on an Equivolume chart the horizontal scale is set by *equivalent amounts of trading volume* rather than by equal units of time. Time as a measure in stock trading is actually rather arbitrary. Putting aside the current movement toward 24-hour worldwide electronic trading, the opening and closing of any local stock exchange is merely a workday-determined convenience for the personnel employed there. The trading day has been of differing lengths at various times, and for a number of years the trading week included partial sessions on Saturdays. A 6-day cycle still exists in some nations. In some countries, the trading day itself is interrupted by a midday meal break, raising the legitimate question—for charting purposes—of whether that day actually consists of one or two sessions.

Charting stocks in a way that portrays volume on the horizontal axis, then, makes more intuitive sense after you have analyzed the alternatives. If a given (relatively inactive) stock trades between $35 and $37 on Monday in volume of 5,000 shares and then trades between $35 and $38 on Tuesday in volume of 40,000 shares, we would probably all agree that the second day's action was more significant. Traditional bar charts do in fact record the higher trading volume, but the Equivolume approach, with its volume-proportional horizontal axis, visually highlights that different, and indeed richer, information for the user.

CONSTRUCTION OF AN EQUIVOLUME CHART

Many chartists will testify with passion that constructing their own charts gives them a much finer and more intimate familiarity with what a stock is doing, than they would have if they simply look a printed chart constructed for them by computer. Thus, in this section we will describe how Equivolume charts are constructed. Price is, as usual, scaled on the vertical axis, and on an arithmetic rather than semilog basis. However, rather than noting the dates on the bottom line and plotting one vertical bar per trading day, the Equivolume chart takes a much different approach. On the horizontal axis, *volume rather than time* is the dimension and the measurement unit. This key difference reflects the underlying insight that volume of trading rather than time itself is more important. As in the example above, a trading day containing eight times—or for that matter, even twice—the volume of another ought to be more prominently displayed. This new charting formulation accomplishes that end.

If days (or minutes or weeks, etc.) are not to be the equally spaced units along the horizontal axis of our chart, how do we decide exactly what units of volume to use? The answer is that each stock's own trading action determines that fact uniquely, for its own chart. In his original (1971) book, Dick Arms suggested that 2 or 3 months of latest actual trading history ought to be used to determine what a stock's typical (average) daily volume level is. His 1994 book modifies that to 30 trading days. I believe that this fine-tuning makes great sense in our currently much more volatile emotional (and thus price) environment. While one can legitimately criticize such an outlook, in practice many market participants— one hesitates to use the word "investors"—think of 3 months ago as ancient history. So using a narrower measurement window for determining what truly is relevant average volume for a stock makes sense.

You can readily access such information in numeric terms (no need to read vertical bars and estimate their exact heights) by visiting a good Web site that documents volume, price, and ex-dividend information. The following address is a good place to start:

http://chart.yahoo.com/t?a5=

You should replace my "SYMB" with the ticker symbol for the stock you are interested in. To gather the information you need for computing the average volume, set the beginning date for 6 weeks plus a couple of dates earlier than yesterday, and the ending date for yesterday. Be sure to specify "daily" data, and then click on "get historical data." If you are willing to settle for a slightly stale calendar month's average volume rather than one up to the latest trading day, you can specify "monthly" data instead. But the following instructions assume you wish the latest 30 days' data for an average.

In your spreadsheet, after your easy download has been completed, be sure to eliminate any trading holidays so that you have a true 30 days of volume data; use the "mean" or "average" function over that range and you will have computed the average daily trading volume. This does not include after-hours activity, but neither do the daily totals of volume you will see in real time in the newspaper stock tables, or at the major charting Web sites that display volume numerically. So your comparison will be fair from the past into the real-time future as you plot your stock's Equivolume chart each day.

Next, following the Arms methodology, multiply the average volume you found by a factor of two thirds. Figure 7–2 is an example, using a period in October and November 2000 on General Motors' main stock (ticker GM). The farthest right column shows the daily volumes, ranging from a low of 579,600 shares the day after Thanksgiving to a high of more than 5.6 million shares on November 3. The mathematical average was 2,988,764 shares per day, shown in the bottom row. Two thirds of that amount is 1,992,508 shares, which we will round off to 2.0 million shares for ease of mental handling. The latter point is important because you will divide each future trading day's actual total volume by the rounded figure. Unless you are terminally addicted to calculators, sometimes you will be able to do that in your head if you are using a rounded number. How much rounding off is reasonable? In extremely active stocks, quite a bit! Note that if you are rounding at the third place from the left, you are affecting accuracy only at the 1 percent level. I would round to some nearest 10,000- or 50,000- or even 100,000-share level depending on how active your stock is. For example, if it trades in the multiple millions of shares a day on average, your two-thirds number can be rounded to the nearest 100,000 or even 500,000 level for ease of future use.

The rounded, two-thirds number you determine as described above will represent the width of one horizontal block on your chart paper. Before we proceed further, I believe a slight adjustment to the pure Arms instructions is appropriate in some cases. If the recent historical window of 30 trading days you are using happens to include one or more days of unusually high trading volume (spikes and severe crescendos are discussed later,

FIGURE 7-2

Equivolume Chart for General Motors' main stock, October–November 2000

Date	Open	High	Low	Close	Volume
29-Nov-00	50	50.9375	49.125	50.5	2,600,400
28-Nov-00	50.5	50.5	48.4375	48.8125	3,452,400
27-Nov-00	51.25	51.75	50.25	50.5	2,247,400
24-Nov-00	51.5	51.8125	51.1875	51.375	579,600
22-Nov-00	51.4375	51.9375	50.375	50.6875	2,431,000
21-Nov-00	52.5	53.375	51.1875	51.3125	3,546,800
20-Nov-00	55.125	55.5	51.5625	51.5625	4,600,500
17-Nov-00	56.75	57.125	55.375	55.875	2,442,100
16-Nov-00	58.0625	58.1875	56.5	56.75	1,904,400
15-Nov-00	57.625	58.5625	57.3125	57.8125	1,871,100
14-Nov-00	57.125	58.5625	57.0625	57.5625	2,702,700
13-Nov-00	55.0713	56.3722	54.6377	56.0625	2,199,000
10-Nov-00	56.8678	57.3015	54.8235	55.1333	2,454,400
9-Nov-00	57.2395	57.9829	56.4961	57.3634	2,233,600
8-Nov-00	57.4873	58.4785	56.1864	57.2395	3,440,900
7-Nov-00	58.9121	59.2838	56.3103	56.4961	5,123,000
6-Nov-00	57.2395	61.2661	56.9917	60.3988	4,166,800
3-Nov-00	58.974	60.0891	56.4961	56.4961	5,643,000
2-Nov-00	60.213	60.213	57.9209	58.974	3,946,800
1-Nov-00	61.5758	63.1865	60.151	60.8325	2,904,300
31-Oct-00	59.9032	62.505	59.8413	61.5758	2,792,000
30-Oct-00	58.7262	61.1422	58.7262	59.3457	2,573,000
26-Oct-00	55.7528	56.8678	55.7528	56.3722	1,808,300
25-Oct-00	56.8678	57.1156	55.6289	55.7528	1,827,600
24-Oct-00	56.0006	57.6731	56.0006	57.1156	2,919,200
23-Oct-00	57.3015	57.3634	55.505	55.7528	2,648,100
20-Oct-00	56.62	60.4608	56.4961	57.797	4,566,300
19-Oct-00	54.1421	58.4165	54.1421	57.3634	3,916,700
18-Oct-00	54.6377	55.6289	54.0182	54.1421	3,238,700
17-Oct-00	57.0537	57.7351	54.8855	55.3191	2,882,800
			Average Volume:		2,988,763

in Chapters 9 and 10), I would eliminate that day or days and compute the average trading on 30 days excluding those extreme highs. My reason is this: You will be charting your stock's volume horizontally in blocks representing multiples of two thirds of whatever recent historical average you computed. If you include one or two days of extremely high volume, those horizontal block units will be so large that nearly all future days will be plotted at an equal, one-block size; that will greatly reduce the richness of the Equivolume chart you construct. In our GM example, we did have one day of extremely low volume (November 24, post-holiday), but its exclusion would have less effect than eliminating a day or two of, say, 10 million plus trading if such had occurred. Excluding that one low day would have raised the average to 3.08 million shares, and after taking two thirds, we would have still rounded to 2.0 million shares per day as our standard horizontal unit of volume.

Once you have determined the horizontal block value (that rounded $^2/_3$ number), jot it somewhere on the chart, perhaps in a left-hand corner so that it will be out of the way and you will not need to rely on memory. Then you can easily find it each day as you update your chart.

Let's consider how to create this Equivolume chart of General Motors starting with mid-October 2000, from the data already detailed above. We established that our unit of trading will be that one horizontal square equals 2.0 million shares in a day. Look at the table and note the daily volumes. Now convert each day's actual volume into complete units of 2.0 million shares or more. Don't round off at this stage. That means that if a trading session produces over 3 million shares in volume, it is still graphed as only one horizontal unit because it is short of a full two units, or 4 million. (Although the Arms books do not sanction such adjustments, I would be inclined to make small allowances at the margin, so that, for example, October 19 and November 2, each with over 3.9 million shares changing hands, might be graphed two units wide rather than one.) Those would be the only 2 days for which I would consider bending the rule about full units of 2 million shares each. As a result, in all just 7 days in this time range would be shown in double-wide plottings, and all the rest would be under 4 million each and therefore would individually get one horizontal unit.

What we have done is to note that 7 of the 30 days in our table generated trading volume of twice or more (but none three times) the basic unit, which is $^2/_3$ of an average day. When we plot the chart, those days will be represented in rectangles twice as wide as for the other 23 sessions. Let us now consider the vertical or price scale. Looking at a 52-week chart of GM at the end of November 2000 would have shown that its price range was from about $95 down to $55 per share—or $40 of vertical distance. In setting your vertical scale for an Equivolume chart of GM at that time, you would want to allow for at least $40 of vertical scale in deciding how much in price each vertical box will represent. If, for example, you were using standard page-size graph paper with four boxes to the inch, and using the paper in the landscape direction, you would have 8.5 inches times 4 or 34 blocks on the vertical scale. Clearly, you would therefore set each block as being worth $2, so that you could get $60 worth of scale from top to bottom. Given that the stock was just off its 52-week low in late November, I would set the bottom of my scale at about 35 (or, if you would prefer even numbers as the bounds for each $2-high block, then at 36). Thus, we have now set the dimensions and scales for our GM Equivolume graph.

As you plot the chart, you will quickly notice that a graph paper square only $1/_4$ inch high does not allow you to make very fine distinctions when drawing the day's highs and lows. In effect, you might need to think in terms of rounding off the actual daily highs and lows to about quarter points since you can fairly easily differentiate within the quarter-inch box in about eight gradations. That will be close enough—no need for a magnifying glass or calipers. Each block on the quarter-inch grid paper will represent two points in the vertical direction and, by total coincidence in this example, 2.0 million shares of trading volume in the horizontal. For some other stock, the side-to-side dimension might be 30,000 shares for a fairly inactive stock, or perhaps 400,000, or maybe 35 million for an active issue like Intel. Each graph will have its own scale, suited to that stock's own volume and price-volatility personality. This is useful since you will be looking at different stocks in equivalent relative-volume terms; accordingly, one horizontal unit will equal roughly two thirds of an average day's volume. Whereas traditional vertical bar graphs use time in days as their unit of measurement from left to right, your Equivolume chart now measures market history not on calendar terms but rather in equal volume units. And volume is a crucially significant dimension of market activity—more so than time itself.

We now would be ready to draw the GM graph in Equivolume terms. Whereas vertical bar charts would be composed of single solid lines with tick marks with white space separating them, your Equivolume chart consists of a series of rectangles of varying shapes, each connected across the volume dimension such that—unless there is an overnight price gap—the left side of Wednesday is the same vertical line as the right side of Tuesday. Using the actual data in our GM example, the first 5 days would cover a bit over $6 (from 54 to somewhat above 60) in the vertical dimension—about three of those $2-high boxes as discussed above—and would cover seven horizontal units (two each for October 19 and 20, when volume was at 4 million shares daily). Thus you see immediately that the shape of this chart differs from that of the vertical bar chart you are accustomed to seeing: One week would cover five horizontal units of space on a bar graph, but in this case it takes up seven on the Equivolume scale. Two days each had trading volume twice as heavy as is typical, and therefore they are plotted twice as wide to show their importance. The full two months of GM trading, detailed on page 102, looks like Figure 7-3.

You will have immediately noticed that there is no plotting of volume on a separate scale at the page's bottom. Instead, volume each day is shown in relative terms by *the width* of that day's rectangle. Price still looks the same as ever in relative terms, except that the vertical lines you are accustomed to seeing have become fatter and transformed into little boxes. Height is price range while width is trading volume. It is a bit of a different way of viewing the world of stocks, but one that is easier to understand and, importantly, one that gives to volume the visual prominence its actual importance deserves. You may be concerned that your graph apparently will be devoid of chronological reference points since

FIGURE 7-3

The First Week of GM Trading

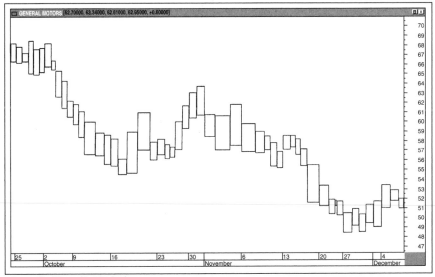

Source: Chart Powered by MetaStock

the scale across the bottom is not marked by dates as a traditional bar chart would be. For that reason, many market students using Equivolume charts will write the month number in heavy letters inside the day's plot on the first trading session of a month (November = 11, for example). Others may simply place month abbreviations or numerals at the top or bottom edge of the graph to mark the start of each new month. This will highlight the fact that over time your horizontal scale is somewhat elastic *in time terms* because it is being plotted in terms of trading *volume* rather than in trading days. Thus, some months will take less graph paper than others to display horizontally because volume activity will not be equal.

KEY FORMATIONS ON EQUIVOLUME CHARTS

It is not my place to explain all the nuances of Equivolume chart interpretation. Those intrigued by this groundbreaking approach should obtain the latest of Mr. Arms's books, which was cited on the first page of this chapter and is also listed in the appendix. I find three observations to be central:

- First, those technicians accustomed to employing trendlines will be pleased to find that they continue to work on Equivolume charts. I believe that is true because stocks exist in a world whose internal meter is actually denominated in terms of volume rather than time units.
- Second, the shapes of rectangles, and even clusters of consecutive rectangles, on Equivolume charts are highly important. The two major and visibly clearly contrasting shapes are tall and skinny versus flat and wide.
- Charted rectangles that are relatively skinny and tall represent price areas in which it was relatively easy for the stock to move rapidly, without much hindrance from volume. One should anticipate that movement in the opposite direction at some future time may also be fairly rapid or violent. By contrast, those plots that are visibly wide rather than skinny ("oversquare" is the term Arms uses) represent significant areas of price supply (if at the upper extent of a price move), or of demand or support if at the lower ends of moves. Such areas will by their nature show themselves more prominently on an Equivolume chart than they would on a bar plot. That draws attention to them and makes study and interpretation easier.

Arms makes a fourth major observation and conclusion from his studies of stocks using Equivolume charts. He asserts that volume begets volume, and in light of that he says the ends of price movements can be approximately measured in terms of the amount of volume that was traded in the formation of the base or supply area from which the price move developed. For example, if 5 million shares change hands while a stock is consolidating between 36 and 40, once the stock breaks out on the upside, one should therefore expect the upward price trend to continue until another 5 million shares have changed hands. This is somewhat similar to the point-and-figure technique of counting the probable ensuing move by counting the number of reversals that formed the base. While again admitting to what some might call a bias in that I am not an adherent of P&F charting, I do find it more intuitive to count in terms of volume (representing people's decisions backed by money) than in terms of numbers of times a stock retraces between two prices.

However, I believe that expecting price moves to be defined by equivalent amounts of volume traded might be somewhat simplistic in the real world of volatile trading we see in the new century. First, such an assumption implies that all buyers and sellers have equal holding-period intentions, which in practice they may not. But in a less theoretical realm, consider this: News about the company, or significant news about the industry or a competitor's merger or legal problems, has a clear effect on both the price and the amount of trading in a stock. If more news occurs after the price breakout than was published during the consolidation phase preceding it, I believe it is logical to expect more trading to take place during the ensuing price move. As an extreme example, suppose that a company issues an earnings warning, or actually reports disappointing earnings, during the ensuing price movement following the consolidation or base period. If the move was up from the base, the upward move will be immediately ended by the bad news, regardless of how much stock had been traded during the upward move. If, on the other hand, the bad news occurs after a downtrend is already in process, the degree of surprise, overlaid by the size of institutional holdings, will determine how much volume hits the stock on the first day after the news, and on the several days immediately following (see Chapter 10 regarding spikes, in this case downward ones). I believe the expectation of roughly equal volume was more plausible in an earlier era when trading volume was much more representative of the buying and selling decision of large numbers of small and relatively equal-sized investors than it is today. Trading on the NYSE is approximately 50 percent in huge blocks, nearly all of which represent institutions' positions moving. Some mutual funds may own more shares in a given company than might typically trade in several days. If they decide to unload, their decision will determine volume. The decisions of relatively small numbers of very large but unequally sized institutional holders are statistically likely to produce imbalances rather than balances in trading volume over time.

In one sense, I do agree with the underlying thinking behind Mr. Arms's equal-volume theory. Volume often does beget volume, and that is true in more than one sense. On a very raw, emotional, gut-reaction level, the appearance of huge trading volume in a stock without any apparent news trigger will cause some traders to join in the selling or buying (whichever happens to be obviously dominant at the moment) on the theory that "somebody knows something." We know that on the downside, frightening price declines on huge trading volume induce thousands (or more) of individual investors to join the panic and sell. It might also be observed that volume will drive future volume in some cases. For example, suppose a stock is trading at $50 and strong rumors circulate, perhaps even supported by hints in a company press release, that the company is about to be acquired at a premium price. Suppose that, say, 20 million shares trade during the phase when the stock is being driven up by such speculative buyers. Now assume that the merger negotiations terminate unsuccessfully and management says it has decided to "remain an independent company" instead. The stock will decline on that news in heavy volume. One might reasonably assume that approximately the number of people who bought on the hope of a takeover will now liquidate their positions upon learning that their hopes have been proved baseless. Thus, volume on the downside might well approximate volume on the upside. Longer-term investors who were willing to part with their stock at perhaps $60 during the rumor-driven price increase may now take advantage of the decline to $50 (or lower) to reestablish their positions and keep the excess cash in their accounts or pockets. Once again, their earlier selling action might be matched by later repurchases. Without the price jump on news or rumor, such holders would not have traded even once.

When surprising negative news hits a stock with an avalanche of trading volume (again, refer to Chapter 10), it seems logical that the shock to the psychology of holders that causes such a wave of dumping might be "measured" by the size of the added volume above usual average levels. One might intuitively suspect that it will take a period of time for the shock to wear off and for stability in the stock to be restored. One might reasonably assume that such a period of time could be measured in terms of either (1) waiting until average trading volume finally returns to its levels just before the shocking news hit, or (b) waiting until excess volume equal to that in the smash or downward spike has traded again on top of normal average trading. Either approach might reasonably be said to measure the time it takes for trading (which of course measures people's emotional as well as rational actions) to sort itself out following the shock to the system.

In sum, I believe that the Equivolume charting method has a great deal to recommend it. The crucial concept of scaling the horizontal by volume rather than time is especially appealing to logic. Readers should not, however, necessarily accept my critique of the concept of equal volumes in consolidations and later price moves; reading the original book is well advised so that one can fairly draw his or her own conclusion.

USING EQIVOLUME CHARTS WITH REDUCED EFFORT

Earlier in these pages, I said it is important to do some actual graphing of stocks by hand in order to capture and internalize the "feel" of what is happening in the market. I believe that is true for Equivolume charts, especially because they will be new to most readers and therefore will take a bit of getting used to and mentally absorbing in depth. That said, we live in a world of electronic speed, and every market participant's time is highly valuable. Plotting graphs by hand now seems to be an activity of lessened value per unit of time spent. Fortunately, it is possible to access Equivolume charts' insights and implications without drawing them by hand. The Arms Companies, Dick Arms's business, has licensed the Equivolume graphing technique to *MetaStock,* the very powerful and versatile technical analysis software offered by Equis, International.* Information on how to acquire access to Equivolume charting capability is provided in the appendix of this book.

Whether you draw them by hand or access them via software or online on the Internet, Equivolume charts provide an added depth of insight into what is driving—and inhibiting—a stock's price movement. Trading volume is what makes stock prices move. A perfect balance of buying and selling pressure in terms of numbers of shares wanted and supplied would create no net movement in a stock's price (assuming that buy-

---

*In 1996, Equis was acquired by Reuters Group plc. The latter firm is also the parent of Lipper Inc., the mutual funds data and analysis firm by which the author is employed at the time of this writing. The author's decision to include significant and favorable discussion of Equivolume techniques was in no way influenced by his employment status, nor was compensation requested, offered, or given.

ers and sellers entered their orders at the same moments and/or that an exchange-floor specialist maintained a very tight market). But the real world we live in seldom sees actual equilibrium in stock supply and demand. News, emotional reaction to world and local events, and even our tendency to respond to market volume and price activity themselves are among many factors that cause buying and selling pressure to vary over time, whether time is measured in seconds and hours, or days, weeks, and months. For the reasons mentioned earlier, these nontraditional charts provide greater emphasis on trading volume and, by the nature of their construction, enable their users to more easily integrate the combinations of volume and price activity that occur in any given period of trading time.

EASE OF MOVEMENT: ANOTHER USEFUL VOLUME-BASED CONCEPT

In addition to, and closely associated with, Equivolume charting ideas, the 1994 Arms book provides investors and traders with another interesting construct for "ease of movement." The basic idea underlying Equivolume charting is that it shows the market student where, in price terms, a stock is having a difficult time moving further up or down. After a rise, a wide single day's box or a series of square or oversquare boxes indicates that a great deal of selling volume was encountered by buyers whose purchasing power was therefore unable to move price up much at all, as contrasted to the upward price effects that buying pressure had created in prior days. Ease of movement might otherwise be called *ability to move* since *ease* seems to connote the opposite of difficulty. The concept Arms gave us is the idea of measuring in fairly simple mathematical terms how freely (or not) price is able to move for a given amount of trading activity. That in turn can be plotted on a graph and used to discern when the forces driving price movement—up or down—are gaining or losing steam.

Here we must introduce three readily understandable terms that Mr. Arms used. The first is *range.* Not surprisingly, that is the distance between the lowest and highest prices of the day. In mathematical terms, it is simply "high minus low." The range is denominated in either dollars per share or vertical box units on the Equivolume chart. For simplicity, I would advise using dollars since that makes the concept much more intuitive.

Arms then defines what he calls the *Box Ratio,* which is equal simply to the day's volume (denominated in horizontal boxes rather than actual shares) divided by the range. If a stock had a range of $3 from high to low and traded 6 million shares in the session, and if 3 million shares equaled one horizontal box worth of volume, the Box Ratio would be two boxes divided by $3, or 0.67. If, by contrast, that same day's $3 range had been established in trading of 12 million shares (representing four horizontal boxes' width), then the Box Ratio would be 4 divided by $3, or 1.33. The higher the Box Ratio, the less free the price movement is, or the more difficult price movement is. If it takes twice as much volume to create a given price range in the same stock on one day as on another, we readily see that there is more congestion, more evenly weighted battling going on between buyers and sellers on the day when more volume occurs within the same price range. Again, then, remember that the Box Ratio is proportional to the difficulty of movement.

The third term is the *Midpoint Move*. Arms says that the commonly used measurement of net price change—namely, from close to close—is somewhat arbitrary and therefore not as indicative of true market movement as the difference between the midpoint price on the first day and the midpoint price on the second. For example, suppose a stock trades on Thursday between 40 and 44, closing at 42.50. Then on Friday it trades between 42 and 44, again closing at 42.50, or "unchanged" in conventional terms. Arms says that since the midpoint of the range on Friday (namely, 43) was higher than the midpoint on Thursday (namely, 42), the stock should be considered to have made net upside progress since its range on the second day had a higher midpoint. To Arms, close is no more important than price at 1:37 p.m. or 10:24 a.m. He considers the proper measure of the day's net movement to be the net difference between the midpoints, either upward or downward. In this case, the Midpoint Move on Friday is +$1, from 42 to 43.

The penultimate step in using the ease-of-movement approach is to compute the day's EMV, which stands for *ease of movement*. This value, which has either a positive or negative sign, is as follows:

$$\text{EMV} = \text{Ease of Movement} = \frac{\text{Midpoint Move}}{\text{Box Ratio}}$$

Essentially, what this formula says is that the day's action in this stock is quantified by seeing how much net price movement occurred (on the midpoint rather than closing basis, remember), divided by the difficulty of movement. Suppose that the difficulty (or "ease") of movement as calculated in the Box Ratio described above was 1.33 for the day because the normal two-point price range was accomplished on more than normal trading volume. The EMV for Friday would thus be 1.00 divided by 1.33 or +0.75. If the midpoint move had been negative, the sign of the numerator and therefore of the EMV ratio would also be negative.

Now that we have each day's EMV, how do we use it? After considerable experimentation including back testing, Arms concluded that the best approach was to compute and plot either a 5-day or a 13-day moving average of the EMVs. Experience has shown the 13-day version to be best since it results in fewer whipsaws or false signals. (Likewise, Arms recommends use of a 13-week moving average when using EMV data based on weekly Box Ratios and weekly Midpoint Moves.) The buying and selling signals given by this strongly volume-influenced ratio are straightforward:

> Buy when the moving average of EMV crosses up through the zero line. Sell when the moving average of EMV crosses down through zero.

What these rules tell us is to buy stocks that have begun to demonstrate on a fairly consistent daily basis that they have a greater ability to move upward easily than to move downward easily. The interaction of volume and price change will determine the numerical value of the daily EMV, and 13 daily EMVs averaged (or more, simply, summed) provide a signal that avoids most whipsaws. Two contrasting examples of good and bad ease-of-movement levels or trends will illustrate the use of this system in a way that should make intuitive sense. If a stock is moving up most days on fairly average volume but is successfully adding fairly large amounts to its value, such that the shapes of the rectangles on an Equivolume chart would be skinny and tall, that would be represented by a positive moving average of daily EMV scores. However, suppose that stock then begins to encounter resistance. It will do one of three things:

1. Its advance will be slowed (tiny net daily gains), resulting in smaller daily EMVs, and therefore the 13-day average EMV will remain positive but decline.
2. Its advance will be stopped, on fairly heavy "churning" volume, so that the daily EMVs will become zero on average, again lowering the 13-day moving average.
3. The stock will begin to decline, creating negative daily EMVs that will rapidly turn what had been a positive 13-day EMV into a negative—and penetrating zero is the sell signal.

If a stock runs up on skinny daily box shapes and then immediately reverses pattern and starts a series of downward skinny boxes, the 13-day formulation of EMV will take about 6 days to turn negative, unless the daily declines are quite large. Thus the EMV approach would fail to provide a timely sell signal. However, the pattern just described is extremely rare. Stocks do not usually move up easily and then immediately begin to move down as or more easily. Much more commonly, volume begins to build and more sellers come in as price rises, causing the daily boxes to go square or wider. That is a supply or congestion area. If the stock is unable to digest such profit taking and again move out of the congestion area on the upside, that area will be called a *top,* and the stock will decline from it. A sequence roughly in line with conditions 1 through 3 above has occurred, and that will define a move from positive down through the zero line for the 13-day EMV line, triggering a sell signal.

This, then, is a brief summation of the EMV approach, which has as its core a strong consideration of volume in determining what the future course of a stock price will be. Where conventional daily bar charts look at formations based on price movement only, the EMV approach takes into account what volume was doing that was causing the price movements. EMV thus is a richer, two-dimensional indicator. Once again, this description is much more abbreviated than that in Mr. Arms's 1994 book, to which interested readers are hereby referred.

SUMMARY

In this chapter, we have concluded our survey and very brief explanation of two important volume-based technical analysis systems pioneered by Richard W. Arms, Jr. Equivolume charts make the volume dimension of trading much more visible and technically prominent than do conventional daily bar charts. And the EMV, or ease-of-movement ratio, moving average provides a fairly simple mathematical means of tracking changes in a stock's ability to move upward, versus downward, more easily. Both techniques are significant additions to a good technician's arsenal, and in my judgment that is true specifically because they explicitly give due attention to the changing amounts of trading volume that cause a stock's price change.

PART THREE

RADICAL NEW CONCEPTS AND APPROACHES

CHAPTER 8

Institutions and the Internet: Enemies Wearing Red Coats

I grew up about a dozen miles from the historic battlegrounds of Concord and Lexington, Massachusetts. Of course, stories of Paul Revere and the earliest events of the Revolutionary War were very familiar locally. One vivid image—and a source of some local, 20/20-hindsight humor—was that the British soldiers were incredibly easy to spot, and pick off, because they wore bright red coats into battle. With that image in mind, I will explore with you two major sources of potential trouble, and two causes of considerable and highly visible trading-volume concentrations: institutional investors and Internet investors. While the former are professionals and those surfing and trading on the Internet are primarily individual investors, in many ways the two groups exhibit the same sorts of crowd behavior. Their patterns of action are self-damaging during periods of market reversal. You can take financial advantage of them because in effect, like those Tory soldiers of over 200 years past, they wear red coats—their presence and direction are easy to spot any time you care to look. Thinking in terms of volume dynamics, our task as would-be successful traders and investors is to notice large crowds of these two types, and then to act contrary to their behavior.

Recall that, back in Chapter 2, we introduced the concept and beneficial thinking of the behavioral finance school of thought on the world of investments. Generations of money managers have been taught, both in the classroom and on the job, that the investment market is a nearly scientific world filled with data and formulas, and it is therefore a comfortingly logical place. Therefore, they were told, learn and trust in the dividend discount model, the efficient-markets hypothesis, and other academic conventions, and go about the business of following the fundamentals, and all will be well. In the past decade or so, the rising dominance of institutional holdings *and now of trading* in the daily marketplace, and lately the growth of the Internet's influence on individual investors and traders, have helped to spotlight and thereby to discredit the mechanistic, exclusively fundamentals-based assumptions of the old school.

Behavioral finance has shed light on the great importance of human psychology and related disciplines in explaining the previously seemingly irrational patterns of price *and volume* in stock market movements. In this chapter we will explore both institutional actions and individual investors' crowd-behavior foibles in terms of behavioral finance explanations. We will see how both groups of investors, unwittingly but quite dependably, form huge crowds and do the wrong thing *en masse* at price turning points in the market. Their footprints are "all over the tape," as veteran observers would say. In our terms, they leave extremely visible trails and patterns in volume data on the overall market—and in individual stocks. As will be developed in considerable detail in Chapters 9 and 10, concentrations of extreme volume most often accompany turning points in price. Institutions and Internet-enabled, Internet-stimulated investors create exactly the prototypical kinds of volume flare-ups that we watch for as signals of price reversals.

THE DRIVERS OF INSTITUTIONS' INVESTING ACTIVITY

Institutional investors—bank trust departments, foundations, pension plans, insurance companies, and mutual funds—typically account for over half of daily trading activity on the New York Stock Exchange, and by some estimates often as much as 70 percent. In the NASDAQ market, too, institutions are clearly the major participants in huge-capitalization issues such as Intel and Microsoft and Cisco Systems. But when a particular type of investing— be it Internet stocks themselves, or new issues, or technology stocks, or biotech companies—becomes hot, institutions flock to that arena almost without regard to the size of the stocks' market capitalizations. Although there remains a fairly small minority still guided by conservative valuation principles, institutional equity managers *must* participate in the currently hottest areas to keep up in the competitive performance derby. Their presence is readily detectable because they trade in huge volume.

Competition

Personal pride of accomplishment, no small thing for people whose life's work involves trying to beat the market, has long existed as a motivation for portfolio managers. Getting an annual Performance Certificate from Lipper as best in their investment class, or being awarded five stars by Morningstar, not only provides ego gratification for a portfolio manager but also gives the fund's marketing company an opportunity to advertise its Number 1 status. Such advertising exposure is a key to attracting additional assets from the investing public—and the management company reaps added revenue of somewhat over 1 percent annually from the resulting additional dollars under management.

Short-Term Results

In the Internet age, keeping secrets that involve publicly available data is nigh impossible. The fund management companies' own Web sites display performance and resulting rankings of their best funds prominently, but that is just the beginning. Each day *The Wall Street Journal*'s mutual funds quotation pages include grades of fund performance supplied by Lipper, and in late 2000 *The New York Times* began carrying star ratings in its pages as well. But even an investor who never sees those broad-circulation dailies need go no further than the Internet for a plethora of locations to find fund-performance data and rankings. Literally dozens of sites provide lists of the currently hottest funds as measured over any of several short time periods. Many sites also provide screening tools that allow any investor or trader to find out quickly exactly what funds of any given type are "doing it" and which are less hot-handed at the moment. Such information is useful in that studies have shown that losing funds tend to remain losers. However, there is little evidence that funds outperform the market over more than short periods when market styles or fads shift. Nevertheless, media coverage of who or what is hot (and not), plus the investing public's desire to own the best and most profitable funds, means that short-term performance is more important today than it has been at any previous time in the mutual fund industry's history.

Unfortunately, career success and current bonus earnings of portfolio managers are in large numbers of instances tied to short-term results—the latter to windows as short as 3 months. For that reason, any but the most confirmed and well-advertised long-term value-oriented managers are virtually driven to play short-term performance games. This means two things to them:

- They cannot forgo participating in whatever is the hot idea or trend *du jour*.
- They absolutely cannot tolerate holding stocks that predictably will act as drags on performance.

This deadly combination of competitively forced attitudes may well go a good distance in explaining why value was trounced by growth in the recent several years of roaring markets: There simply was no time to be patient and hold value. Doing so was a fool's game when measured by the yardstick of short-term performance and personal compensation.

THE IMPACT ON THE MARKET OF INSTITUTIONS' INVESTING PRACTICES

What does all this have to do with our primary interest, the noting and profitable use of volume data for purposes of identifying price tops and bottoms in individual stocks? It is a central, and predictable, and measurable force that drives massive and concentrated surges in trading volume in stocks that experience either good or bad news. We will expand on and demonstrate in detail the resulting volume patterns in Chapters 9 and 10. For the present, let us merely say in the strongest terms that the competitive performance derby forces portfolio managers to act as herd animals do: They all "must" get out of stocks at the same time on any hint of problems or lack of future smooth sailing. And, although greed is less instantly crystallized into buying action than fear is into selling behavior, portfolio managers are effectively forced to form crowds in the hottest stocks and concepts. Thus, whether the news on a stock is good or bad, it generates very concentrated buying and selling action by portfolio managers who collectively own huge percentages of a company's shares. Moves in price and especially volume changes are extremely large and highly visible in our age of instant screening and screaming headlines.

Buying Stocks

Like those Tory soldiers wearing red coats, portfolio managers find it very difficult to hide. The more successful a fund has been recently, the more assets it draws. The larger a fund's size, the bigger the position it is likely to hold in any given stock. (Some degree of concentration in holdings is virtually required since a fund that keeps adding many hundreds of different positions will by definition tend to act more like the broad averages and therefore will have greater difficulty in outperforming the averages or beating other funds.) In a time when everything, including portfolio activity, is speeding up, fund managers will find their performance numbers hindered if they try to accumulate desired stock positions gradually so as not to be noticed and not to move the market. Some competitor(s) will surely say, "damn the torpedoes" and order the immediate purchase of a couple of million shares. Thus, the race is on when the news is good. Portfolio managers all try to buy the same stocks, the hot groups or concepts, at the same time. Well, we who watch volume can readily observe their appearance and their building into a crowd by tracking the trading volume they generate. Chapter 9 will show how to measure—simply and easily—the formation, maximization, and dispersal of the buying crowd. While the colonists were exhorted not to shoot "'til you see the whites of their eyes,'" we as investors must watch closely until the number of red coats stops increasing—and then immediately take action to sell what they have been buying. Remember, once the size of a buying crowd tops out, there cannot be enough new buyers to keep price from falling back. When all the big buyers are satisfied, who is left to buy in size?

Selling Stocks

What we have been describing in terms of multiple portfolio managers rushing in at one time to buy stocks is true even more intensely when bad news occurs and selling is perceived as appropriate. Look at it this way: If you are a portfolio manager and see some attractive action in a given stock or group, you of course suspect that the stock(s) involved will do well in the short term. You may well have legitimate doubt as to whether the presently popular issues will have staying power or continued momentum. At the very least, there is room for doubt, and there may be a choice among several individual stocks as means to play the trend. And finally, you do have the option of deferring action or deciding not to play at all. Maybe the day's hot stock would help your performance over a sustained period, but maybe not.

In contrast, when you own a stock that is in the unfortunate position of experiencing a "negative surprise," as the Street calls it, you are absolutely sure of the result and know the only (short-term) rational course to pursue: You must sell immediately. There is no doubt about the stock; if it is in your portfolio, you have a definite problem and a decision to make. You know that dozens or even hundreds of your peers are simultaneously agonizing over this exact same painful reality, that a stock is going to tank. What to do? It is very difficult to be the patient one who says, "I can tough it out because I know this is a great company with only a single, short-term, minor problem." First, you cannot be sure there will be no further bad news. You can only hope. Second, you know that the price pressure will be extreme for at least a day or two, and at a minimum you strongly suspect that selling immediately will put you in the front of the line and thereby probably get you a less-bad price and a smaller loss than others who hesitate. If you sell immediately, you will get out of the way of likely additional sellers in coming days, and possibly some further but unspecifiable bad news from the company or from another in its business. You reason that you will have a smaller loss than any competitors who may possibly hang on in hope.

And, of course, the sooner you sell, the more time you have to work with the cash proceeds, trying to recoup your setback in some other promising issue. Remember, there is no time to waste in this performance race since public measurement occurs daily and official measurement occurs quarterly. And, speaking of quarters, it will be less painful if you have erased that embarrassing stock's name from your list of holdings before the next meeting of the directors or trustees, and before the next shareholder report is mailed. Finally, it will be personally less painful to remove the sight of that offending stock from your own view sooner rather than later.

For all these reasons, selling crowds are larger and their price impact is more severe and immediate than is observed with buying crowds. While it is definitely true that fear is a stronger and more urgent motivator than greed, what we have seen is that the motivation—what a kind word for a terrible thrust forcing action—for selling is more acute and immediate than that driving buying on unexpected good news! As we shall explore in great depth and detail in Chapter 9 and even more so in Chapter 10, in the case of downside price and volume explosions, selling by a huge crowd will create some predictable and clearly measurable volume and price patterns. And these can be highly useful to us as investors and traders who are willing to wait for and then gain from advantageous price situations rather than buy and sell at otherwise randomly chosen times and prices.

Selling action by crowds in individual stocks tends to be much more intense in terms of volume explosion than is urgent buying. What is interesting—and this will be covered in greater depth in the chapters that follow—is that selling in the overall market that constitutes a classically described "selling climax" tends to last over more days and to build to a crescendo. When making decisions about individual stocks, one must carefully discern, even in the intense emotional heat of the moment, which kind of selling is driving a stock down violently. The reason is that the emotional aftermath is extremely different in individual-stock high-volume smashes than in overall-market collapses. To return to the analogy of the British soldiers of yore, when you see a massive number of red coats—and they will indeed be impossible to miss!—it is crucial to take the right action at just the right time once their numbers have peaked and started declining. Fire much too soon and your position will be overrun. Fire a bit prematurely and you may face a long recuperation period from a nagging but nonlethal injury to your capital.

THE INTERNET: A GREAT TOOL BUT A TERRIBLE MASTER

Like fire, the Internet is a very powerful tool for good, but it can also turn against us and cause huge damage and destruction. The individualized outcome depends on how, and how carefully, each of us uses it.

Here are several ways the Internet is a great boon for investors and traders:

- It can save you a great deal of time (and gasoline) in locating important information.
- You can get a lot of information from brokerage firms and mutual fund companies without exposing yourself to selling pressure tactics as a by-product of your inquiry.
- Huge amounts of crucial technical analysis information that once cost hundreds of dollars or more per year to have delivered (slowly!) by mail or online can now be had at no additional cost beyond an Internet subscription—and that can be gotten free as well!
- The Internet is never closed, so you can trawl for information 24 hours a day.
- Brokerage accounts utilizing the Internet's speed, huge bandwidth, and anonymity can allow the careful self-directed trader or investor to implement decisions without possibly crucial delays while phones are busy or account executives are "out of the office."
- Speaking of brokers, an Internet account prevents you from having to deal with the inevitable pitch that you buy the product of the month. This frees your mind from required self-defense so you can think about strategy and tactics.
- Internet brokerage firms have collapsed the commission structure to the extent that you should now be able to dismiss transaction costs as a reason not to make a contemplated move. If you still

find yourself worrying about commissions, you need to change brokerage firms so fees will become a nonissue.

Thus, without question, actual results depend on how, and how carefully, investors use the Internet.

In this chapter and elsewhere in the book (especially in the appendix), you will find numerous references to useful Internet investment and trading resources. In each case the address (or URL) is provided along with a description of the content and an explanation of the importance and use of the information found there. Like carbon paper in its time, electronic typewriters in theirs, the first fax machines in the 1970s, and more recently e-mail, the Internet has become one of those things we cannot imagine life without. As investors and particularly as traders, once we go there, we cannot imagine ever going back to the old way—and cannot imagine how we previously functioned in its absence. Implementing investment strategies and tactics based on understanding and acting on volume dynamics will be of considerably diminished power if you try to do it using a telephone and a traditional broker. Needless to say, I am assuming throughout these pages that you *are* Internet brokerage equipped!

The Downside of Internet Access to the Market

Having skipped over Caesar and instead praised the Internet, I must hasten to raise some cautions about its use. We will look at each of these in some detail, with the understanding that together they are inextricably connected with reading volume dynamics as it describes and measures crowd behavior. A major reason we dove into behavioral finance, contrarian strategy, and crowd behavior early in this book is that they are the reasons that watching volume actually works as a way of timing purchases and sales. The Internet has intensified the effects of emotional behavior by individuals and has speeded the formation and increased the size of investor and speculator crowds. Therefore, it behooves any serious student of the stock (and option) markets to examine and truly integrate into daily behavior the effect of Internet trading on volume and prices.

Recall from Chapter 2 some of the findings of anthropology, psychology, and contemporary sociology that describe human behavior. We weight and act on most-recent news more than is truly justified; we are strongly impelled to action by vivid experiences; we seek safety rather than risk; we are group animals; we respond strongly to reinforcement, whether it be positive or negative in nature; we tend to make irrational and inappropriate judgments and decisions when under high stress; we seek authorities, especially in areas where we believe our expertise to be sub-par; paradoxically, both shame and overconfidence are deeply ingrained mental attributes. Finally, ours is an up-tempo and instant-gratification-oriented society. These human traits, failings, and weakness biases are, mostly inadvertently but sometimes deliberately, brought out for self-destructive use against Internet-empowered investors, exactly because and when they use the Internet.

The Safety and Comfort in Groups

Anthropologists have documented how early *Homo sapiens* was naturally driven to act in groups rather than individually. Conditioned not to strike out on risky solo adventures, cave dwellers learned to accept the will and apparent wisdom of the group. It was one step from there to preferring to follow a leader, an authority figure, over exercising individual thinking and will. Thus we came to be seekers of authorities, especially in areas where we believe our expertise to be subpar. In modern Western societies, one of the clusters of greatest deficit in education and training consists of economics, money, business, and personal finance. Therefore, people tend to seek leaders or perceived experts to guide their thinking and actions. Telephone switch hotlines run by widely followed stock and mutual funds advisers are examples of the ease with which huge crowds of followers are willing to pay and follow a leader in the personal finance area. Annual "best funds for the new year" stories (and entire editions) published routinely in magazines are extreme examples of how people will buy whatever perceived experts say despite the fact that it is impossible to deliver: The performance of a fund can be calculated for the past, but it cannot be forecast into the future.

Enter the Internet. How could anyone conceive of a more efficient way of jumping around to seemingly limitless numbers of perceived experts' Web sites for news, insight, and guidance? What a "find" for those who want to be led! And since so much of the investment opinion and information available on the Internet is free, there is nothing driving the user to make a sober appraisal of value received, as one does before writing a check to renew a periodical subscription. In addition, the content offered on the Internet is provided via what itself is seen as an authoritative medium: the computer. In times past, anything we saw on radio or TV (recall Orson Welles's Halloween 1938 *War of the Worlds* trick on nation-wide radio) or read in the newspaper was believed trustworthy content. Baby Boomers experienced the miracles of the dawn of the computer age and its growth; later-born earthlings entered a world wherein computers were a daily fact of existence no more to be questioned than space stations or telephones. We understand that computers derive their output from databases. And it is but one simple jump of logic to assume as a matter of course that whatever comes from a database must be true. Thus the computer itself is seen as an authority per se. So when the computer delivers Internet content, mere mortals tend strongly to rely on the output unquestioningly—even if that content is actually mere opinion!

What does all this have to do with trading volume as a guide to investment and trading moves? Paul Revere received his critical information by lantern signal and then spread that news to individual towns' leading citizens at the speed of horseback travel. Paul Julius Reuter relied on carrier pigeons in the 1850s to send financial news between Germany and Belgium where telegraph lines did not yet connect. Suffice to say that the Internet is more efficient and infinitely faster than any prior means of mass communication. For our purposes, the key result of this immediacy of idea and fact transmission is that huge numbers of people come to the same conclusion all at once, and act—*as a crowd*—all at once. A crowd of traders all trying to do the same thing creates huge volume associated with and driving a given price move. And, as described in Chapters 9 and 10, subsequent price patterns are predictable once a crowd has acted and starts to disperse. The Internet, functioning as a transmitter of the facts and opinions of known or presumed authorities (corporate spokespersons, brokerage analyst stars, and stock pickers of all stripes), has become an agent of crowd creation. Its electronic speed and transglobal reach have immensely telescoped the time news takes to generate a crowd and the time the crowd takes to assemble and then to complete its acting. But it all begins with humans' willingness to seek leaders or authorities.

In most cases the Internet's transmission is innocent enough. In a few instances, however, individuals of dark motive have figured out the dynamics of information and opinion spreading and its predictable resulting impact on stock prices in generating huge trading volume. Although not always clearly discernible as such from the outset, such people are the touters and scam artists that the Securities and Exchange Commission is very visibly pursuing and prosecuting. But even where the information is factual and those who spread it have nothing but the purest of motives in doing so, the Internet's power to attract a crowd is a force that will usually hurt investors who are acting with the crowd. One should always ask, "Am I joining a crowd by doing this trade?" and then refrain from the action if the answer is yes. Watching changes in volume, even on an intraday basis, makes determining an accurate answer quite easy.

The Excitement of New News

The subtle but strong force of the Internet only begins with its speed. Psychologists have shown through experiments that we humans tend to place unduly high value or emphasis on **information received most recently.** One amazing demonstration of this was accomplished in Las Vegas. A huge wheel with lucky numbers on it, ranging from $50 to several hundred, was spun in the presence of onlookers. These folks were then asked to estimate the number of member countries making up the United Nations. Time after time, the responses were biased higher or lower by the number last shown on the wheel. Internet users can literally continuously expose themselves to new information, whether by actively surfing various sites or merely by standing still and letting the news ticker roll before their eyes. A company reports good or bad news, and the brokerage analysts and other commentators pronounce opinions reinforcing that news's implications. The snow-balling price action also tells the observing investor to rely on this latest revelation and immediately buy or sell—in line with the latest direction.

The enormity of news-driven trading volume itself becomes yet another piece of new "information" to which an Internet-enabled investor or trader is exposed, adding yet one more piece of current input likely to trigger a response. Here are just a few of the popular Web sites where millions of individuals go to get information (some of it no more than opinion) that is highly current and therefore likely to excite them to action:

biz.yahoo.com/research/earncal.e.cgi?s   This site anticipates EPS news.

bigchartss.com or **quote.yahoo.com**   These sites provide charts and news items. In particular, the chat rooms at Yahoo, because of its extremely large built-in following, reflect crowd opinion and excitement.

CBSMarketwatch.com   Due to its immense TV audience feed, this site has attracted a large crowd and holds the potential for inviting touters slipped in among the serious discussants.

TheStreet.com   This site has a large following because of its message boards, as well as its constant stream of news and staff editorial postings, combined with easy access to charts and lists of hot stocks.

ClearStation.com   This site has great appeal because it seems to provide a feel of the day-trading community's mindset.

SiliconInvestor.com   This site is perceived by many as "the original" Internet investing forum. It is focused on the exciting world of technology stocks.

icefi.com   The Internet Closed-End Fund Investor forum acts as a gathering place for those watching takeover attempts and other news in such funds.

MotleyFool.com   This site appeals to a steady and growing clientele of fairly new Wall Street participants who are directed to the site by its wildly popular books. It tends to be somewhat of a momentum- and trend-following site, and it is therefore useful for sensing crowd opinion.

The Technicolor Picture

But newness itself is not the entire story. Increasingly, what we see unfold before our eyes on Wall Street, viewed in living color and in real time, is extremely vivid. No longer need we wait for the TV news at dinnertime or later. We are witnessing actual pieces of business and financial history, now including executives' press conferences, live. News of an accounting fraud, a billion-dollar writeoff, a gigadollar merger agreement, or a well-known company dramatically bettering or missing its quarterly earnings target is all over the screen in front of us. It is hard hitting and either exciting or wrenching in its emotional impact. Psychologists refer to this as **vividness:** The more vivid a piece of input is, the more likely a person is to react—and to react immediately and strongly. Almost 20 years after the fact, scare-tactic 1964 political ads showing an atomic bomb explosion had considerable effect on voters. That is vividness in action.

Thus, no matter how we try to gird our minds and emotions against the possibilities of undue emotional impact from Internet-delivered news, we are exposing ourselves to the very vividness of the events themselves. When in real time you are watching a stock's price jump (or plummet, and remember that the downside will be more violent than any rally because fear is a stronger stimulus than greed), you are seeing vividness in action. The sharp price change itself, especially when accompanied by incredible trading frenzy (volume), makes taking action often very tempting. If you have ever had the misfortune of owning a widely institutionally held stock and seeing a 30 to 50 percent price destruction caused by bad news, you understand vividness in its most brutal and sudden form. The vividness of the huge price and volume action overlays itself atop the immediacy of the latest new information, powerfully urging traders to act immediately. When they do, they become part of the crowd that creates, by its own action, a volume spike or a volume crescendo. Without the Internet, events in the real world and on the tape would be less vivid and the crowd reaction would be slower to form and smaller in total size.

The Power of Rewards

And yet we are not done with our catalog of ways in which the Internet experience causes us to respond to emotional stimuli. I need not provide any specific examples of the many behavioral experiments showing the effects of **reinforcement.** In a nutshell, we know that repetition of the same stimulus, combined with reinforcements, strongly increases the likelihood that we will change our beliefs and therefore potentially take or alter our actions. Here is an example of the ways that Internet use provides investors with greater reinforcements than that which a laid-back, read-the-magazines player receives. Suppose we see some item of corporate news, and within perhaps 20 minutes several major news agencies and Web site editorial bodies such as TheStreet.com and CBSMarketWatch.com all file stories repeating the information and perhaps expanding on why it is important. We see a rather sharp move in stock price, up or down. That convinces us that others are taking this news item as significant because obviously the supply-and-demand balance for that stock has been altered markedly. Not much time passes before we see followup releases quoting major brokerage analysts as having changed their opinions by a notch or two. Wow! These professionals are so deeply affected by this news that they've changed their outlook on the company in a matter of hours or less. That certainly adds weight to the mountain of evidence we are seeing pile up. And the volume of trading itself tells us that probably both thousands of individual investors and dozens or hundreds of institutional money managers are all on the same page—selling at any price or buying en masse. Each big block functions as just another piece of evidence—reinforcement—pushing us toward action. And of course taking action in line with all the parallel indications we are watching means we will be joining the crowd. Totally innocently, but nevertheless extremely effectively, the Internet has acted as a reinforcement engine.

The Fear of Being Alone, Out of and in Front of the Crowd

Sociologists well know what **group animals** people are. A lot of it goes back to our need to band together for hunting and self-defense in cave-dwelling times. Whatever the causes, a very large majority of people are most comfortable when they are in sync with other people and feel truly uneasy when they are alone and out of step. Such is the basis on which fashion trends in clothing and cars create billions of dollars in sales of goods to replace perfectly functional older versions merely because they are no longer in step with the times, which really means in favor with the latest whims of the group. Think back over your personal investment experience as relates to the opinions of others. How did you feel when you ran opposite to the prevailing party atmosphere during the dot-com boom in early 2000 and your friends and colleagues brushed off your "old-fashioned" notions of value and reasonableness? You said those stocks they loved were overpriced and true accidents waiting to happen—and in response you were verbally beaten nearly senseless. You wished you'd kept your mouth shut, right? And did you ever have the courage to put your money on the line during a market crash? Good for you. But what happened when you told someone else you were doing that impossibly risky thing, buying when clearly the whole world wanted to sell? You were summarily and loudly dismissed as crazy, right?

Those belittling feelings are unpleasant, often enough so as to make us reverse our actions despite the correctness of our first judgment. Why do we do that? We can't stand to be out of step with the group. Well, on the Internet we can always readily know exactly what the group thinks. Read it in the chat rooms, see it in the analysts' quoted opinions, note it in the volume and price before our eyes, and of course trace it visually in a stock or index price chart as it is updated every minute to show the straight-line price move in process. We know exactly what the group thinks without asking anyone personally, and we are sorely tempted to join the crowd in its opinion and action. The Internet grabs yet another victim!

The Lure of Anonymity on the World Wide Web

Functioning as an investor or trader on the Internet, for any one of the reasons noted above, can readily become an activity hazardous to your financial health. Together the constellation of influences can be nearly deadly unless we are in control of our emotions, watching for undue but subtle influences, and obeying our tested personal rules and disciplines. There is yet another by-product of the Internet investing experience that drives us to make bad moves: **stress**. Psychologists have long observed that we tend to make irrational and inappropriate judgments and decisions when under high stress. For investors stress can go over the top from a rapidly falling price, bad news a company has just revealed, or the pressure on the market of a crowd in action.

Stress comes from other sources too. Visit a chat room and read the various opinions on any given stock. These are hardly the considered and carefully worded judgments that one would read in an academic paper.

No, these are people screaming at each other! I'm right and you're wrong. The company is going to fail. The company will be the industry leader. The stock is going to 1,000, or to zero. We often feel as a substitute teacher does upon entering a classroom of riotous second graders uninhibited by any supervision. That intensity of market action and opinion alone will raise your blood pressure when thinking about a stock—or the overall market—with the "assistance" of the Internet. Thus in yet another way our investing or trading time on the Internet threatens to be a time of financial self-abuse because we are likely to do things that are not wholly rational *in response to the stress* that the Internet experience itself introduces.

Believe it or not, the list of ways the Internet causes crowds to form and do the wrong thing all together is not yet quite complete. Trading on the Internet allows large crowds of people to simultaneously seek individual **comfort zones**. Recall our diagram and discussion of comfort-zone seeking in Chapter 2. Buying high, holding what has zoomed to silly levels, selling low in panic, and failing to buy clear bargains are all manifestations of investors and traders seeking comfort or avoiding *dis*comfort. Each of those financially damaging behaviors is encouraged or perhaps literally triggered by the combination of influences recited in recent pages. And the fact that we are alone in our office or den makes us feel like individuals rather than like members of a crowd. If we had to yell and gesture wildly to get our orders executed in a physical crowd of humanity, as floor traders do, we might see the madness of the mob and think twice before buying or selling in tandem with it. While our pulse may be racing, we quietly point and click and our order is entered. We feel immediate catharsis in the knowledge that we have now accomplished the "right thing"—that action that relieves our prior stress and discomfort. And of course time will soon show that we have anonymously joined a crowd in a foolish move.

Another aspect of anonymity that trading via the Internet provides is also worth mentioning. Psychologists know that shame is a major inhibitor of actions and can be the driver of complex avoidance behaviors in some people as well. In parallel fashion to the way our physical and quiet Internet-trading isolation shields us from knowing we are part of a trading mob, the ability to take action without any other human being knowing it provides cover for us in otherwise awkward times. In just the same way that brokers have learned not to remind their clients of deep loss positions because of the pain (via shame) these bring, we as individuals can quietly click away an embarrassing and troubling loser. No need to phone Bob or Betty Broker and say, "You know, I've realized what a stupid mistake I made in buying that Tulips2You.Com *after* its IPO back in 1999. I should have listened to you and not paid so much. I think it's time to admit my folly, take my loss, and move on." We avoid shame with the silent click of the mouse. And shame may also exist in the form of buying high, joining the crowd late, when one feels sheepish for not having seen what a great opportunity was available 200 points lower. Of course, when enough individuals exercise the same capitulation at one time, their single actions collectively will create a crowd's volume of trading, probably signaling at least a temporary price reversal once the crowd is finished.

The Shame and Overconfidence Drivers of Emotions

Strangely, in the infinitely complex web of the human brain, shame and overconfidence can coexist! Psychologists know from numerous experiments that we tend to overestimate our capabilities. For example, when written questionnaires are answered, about 90 percent of males will pronounce themselves above-average drivers. In investing, people have a tendency to filter their memories conveniently: Their batting averages and slugging percentages become magically higher in memory and estimation than the actual record would show. Professor Terrance Odean has concluded, after examining actual trading records of thousands of investors supplied (with names deleted) by a large discount brokerage house, that investors tend to trade too often and that at least part of the reason they do so is that they inaccurately (optimistically) predict their likelihood of success. With the Internet, we have seen commissions decline to $10 or well below at many firms. This wonderful reduction in costs of transacting has brought with it, however, a huge reduction in people's consciousness of the cost of making a move. If they were faced each time with an old-fashioned dollar commission in three digits—each way—it is likely they would have lower confidence in their ability to make a trade profitable enough to overcome those high costs and pay themselves as well as their brokerage firm. Thus, the Internet has helped us to implement actions initially encouraged by our tendency toward overconfidence.

For all the greatness of the nation, Americans are also spoiled creatures on the whole. Most alive today, your author included, have not lived through such a trauma as the Great Depression. Our last personal experience with war was the armchair "enjoyment" of watching the Gulf conflict in early 1991—an efficient and rapid and startlingly pleasant victory gained mainly by remote control from computer missile-launching consoles. We are indeed a mass culture of instant gratification, people who expect results and expect them now. In the years 1999 and 2000 we began seeing corporate CEOs and chairmen forced to resign over failure of one or two quarters' results to meet prior forecasts. We have come to expect electronic speed in everything. Residents of Manhattan can get, at an added price of course, same-day delivery of books ordered from a popular mass Web site. It is easier and faster to buy a new TV or automobile than to have an old one fixed. All of this creates a mindset expecting immediate action and quick satisfaction.

The rapid gains in IPOs' aftermarket prices in 1998 and 1999, and indeed the 25-percent-plus annual gains in the S&P 500 for 3 years running, caused millions of investors to believe at least subconsciously (against all of history's evidence) that rapid and uninterrupted gains were an American investor's birthright. And much of the good times at that extended party were achieved while pushing keys and clicking mice to exercise our Internet brokerage accounts. Thus we have been subtly conditioned to have favorably biased expectations when transacting on the Internet. Having positive expectations enables people, in large numbers, to trade more often than they ever would have in prior times. Therefore, there are more participants available to join a crowd in buying or selling in a frenzy—leading to volume crescendos and volume spikes. Our job if we wish to be successful is to take advantage of the opportunities the Internet provides while guarding against the easy trap of joining the trading mobs it enables and emboldens.

The Weight of the Time Spent Seeking Information from Internet Sources

Finally, people carry over to their Internet-centered investing habits a subtle but real subconscious attitude created in earlier decades when shopping involved visiting a physical store and taking the time of a knowledgeable salesperson: We feel uncomfortable leaving without having bought something, to pay and thank that proprietor for his or her time and trouble. The Internet provides a vast store of information and powerful tools, rendering buying or selling so very easy. We have spent our time and mental energy there, and have thought about taking action. It seems so unfulfilling, so empty, to leave with our portfolios unchanged. Within limits, brokers know that the more people they reach and the more times they speak to each one, the more likely they are to receive an order. The same dynamic applies on the Internet, even though we have no real need to feel guilty for inaction and no individual we feel directly obligated to. Once again, added encouragement for more people to transact investing business more often than in the past. Thus volume is greater than it would otherwise have been.

SUMMARY

We have seen in these pages how institutional investors and the Internet—separately but in many ways similarly—function as two major influences on market activity. Both create huge amounts of trading volume. Both, for somewhat different reasons but with the same net outcome, therefore act as beacons that highlight the formation of crowds—happenings made simple to note and measure through the widespread and free availability of real-time stock charts equipped with plotted volume. We noted the wonderful and inexpensive tools that the Internet gives individual investors. But then we analyzed the numerous ways, some obvious but many more that are psychologically subtle, in which the Internet tends to push the many unwary toward simultaneously joining the mob in registering an investment opinion by buying or selling. We observed that the immediate global dissemination of facts and opinion—and vivid stimuli in the form of rapidly moving stock prices seen on dramatic charts—has shortened the time it takes for news to be reflected in prices. That implies that market participants face very short reaction times to take advantage of contrarian opportunities to sell at advantageous prices. Along the way, we noted that volume records the size and intensity of the crowd participating. In the next two chapters we will describe, and then explore, the huge psychological fallout of two very important volume patterns: crescendos and spikes.

CHAPTER 9

Volume Crescendos: Beacons of Crowd Activity

Recall that in Chapters 1 and 2 we established the importance of trading volume as a means of monitoring the emotional content of the collective investing public's trading decisions, and as a way of literally measuring by proxy the size of the trading crowd involved. Being able to spot crowds (or "mobs") is important because their actions signal price turning points. We know that "the crowd" in the sense of the quiet majority can be correct during the middle of a price move as long as it remains calm and it is not overwhelmingly large or noisy. But once considerable numbers of individuals in the crowd become agitated and take parallel action in a concentrated time frame, the crowd has become an active mob, and that shift in its nature signals the imminent termination of the price move. The reason this is inevitable, of course, is that stock prices change in response to shifting balances between supply and demand. When a severe and urgent imbalance of orders arises, price moves sharply in order to accommodate the heavy preponderance of buyers or sellers. In order for price to continue in the same direction, it becomes necessary for an even larger group of urgent buyers or sellers—whichever was pushing the price so sharply—to be willing and able to keep pushing the trend further.

We can monitor the size of the crowd that is moved to action simply by watching the trend in volume. Once the volume of trading ceases to increase, momentum in price change will have reached its peak. It literally takes more selling or buying, as the case may be, to keep price going in the same direction. Once the size of the actively participating crowd trying to do the same thing at the same time no longer increases, price will reverse. Then the urgency, or "excitement" in the sense of stimulus, begins to decrease. When that happens, computer-drawn charts and momentum software immediately signal a "change in momentum," and those following such tools know that the trend is over. To the extent they have been involved, they tend to close or reverse their trading positions. Thereby they drive price to start moving in the opposite direction. As more participants and would-be participants note the end of the move, the urgency of their inclination to join the action dissipates, and the volume of trading declines. What was a crescendo of volume and price begins to morph into a parabolic shape and the parabola becomes a wave.

In this chapter we will describe the kinds of changes in group opinion that cause a crescendo of volume to appear. We will trace the thinking of both buyers and sellers as events transpire—and here price change itself is one of the important events. Then we will examine what happens, and how participants feel, after the strong crescendo has ebbed. This aftereffect is important because it has significant and direct implications for subsequent price action. We make profits by being positioned on the correct side of the market for price moves that occur: We take our cues as to which side to be on by watching the patterns of trading volume, because they tell us what the crowd has recently done *and is no longer doing.*

UPSIDE VOLUME AND PRICE CRESCENDOS

It is important to distinguish at the outset of our discussion here a sharp differentiation between volume *crescendos*, which we will discuss here, and volume *spikes*, which constitute the subject matter of Chapter 10. A *crescendo of volume* occurs over a period of several days, often about five or so. It is at first a gradual buildup of daily trading volume, which then accelerates such that volume on each succeeding day grows as the size and excitement of the crowd swells. After several days, however, the story causing the trading becomes widely known, and the number of new participants wanting to take action in the dominant price direction no longer grows. At that time, the crescendo reaches its highest point and is poised for a gradual reversal—if you will, an emotional unwinding. The volume, plotted as bars over a period of consecutive days, is as shown in Figure 9–1.

The plot of volume in a spike situation would not have any of the left-hand half of the shape in the figure. A volume spike begins with a single day of huge volume (perhaps 5, 10, or more times normal) and is followed by the declining or decaying shape seen in the right-hand half of

FIGURE 9−1

Volume Plotted as
Bars over a Period of
Days.

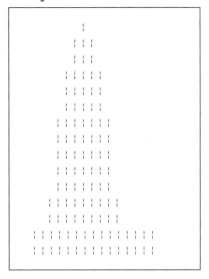

the schematic diagram. The two patterns must be clearly distinguished since the events that drive them and to a considerable extent the emotional aftermaths they leave in their wakes are quite different. This chapter deals with the crescendo pattern only.

Of course, we cannot expect the crescendo in volume to display a shape that is perfectly mathematically predictable in terms of how much it increases per day (Figure 9–2). Multiple external events relating to the stock itself, as well as overall market-mood-shaping news, will affect the size and confidence of the crowd each successive day—perhaps extending its courage (or panic) and extending the formation, or dampening the emotional electricity and thereby shortening the length of this process. Likewise, one should not expect the back side (the right-hand portion) of the volume plot to be perfectly symmetrical with the front side. But once the decay in daily volume starts, it should be expected to take some time to play itself out before trading activity can return to its normal average levels. If, for example, the volume crescendo drove and accompanied a price rally, it will take time to convince late-arriving would-be buyers that there is no use in hunting a bargain since the move truly is over and the stock has lost any hint of upside life. Such bargain hunters may be buyers in moderate number early on the way down in price and volume, but they will quickly become discouraged or scared as price erodes unrelentingly. They will sell out, creating a small amount of still-above-average volume. The unwinding process takes some days or longer to play out fully, until "no one" is still interested in bargain hunting at newly established lower prices.

Crescendos in volume that coincide with an acceleration of the previously existing price trend, exactly because they document the formation of a strongly opinionated trading crowd, cannot occur without predictably *time-coincident crescendos in price.* Crescendos in volume can and do drive, and occur at the same time as, parabolic-like moves of price in both directions: up and down. I cannot emphasize strongly enough that both traders and, yes, even investors must act immediately on noting a price-culminating volume crescendo that has lasted for several days and whose volume is now failing, one day, to exceed that of the prior trading session. One usually need not wait until the close of business to conclude that the latest day was in fact a lower-volume session than its immediate predecessor. Almost always, by about 90 minutes into the new day, one can see that today's early-morning action is less hectic than that of 24 hours earlier. One can accurately predict that the volume total by the end of the day will indeed be below that of yesterday. Mentally, you are taking a moving average of total trading whose time window equals the $6^{1}/_{2}$ hours of a normal trading session. The first hour or two in the new session will almost always reveal whether the crowd is still growing or has already peaked.

If you have been lucky or smart enough to be riding the price action driven by the volume crescendo, there is no time for celebration, ponder-

FIGURE 9−2

AMR Corp: Major Volume Crescendos
at Late May 2000 and In January 2001

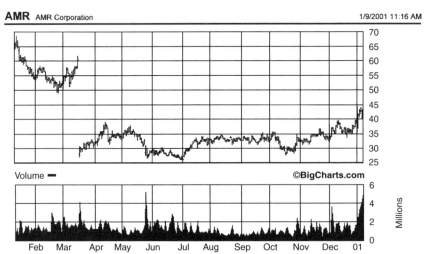

ing, or quiet reflection. You cannot take the weekend to think about it: *The move in price is over because the volume is no longer expanding.* The time to sell is now, not some time in the future. It may be frustrating, on the basis of long-established thinking that focuses on price, to accept the fact that there is no dependable way to forecast in advance the extent of the price move. Price change is a function of the dynamics of supply and demand, so the time for a price reversal is determined by when the crowd's interest ceases to increase. One cannot, either, predict mathematically the exact pattern of daily volume change and thereby know in advance when the volume may peak; observation in real time is required for discerning when the excitement crests.

Remember our discussion, in Chapter 8, of how the Internet age has marked a shortening, a telescoping down if you will, of the length of time it takes for information (and therefore resulting opinion and emotion) to reach and penetrate every interested investor's and trader's mind. Because of that inescapable fact, we must be ever more vigilant in noting crescendos in volume. Many other market participants have computer tools exactly like ours, and therefore "everyone" who is interested will be observing the same volume and price changes as we are, in the same short time frame. The Internet age has brought with it a shortening, a contracting or concentrating, of all phenomena in the trading markets. For that reason, like it or not you must be prepared to take action sooner than you previously would have. In effect, the Internet as the information tool and trading milieu of millions has made more of us need to become shorter-term oriented than we previously thought ourselves, or really desire, to be. The pace of the action has quickened and therefore the time for action to lock in profits and prevent losses is sooner than it would have been in the early 1990s or in prior decades.

A volume crescendo corresponding with a downward sweep in prices after prices have been moving lower for some time *marks the end* rather than the beginning of a price decline. *Beginnings* of price declines accompanied by high volume are virtually always driven by adverse news, which by its nature causes an immediate universal reaction and therefore a sudden *spike* in volume rather than a gradual buildup of trading activity. When stock prices have been eroding and are now lately careening lower, a rising number of investors who previously kept stiff upper lips will capitulate and sell. Bargain valuation gives way to personal discomfort, driving people to feel a short-term need to sell "at any price." Over a period of several days, a rising number of investors will succumb to such panic, abandoning their previous rationality and resolve. At some point, four things happen that signal termination of the downside waterfall in

FIGURE 9-3

Worthwhile Price Bottoms (Arrows) Marked by Multiple-Day
Volume Crescendos

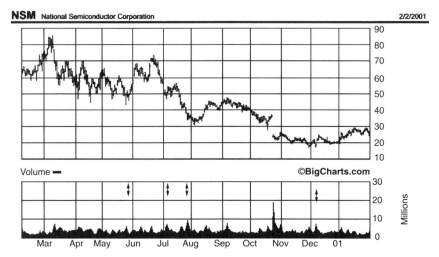

price: First, the pool of those investors who are prone to panicking and abandoning their erstwhile resolve as long-term holders will have been exhausted as rising numbers give up each day. So the potential of more sellers' throwing in the towel is literally reduced as time goes on. Second, some number of would-be panicked holders will actually become numbed by the severity of their financial and emotional pain and will therefore be unable to take action. Figuratively, they will pull the blankets up over their eyes and stop watching. Again, a subtraction from the pool of possible further sellers. Third, margin calls will be sent out and acted on, and when the added selling they cause is already a past factor, they will cease to add to the previously rising tide of panicked selling. Finally, at some point the price of the stock in question is cut down so low that bargain hunters appear, and their buying helps to slow and reverse the panicky price slide, thereby relieving the pain and panic of remaining holders who then cease to be potential sellers. The battle turns, albeit tenuously, to the side of the bulls once the panicky sellers have been found and exhausted. Some old Wall Street wags refer to this process as "stock moving from weak hands to stronger hands." Figure 9–3 shows 4 volume-crescendo bottoms.

Likewise, volume crescendos accompanying (and of course, actually driving) upside price crescendos sustained over a number of days such as a week or longer are much more likely to mark the conclusions of previously existing price advances than their continuations. Volume and upward-price crescendos reflect the capitulation of previous doubters who finally "must buy," as and after the climate of information and opinion has become widely known and very bullish and excited (Figure 9–4).

Crescendos in volume in the life of a single stock, an industry group, or even the whole market, are not mysterious, inexplicable phenomena. The sequence of information and opinion and then emotion that moves a large number of people to buy or sell a stock is not some magical combination of ingredients we cannot analyze and predict. It really is quite an orderly series of days whose dawning brings a slightly changed but progressing net attitude on the part of investors and traders. (The more seasoned a stock is in the hands of the investing public, or the shareholder family of a given company, the greater the number of days it will take for a crescendo to play out. In recent-IPO situations, the information sequence leading to an emotional reaction is shorter and the entire process is more volatile, so you should expect that lengthy crescendos will be rare in such stocks.) Well-established companies have shareholder families that, on average, are less tuned in minute by minute on the Internet than those of recently public companies in hot industries. The latter have tens of thousands of holders who know the stock and its moves better than the company and its products, markets, or strategies. If the typical shareholder is older and longer related to the company's stock, it will take more days for a crescendo to develop and run its course than if the typical shareholder is young and less tied to the company per se and is watching the stock on the Internet several times (or even continuously) during each trading session.

FIGURE 9–4

Three Volume Crescendos Marking Highs of Price Waves Within Six Weeks

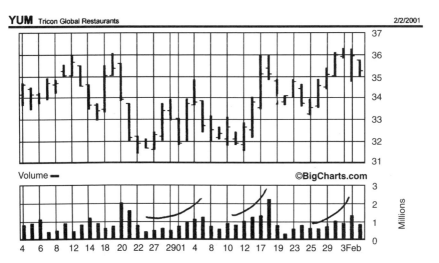

Let us look at the development of shareholders' and traders' thinking over a period of several days as a crescendo in volume and price arises and finally reaches its high point. First, we will trace the development of a crescendo in volume *driving a rally* in price. Opinion is gradually becoming more favorable each day.

Day 1
Some event or fairly minor piece of news, perhaps an initial brokerage recommendation, raises a stock's price a bit on trading volume that is above that of the prior day. This trigger is more likely to originate during the market's trading day or perhaps just before the opening, rather than after the close the prior day. The reason is that a prior-evening event would give a lot of traders who do their surfing and thinking at night the chance to make simultaneous decisions that would be reflected at the opening and would immediately trigger a large volume burst and probably an opening, upside price gap—in effect a price spike rather than a start of a crescendo.

Day 2
Those so inclined find our stock on the list of issues with the most unusual increases in volume. That brings their attention to the story that triggered the volume and price increases on the prior day. These people correctly perceive the story as positive and yet not striking or overwhelmingly urgent. They look at the recent price chart and see that the stock has acted well, and that on day 1 it seemed to accelerate on (a good sign) higher volume. They buy it. People who saw the news on day 1 but took no immediate action now also notice that the stock is continuing to rise and perhaps also observe the rising volume. They feel the stock is proving its staying power on the upside, so they also place buy orders, mainly at market rather than with limits. Maybe a few chat room postings take note of the stock's 2-day run-up. The story is thus spread further. In all, the first couple of days have brought in buyers in rising but still less-than-enormous numbers. Day 2 finds the stock closing higher again, with volume likewise greater than on day 1. The gains have so far been pleasant, but moderate enough so as not to prompt many previous holders to become sellers.

Day 3
An increasing number of information channels are now taking notice. Maybe the stock's well-above-average volume triggered a mention on an investment TV network. Perhaps the company was contacted, and management duly responded that they "know of no reason for the recent rise

in price and volume" or, even more intriguing, said, "We have no comment on our stock's action." The latter would of course immediately make some conspiratorially minded traders suspect fire where there truly is not even any smoke. They read an innocent "no comment" to mean that there is indeed something brewing that management is not ready to talk about, and they interpret the rise in price and volume as putative confirming evidence that "somebody knows something." They jump on board with buy orders. A number of people who saw the action starting more modestly on days 1 and 2 now cannot stand aside any longer; they also buy the stock. On day 3 the cumulative rise in price, now approaching double digits in percent, begins hitting the radar screens of technically oriented momentum traders both small and large. These players are quick to act, and many of them have personal networks with whom they share their latest hot discovery: This stock is looking like something is brewing. Look, it just will not stop rising, and the volume, at x million shares, is way above normal. Brokers who have technically inclined, trader-oriented clients are on the phones and stirring up further buying interest. By the end of the day, a nice price gain is recorded, the stock closes on virtually its highest tick, and volume has perhaps quadrupled over the past 3 days. Very little heavy selling pressure has yet coalesced since, after all, this run has been pleasant but has gone on for only 3 days now.

Day 4

Happily, as events would have it, the stock made a new 52-week high yesterday, or does so this morning. Web sites track current-day highs and lows in real time, so their activist spectators have no need to wait for the next morning's newspapers. That would be so painfully twentieth century! A couple of the hot-story Internet news agencies, perhaps Motley Fool or The Street or CBS Marketwatch, run articles noting our stock's recent pleasant price rise on high volume. Maybe a few others in its industry group are also cooking along, and this begets stories in which favorable fundamentals or prospects are recited as likely justification of the price rise. Volume is really heating up, as just about anywhere a person might look the stock is mentioned, and those who follow the old-fashioned tape keep seeing that symbol dancing across in front of their noses. They catch up with the story and also jump on board. One or more brokerage analysts make favorable comment about a stock they already liked. At least one of them now is also effectively forced to raise his or her price target (since not doing so would constitute a verboten "sell signal" now that the price is above target). Such raised targets beget buying by the customers at those firms, and the rises in target are duly reported in the online media, adding gasoline to a now-raging fire. A check of the Web site chat rooms shows that rumors are flying furiously. Maybe it's a great new product; perhaps they will be taken over by Conglomerate X. The volume is so heavy that all have come to believe someone else must know something. Volume has nearly doubled from day 3's lofty levels. This means that a large number of sellers have started appearing, drawn out by the easy and quick paper profit of recent sessions. Many are longer-term holders, but a few might be traders who bought on day 1 and are happy with more than a 10 percent gain in a few sessions. Yet, despite the fact that selling equals buying, price evidence shows that the pressure is still on the bulls' side. The stock's run-up drives out some short sellers who feel they must cover before their losses snowball excessively. A strong close, if the traders are really in luck, gets a nodding notice on the *Nightly Business Report,* carried nationwide.

Day 5

Everyone who is not asleep knows by now the name and symbol of our stock. The huge volume itself, now maybe about seven times normal, has tweaked more technicians' PC screens and they take notice, joining the buyers. Rumors continue to swirl, and the company remains "suspiciously silent"—surely a blockbuster news item is but hours away! The shorts are beyond nervous and are in the process of being mercilessly squeezed. A couple of smallish mutual funds that trade in momentum issues add their medium-sized buy orders as fuel on the fire. But now, after an hour or so, what had been a nearly straight line price rise starts to flatten out. Volume is still heavy, but price is having trouble. Obviously the extended price run has enticed an increasingly large number of longer-term holders to give thanks and take their rapid and unexpected profits. But the selling does not knock the price down much, and clearly a tug of war is under way between the bulls and bears. The playing field is no longer as lopsided as on the prior day. A pullback of a point finds fresh buyers who were unwilling to pay the opening price but still ache to be on board for the ride. Today will see more interim price moves up and down, with the close mildly on the upside and yet with volume still modestly above day 4's bloated total. But price momentum has slowed down. There are no TV mentions this evening because the price change was small.

Day 6

The hottest-money chartists now see that clearly our wonderstock has broken its extremely sharply upsloping trendline. They are sellers at the opening. After a little pullback, the stock finds enough remaining unsatisfied buyers who had put in limit orders a bit below market in hopes of being prudent by not simply buying at market. A small rally ensues. Maybe another momentum-driven institution cannot stand being on the sidelines and enters its purchase order. Volume is still heavy but not as frenetic as on day 5. The stock fails to make another new high price, and clearly volume has started to wane. Maybe, just maybe, there really *never was any* story after all. Larger numbers of traders who joined in for the ride but have no long-term desire to own the stock cash in their chips, scraping off a small profit for a couple of day's risk exposure to their capital. The volume crescendo, it is clear by early afternoon, has run its course and is going to unwind. More traders sell out, and the stock closes lower on volume well above average but still below the peak hit on day 5. The next few sessions will see more people unwind their positions, give up hope for hard news, take small losses, and slink away to find some other hot game to play. It will take perhaps 2 weeks' time or more for the smoldering embers to finally be extinguished as volume finally returns to roughly normal levels and price accordingly settles at some equilibrium level. The parabolic rise in volume has been mirrored, more or less, on the downside. The phenomenon has passed.

Note that our example describes a generalized process. It should not be taken as meaning that literally some particular event occurs without fail on a certain day. But the 5-day length is quite typical if not at the outer limit of the extent of these moves. Internet transmission of information is working to shorten the length of the process if anything. Adverse general market news or a weak mood among traders might shorten the process, so 5 days is not guaranteed. Understanding the sequence of the types of players to become active participants by entering orders is what is important to your internalizing of the essence of a crescendo. Volume will always tell the tale—a day-over-day decrease in volume spells the end.

What is most important to note from the above description of a rise-culminating volume crescendo is the debris it leaves behind. The number of shares outstanding is exactly unchanged, of course. But in the process we have just described, stock has moved, on balance, from longer-term holders to more shorter-term hands. This has a profoundly important implication for future price potential on the upside—and the portents are stronger to the degree the volume of trading was greater. We now have a collection of recent buyers who (a) are short-term owners rather than buy-and-hold believers and (b) are looking at a losing position, perhaps down several points in a few weeks or so. To a smaller extent, there are also some longer-term shareholders who observed the pleasant price action but never quite mustered the gumption to place a sell order to take advantage of that rise. These people now have in mind the now-unavailable higher prices at which "I could have sold, and should have, and almost did."

Both types of holders have been emotionally affected by the price rise on high volume, and for both a similar mental dynamic takes shape: If and when that stock gets back near its price peak, which we as students know was driven by that volume crescendo, these holders will be "smarter next time" and will sell out. Some will have placed actual limit orders, and others will stay on mental alert for such a rise. The net effect of such thinking and actions is to make the crescendo-created, high-price area become a significant overhead supply zone. Remember, there are literally millions of shares (perhaps tens of millions in a normally heavily traded, large-cap stock) in the hands of those who are looking to sell to get out even (the late-buying traders) or to sell to recapture the previously available higher price (the earlier holders who overstayed). Therefore, a price high driven and created by a volume crescendo represents a significant turnaround level for the stock for a considerable period afterward. Overlaid on future routine market movements and general economic news is the recently created overhang of disaffected holders—a combination of unhappy traders with no inherent or enduring interest in the company and some number of wish-I'd-sold-then longer-term holders who vividly remember and regret their lack of selling agility at the peak. Old-time market watchers refer to such an army of potential sellers as "weak hands"—owners who have no strong motivation to hold.

What will it take, with that crescendo-induced lump of overhead supply looming in the wings as potential sellers, to allow the stock to move up through and then above the high price made during such a crescendo run? In short, a lot! Major positive news, preferably the type that no one expected, could do it. A series of moderately good earnings, dividend, product, or similar announcements would probably have a salutary effect over time. A very strong overall market, almost certainly requiring the accompaniment of strong price action in this industry group itself, could over time help to raise the stock and eat into the crescendo area buyers' supply of shares for sale. Absent some truly major and striking good news, the implication is that *a considerable amount of time will be required.* The implication for holders, regardless of their personal disposition toward loyal long-term investing, is obvious: This stock will represent dead money or underperforming assets in the market for some period (probably measured in months). My purpose is not to make all readers into short-term traders. However, I point out the psychological fallout of an upside crescendo event so that anyone who thinks about it will realistically conclude that—especially in a strong overall market where other promising stocks represent opportunities to consider—such a stock has an emotional ball and chain attached. Whether you choose to hold or to sell is your business; I have done my best to issue an intellectually justified warning about likely stock performance, which will be disappointing barring some enormously positive corporate surprise.

DOWNSIDE PRICE CRESCENDOS ON ACCELERATING VOLUME

Just as a volume crescendo and accelerated price increase that follows a previously existing price uptrend signal the end of the price rise and a coming price decline, waterfall-shaped price collapses accompanied by a volume crescendo *after a stock had already been declining* signal the end of the bearish phase and a price reversal to the upside. Many long-time market observers refer to these phenomena as *selling climaxes*. Let us next examine these situations. In some ways they represent the mirror opposite of what we described above for bullish blow-offs. And yet, because there are psychological differences between the intensity and behavioral manifestations of fear as contrasted with those of greed, some differences also exist. Let us examine selling climaxes closely then.

As was the case when we began looking at upside volume and price crescendos, we must immediately state that a downside collapse in price driven by a crescendo in volume is to be clearly differentiated from a sudden downside gap or 1-day collapse in price occurring on suddenly tremendous volume. Such downside spikes will be discussed in Chapter 10. Here we speak of volume crescendos accompanied by accelerating price collapses that last for several days. Such volume/price combinations almost certainly occur only as the culminations of preexisting price declines or bearish phases. The reason for that is this: If something negative occurs in the news background (company, industry, or world news) and a stock has most recently been trending upward in price, a collective reaction of investor and/or trader shock or surprise will almost certainly drive an immediate downside price gap. The suddenness of change from positive thinking to negative opinions in itself creates such an immediate overload of selling orders that price continuity is basically impossible and a gap is predictable.

Our subject here, rather, is the culminating (rather than starting) price collapse accompanied by a volume crescendo. Circumstances likely to drive such a behavioral combination include further negative company or industry news following a previously dreary phase, or an overall market washout that will later be seen as a selling climax creating an important market bottom. As noted above, in many ways the string of several days' increasingly bearish opinion and resulting selling action is quite similar (but opposite in direction) to the 5- or 6-day sequence described above. What is different is that fear becoming terror is a stronger and therefore more compelling driver of human behavior than is optimism and greed. For this reason, downside price collapses accompanied by crescendos in trading activity can sometimes last for more consecutive days, and in most cases result in a larger (although later known to be only temporary) percentage decline in price. Some observers have explained the cause for this difference by noting that it takes optimism and as a result a somewhat constant flow of buy orders to keep a stock's price steady or rising, but a stock can drop seemingly "of its own weight" if buying interest dries up—let alone if nervousness or panic creates a rising flow of sell orders.

We will not actually walk through a series of pro forma daily descriptions of events and participants' emotional and behavioral responses during a price waterfall. Having read and mentally pictured such a sequence surrounding an upside culmination and blow-off, you can readily imagine the downside equivalent. The main difference is that its intensity soon becomes greater and reaches a point of severe panic. Not exactly tied to a perfect daily progression but definitely predictable in terms of a developing order of occurrence, the reactions of shareholders in a first declining and then sharply collapsing stock run along a continuum as follows:

> lack of notice   distaste   building concern   revulsion
>   anger or self-doubt   fear   irrational panic

In some cases, much as a body goes into shock or passes into unconsciousness when assailed by severe pain, a person observing his or her wealth evaporate rapidly and due to causes entirely beyond his or her understanding or control may retreat in denial and horror and actually remove himself or herself from further observation somewhere along in the sequence laid out above. If the person is sufficiently deeply injured so he or she remains in hiding for enough days, he or she may luckily not peek out at the world until the irrational panic stage on the part of other investors (the crowd!) has played out fully and price recovery is in process. This is unlikely since the more severe a general market decline becomes (or the more spectacular an individual stock's collapse is), chances are very high that the media attention to the incipient disaster will be unavoidable even for those trying their best to isolate and ignore. Predictably, such re-entry into the ranks of those actively watching the market's meltdown will tend to occur at the very late stages, when wealth destruction is most rapid and horrible and therefore the likelihood of suc-cumbing to panic is greatest.

Sheer numbers of investors and traders falling prey to their pain and irrational but understandable fears rise in a sudden wave, and the final selling climax is an awesome display of falling-knife prices on huge vol-ume. Many, those who have previously held fast with albeit shaky con-viction that the world is not ending and they can outlast the current sharp pain, collapse seemingly as one under the terrible weight of fear and grief. They figuratively scream as with one voice, "I can't stand it any more! Sell me out!" even though and even as they know intellectually that the current price is a bargain in value terms. The need for emotional relief of pain overwhelms any rational resolve to tough it out.

We have been describing here the collected individual reactions of stock investors. Mutual fund owners are human beings feeling the same sequence of emotions and rising fears (perhaps a bit more rapidly, as they tend to be a more risk averse lot). Their redemptions of fund shares, now ever more readily enabled by Internet account access and funds-super-market connections, can drive portfolio managers to sell stocks to gener-ate cash to meet fundholder liquidations. Whether or not they personally feel a sense of panic, fund managers thus by proxy behave like gravely scared individual investors. Selling begets selling until at some point all the potentially shakeable sellers have been moved to bail out. Stock has moved from weaker to stronger hands. Once the price waterfall incredibly finds a bottom, the very cessation of decline itself provides a catharsis that dries up the selling so that even a moderate trickle of buying can drive a sharp bounce in price. The crisis is thus completed and passes.

Margin account holders of stocks find themselves pushed along the continuum of emotions to likely selling out even faster. Knowing their capital is evaporating fast because of the leverage they are carrying, and being aware of the real chance of a margin call "if this goes on much longer," they are quicker to sell in panic and tend to exit a bit sooner than nonmargined holders will.

Potential buyers of a stock move along a sequence of thinking and emotions like this, as prices evaporate:

contented distance	rising bargain interest	
shaken confidence, waiting	revulsion	deliberate withdrawal

Few will have the contrarian's resolve and necessary courage to step in and buy before the price bottom is actually reached. Some might buy in nib-bling amounts on limit orders only to find they quickly have paper losses; these will either (1) liquidate quickly or (2) ride out the frightening episode without the courage to buy more at lower levels. Many more would-be bargain- hunting buyers will simply wait out the decline. On the way down they will let a combination of growing fear, plus knowledge that waiting longer means bigger bargains to be had, keep them from jumping in to buy. Most will not have courage enough to buy at the bottom, but they will gradually come to believe in the turn once it has already passed them by to the tune of several days and probably 10 percent or more in price gain already missed.

The crescendo of volume will affect both holders and would-be buyers as they observe it. Holders will see the daily rise in transactions as a sign that something very serious is taking place and that multiple thousands of other stockholders are selling out. This evidence of mass opinion will drive lots of remaining holders to succumb and join the rising mob as it heads for the exits. Volume balloons accordingly. Would-be buyers may at first sniff out increasingly interesting bargain prices, but as they observe the huge buildup in trading volume, they too will be impressed by the presumed knowledge of the large number of sellers, and that perception will send them to the sidelines to wait out the decline. Few will have the courage to buy in the final avalanche of selling as volume explodes in a huge frenzy of panicky selling orders from the crowd. Only when they note that volume has quieted down will they be convinced that the rush to exit has ended and therefore be willing to buy.

It is important to note that, for readily understandable psychological reasons, price behavior after a volume crescendo has played itself out will differ as between post-blow-off and post-panic events. After a "buying panic" and upside blow-off are over and past, remember that there will have been created a large pool of shares available for sale if and when higher price become available. That stock is in the hands of recent, weak holders. Therefore, price will tend to be flat or continue to decline—or in a strong bull environment it may rise but only moderately—after an upside volume/price crescendo or parabola has occurred. By contrast, after a truly scary panic sell-off on huge trading volume has visibly been completed, price has a greater chance to rise smartly. The reason is that the emotional process that constituted the selling climax will have already taken stock out of weak hands (those shakeable enough to sell) and will have placed it in stronger hands (those of buyers with courage despite the carnage all around them). After the high-volume selling and initial price bounce-back have occurred, there are relatively few weak holders in existence, as those were already persuaded to dash for cash during the days of crisis. Therefore, postcrash buying meets with fewer early sell orders and price is able to begin a fairly sustained recovery. Price will rebound sharply at first and then at a more gradual angle.

RELATIVE LENGTHS OF VOLUME CRESCENDOS WITH RISING AND FALLING PRICES

Random-walk theory would predict that runs of consecutive days' rising prices and of consecutively falling prices should be about equal in number over long time windows. Actual experience is that consecutive days of declines tend to have a greater probability of extending a bit longer than advances. Volume tends to build in a crescendo during severe price declines for a bit longer as well. I attribute such departures from statistically predictable behavior to one simple aspect of human nature: Fear is a stronger driver than greed or optimism. Imagine, for example, thinking by individual investors over a weekend as they review the weekly Sunday stock tables, or as they check out their portfolios' values or the appearance of key stocks' charts on the Internet. If the market has gone straight south for the prior 5 trading days, and it quite often will do so with an especially nasty acceleration on Friday afternoon, bargain-seeking individuals will be fairly unlikely to have the courage in large numbers to cause a rally at the opening on Monday. Fear begets selling and lack of buying, and the decline easily degenerates into worse panic on Monday and perhaps into Tuesday as well.

By contrast, envision a good week for the market when a large plurality of issues advance and a heady percentage gain is seen in many. Of course, there will be some buyers eager to mount the apparent bandwagon on Monday. But their numbers and their urgency will not match those evident after a week of sharp declines. Some cautious owners will take their fortuitous profits. Therefore, a run of selling on rising volume is more likely to extend a bit further than a run of rising prices on rising trading activity. This general pattern has persisted over the past several decades; it will be interesting to observe whether the newly widespread public participation in the stock market, coupled with Internet speed in the spread of information and opinion, might in coming years serve to spread both bubbling overoptimism and, in its turn, widespread and speedy panic in runs counted in fewer days than earlier. That change surely is one potential effect of an Internet-traded stock market in the twenty-first century.

RECENT PRICE HISTORY DETERMINES CRESCENDO'S PREDICTION

In the prior pages of this chapter, we have been dealing with the occurrence of volume crescendos that coincide with price patterns that are *continuations or accelerations* of recent price trends. Such crescendos usually are urgent signals that a *price reversal* is taking place as soon as volume fails to increase for another day. Those volume crescendos that emerge coincident with price acceleration of the existing direction represent an emotional peaking, or an exhaustion of interest in the stock in its old direction, implying that the price trend will now reverse. But an entirely second group of volume crescendos exists, and these typically forecast *continued* price movement. Volume crescendos that coincide with price moves that are clearly visible reversals of prior price direction, or that coincide with a price breakout from a congestion zone, by contrast, represent the *beginning of a new move*. In these latter cases, one must be patient while the volume crescendo is forming (so as not to join the crowd and buy too high or sell too low immediately). One must then also wait while volume soon afterward quiets down, on the right-hand side of the parabolic wave, as that period of time will represent a resting, or countertrend, correcting phase in price. Once volume has palpably quieted down, positions may be entered in the direction that price took in its breakout while the crescendo was forming. Long-time technicians will recognize this as a volume-centric explanation of the advice to enter buy orders only after a price breakout *and pullback* have occurred. The various circumstances and implications of volume crescendos, then, are summarized in Figure 9–5.

FIGURE 9 – 5

Various Circumstances and Implications of
Volume Crescendos

Price Trend Before Volume Crescendo Appeared	Price Trend While Volume Crescendo Builds	Implied Subsequent Price Direction
Rising	Up, accelerating	Down
Rising	Breaking down	Down
Flat or congested	Breakout to upside	Up
Flat or congested	Breakout downside	Down
Falling	Accelerating downward	Up
Falling	Reversing, up	Up

SUMMARY

This chapter has examined in depth the psychological processes at work in times when volume crescendos occur, particularly when those crescendos drive extending, culminating price moves after a previously existing trend. Chapter 10 will explore the somewhat different dynamics during and following volume spikes—again looking separately at times when those huge overnight bursts of frenzied trading drive sharply rising, as opposed to frighteningly falling, prices.

Volume Spikes and Their Psychological Aftereffects

Chapter 9 described *crescendos* in volume, as associated with both sharp and accelerating rises and with waterfall declines in price. Here we will examine in some detail a somewhat similar but clearly differentiable phenomenon, the *volume spike*. Once again, we will look at spikes separately as they relate first to rises and then to collapses in stock prices. Some of the concepts brought out in Chapter 9 have application here as well. But, as you will see, there are some key differences between the phenomena themselves—the spike versus the crescendo—and especially between their psychological aftereffects on investors and traders, and therefore on subsequent price behavior.

DEFINITION OF A VOLUME SPIKE

A volume spike is a sudden and extremely large immediate increase of trading activity from one day to the next in any given stock. In a large majority of cases the spike is driven by some news that has occurred since the prior day's market close. In such situations, it is predictable that price will gap away from the prior day's closing level at the opening of the new day's trading. Most companies announce major news outside normal trading hours, thereby minimizing the number of instances where spikes begin during midsession. Spikes in volume record such huge and sudden shifts in investor opinion that they essentially cannot accompany small price changes; if the event driving an observed large rise in volume were one with ambiguous meaning such that investors' buying and selling decisions were well balanced, there would not be an explosion of volume at all. In general, you can think of volume spikes and the price changes they drive as being associated with sudden surprises. Except for unpredictable and catastrophic world events, the surprises we will be describing tend to occur between trading sessions and are single-company specific.

Exceptions would be the assassination of a major world leader, a natural disaster such as a huge earthquake, or (much as we hope it will never occur) a surprise terrorist bombing using chemical weapons. Other major events tend to be somewhat expected, at least in the short run. For example, the largest hurricane ever recorded would be visible on TV-broadcast weather maps at least a couple of days before it did its damage. Investors might react over a few days with growing fear in advance, likely forming a crescendo rather than a spike in volume. A declaration of war, likewise, would have been preceded by advance indications that the underlying situation was worsening. While a formal declaration of war was not involved, the many months' buildup of forces before the Desert Storm conflict in January 1991 was an example: Investors gradually realized the seriousness of developments and sold down in preparation for armed conflict.

EVENTS THAT DRIVE VOLUME SPIKES

Many of the company-specific kinds of events that drive volume spikes are negative in nature, but some are positive. Let us begin with the latter, listed below:

- An analyst's picking up coverage with a strong buy recommendation
- One or more significant upgrades of analysts' opinions (sometimes with raised price targets)
- Receipt of a major contract (defense systems, supplying of subsystems to prominent company)
- Granting of a major patent
- Announcement of a major corporate strategic alliance with a prominent partner
- Discovery of a major drug for treatment of widespread diseases (cancer, heart disease, etc.)
- Granting of FDA approval for a drug or device that is extremely important to a given company
- Victory in a major court or administrative proceeding, especially if not reversible on appeal

- Corporate decision to restructure or divest, not previously anticipated
- A troubled company's hiring of a highly regarded executive as chair or CEO
- Previously unanticipated news that a company has put itself on the auction block
- News that a company has received (and, often, agreed to) a premium-priced takeover proposal

Although we will fully explore positive-news-driven volume spikes before tackling their negative counterparts, let us first list major negative news surprises:

- Earnings disappointments, either actual declines or shortfalls against analyst expectations
- Management warnings of future revenue and/or earnings declines or decelerations
- A dividend cut by a company whose stock many investors count on for its income stream
- Announcement of revisions of past earnings statements or balance sheets
- Any hint of severe financial distress such as might lead to a bankruptcy filing
- One or more significant downgrades of analysts' opinions (sometimes with lowered price targets)
- Denial of a major patent previously expected to be granted
- Product-defect and/or liability litigation initiated against the company
- Dramatic explosion, fire, or similar event with loss of life and/or potential environmental liability
- Loss of a major contract or customer relationship
- Crippling strike against company or a key supplier
- Large product recall
- Delays or early glitches associated with a widely anticipated new product that will impair earnings
- Unexpected death or voluntary resignation of a significant corporate leader (or more than one)
- Termination of a major corporate strategic alliance with a prominent partner

- Failure in trials of a major drug or medical device for treatment of an important disease
- Denial of FDA approval for a drug or device that is extremely important to a given company
- Loss in a major court or administrative proceeding, especially if not reversible on appeal
- Termination of an agreement under which the company (or a major division) was to be acquired
- Withdrawal of needed financing (stock or bond sale, line of credit)

IMPORTANCE OF SEC REGULATION FD

On October 23, 2000, the U.S. Securities and Exchange Commission put into effect Regulation FD, which attempts to "level the playing field" in terms of timing of information availability among investors. The chief concern of the SEC in adopting this controversial new ruling was that individual investors were in a practical sense systematically excluded from receiving timely disclosures of corporate information as quickly as institutional investors and brokerage analysts get them. The subject matter was not predictable or routine disclosures such as quarterly earnings or dividend announcements. Rather, the SEC's concerns centered on such things as hints, nuances, and seeming trivia that analysts tend to garner in the course of conversations with company managers or spokespersons. Included, but certainly not alone, in the latter category are what the market has come to consider all-important revisions in guidance as to earnings for the current quarter or year. Regulation FD (for "fair disclosure") basically made it a serious offense for public companies to provide or allow any selective dissemination of information that investors might find important. In effect, anytime corporate representatives speak to a securities analyst they now are much more constrained than in the past when answering specific questions on which they have not previously made a public disclosure.

The net effect of Regulation FD has been a chilling of communication, involving decreases in both openness and frequency. Without commenting on the seriousness of the prior problem or stating a personal opinion on the virtues of the new rule, I am strongly persuaded as to one effect it will have: *There will literally be more surprises, leading to more volatile stock price behavior, with an increased likelihood of volume spikes,* as both institutional and individual investors react simultaneously to less frequent and therefore more dramatic disclosures by public companies. Therefore, understanding what this chapter will cover has become even more central to investment and trading success than was the case before October 2000. Regulation FD has literally changed the rules of the game in a way that will make volume spikes and related price discontinuity more frequent and more severe. When essentially no one has had previous inklings of notable corporate news, by definition the size of the crowd that is to be surprised is increased. Larger crowds reacting to greater changes in generally understood assumptions means we can expect more volume (and price) spikes.

It seems logical that an unintended by-product of the Regulation FD climate of information dissemination may be this: Fewer news releases are likely to occur during the trading session. Publicly traded corporations receiving the most cautious guidance from their lawyers may conclude that it is safer to release news after the market closes or before it opens in the morning, so that news-media dissemination has a greater chance of reaching "all" interested investors at the same time with reference to stock trading—that is, while trading is not occurring. The most cautious of counsel may suggest that failing to take into account the fact that many (primarily individual) investors are unable to receive corporate news during the trading day could imply that making a release during that time window runs an avoidable risk of failing to exercise maximum effort to give all investors the same information at exactly the same time. For purposes of our discussion, this again implies an increase in the number of overnight price gaps accompanied (driven!) by volume spikes. (In turn, that sort of a climate has implications for the value versus danger of using good-till-canceled orders, but that is a subject for another forum since our primary focus here is the effects of volume on trading, prices, and profit opportunities.)

BACK TO EXAMINING SPIKES

Having explored Regulation FD's implications, let us return now to consideration of volume spikes, first as accompanying and driving upside price gaps. Here, however, we must begin with exploration of an exception to the following discussion. That exception involves news of the proposed acquisition of a firm. There is a fundamental difference in what will drive stock price behavior in post-merger-announcement situations versus all others. The difference is one of certainty of information about future stock price, one of fact versus opinion.

Stock prices, except when a pending sale of the company is involved, are driven by the balance of *opinion* as to suitable price (I hesitate to use the word "value"). Investors have opinions as to earnings and dividends, appropriate P/E multiples and yields, and possible future news events (plus, for technical analysts, the implications of price and volume patterns on the stock's chart). The collective optimism and pessimism about these factors sets stock price. When a corporate merger (especially one for a cash amount per share) is pending, an entirely different list of drivers sets stock price: amount of future payment, time to fruition, prevailing risk-free interest rates, and perceived likelihood that the deal will be either scuttled or bettered. It is this focus on facts that produces much smaller fluctuations in stocks that are awaiting a payout due to acquisition, as compared with all others. In effect, subject to judgments about possible breakoff or improvement in the agreed deal, the current price of a takeover stock is the discounted present value of the future payment per share. This can be illustrated over and over by examining the prices of such stocks. For an illustration see figure 10–1, a chart of Bangor Hydro (ticker, BGR), a Maine electric utility that announced its agreed-to acquisition for $26.50 cash per share by Enera, Inc. Observe the very small daily price ranges and reduced trading volume after the first few sessions following the news—news that of course was greeted with an upside price gap driven by a spike in trading volume. An interesting contrast is provided by comparing the BGR chart with that for the same period of Maine Public Service Company (Figure 10–2) whose stock reacted favorably to the BGR news on speculative hope it too might be acquired. Here, for six months from July 2000 on,

FIGURE 10–1

Bangor Hydro-Electric: Example of Volume Spike on Takeover News.

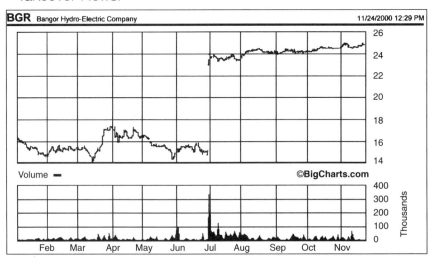

FIGURE 10-2

Maine Public Service Company: Volume and Price Spike on
News of Competitor's Acquisition

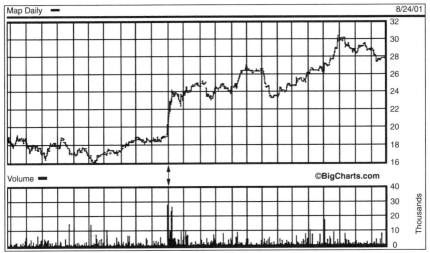

we see the ebb and flow of investor hopes in a climate where no company
announcements justifying acquisition hopes were made.

An acquisition in which the surviving company will pay shareholders
of the merged-in company mainly or entirely in stock presents a somewhat
different situation. Here, the ratio of shares (and any cash) to be received
for each existing share is known. But the value of the "currency" to be
accepted—the stock in the acquiring firm—is not a constant like a fixed
dollar amount. As illustration, see Figure 10–3, a graph of PaineWebber,
which was being bought by another publicly traded company, Swiss banking and financial services conglomerate UBS AG. PWJ stock gapped up on
a volume spike immediately when the deal was announced, but its further
price action was a mathematical function of the price of the acquirer's
shares rather than a simple discounted present value of a certain cash
amount. Both types of takeover situations, however, represent in common
a considerably different set of controlling drivers of price action than are in
force when nonmerger news drives a price gap on a trading-volume spike.
When a merger is involved, people's emotions are thrown out and the simple likelihood of the deal's actually being done, and the discounted present
value of the currency involved, will rule further trading. Other corporate
news, unless it seems to threaten the deal itself, becomes irrelevant to price.
In nonmerger situations, after a spike-creating event occurs, further stock
price action is driven by changing investor expectations, including psychological reactions to events and expectations. There is no single, widely

FIGURE 10-3

PaineWebber: July Price and Volume Spike on Acquisition News

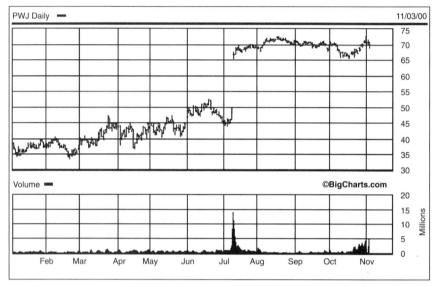

accepted future dollar value per share about which all market participants can have little debate. Therefore, when we discuss postspike price performance below, stocks involved in takeovers and mergers are excluded.

UPSIDE SPIKES EXCLUDING MERGER SITUATIONS

Having disposed of narrow but glaring exceptions to the rule, we now turn to what volume spikes driving large upside price gaps do have in common—and therefore what the price aftermath of such phenomena is likely to be. It is important to remember that nothing happens on the stock market until action has first taken place in the minds of investors and traders. Price change occurs to accommodate an imbalance between demand for shares and their supply. Supply and demand exist because people enter sell and buy orders. People enter such orders because of their (changed) expectations about future price action. Expectations about future price action, in turn, are driven by what investors perceive. Chief among the inputs that might drive entry of buy and sell orders are world events, economic trends, interest-rate levels and directions, and general market moods, plus of course industry-specific and company news. The above are considered the province of fundamental analysis—with general market mindsets seen as determinants of whether P/E and other valuation measures are likely to become more or less bullish.

Certainly not to be forgotten on any list of factors influencing decisions about whether and when to buy and sell stocks are technical-analysis factors—stock price action and volume data themselves. While a good number of investors profess with almost religious zeal that they are long-term buy-and-holders, it is undeniable that market movement itself, when it becomes extreme, can drive people to do what they had not earlier planned or intended. As an example, the week of April 10 to 14, 2000, was one of rapidly evaporating stock prices. Data compiled by Lipper Inc. and others, based on information supplied by mutual fund management companies, indicated that during that temporary meltdown, even S&P 500 Index-type funds experienced net redemptions. The vividness of a price collapse over several days was enough to shake the faith of even the faithful! Thus, price action itself can and does trigger buying and selling decisions. A similar meltdown in faith culminated in the morning of March 22, 2001.

Volume of trading can also contribute to decisions to take action. Certainly technical analysts who are watching for breakouts are watchful for buildups of volume to presage and then confirm price action. Even some individual investors who would not classify themselves as technicians can also be influenced by trading volume. For better or worse, we humans tend in the majority to be group animals. When a large preponderance of people are doing one thing, it becomes increasingly difficult for others to resist acting likewise. That is a large part of the basis behind changes in clothing fashions and hair styles. Children's toys succeed or fail in a commercial sense by gaining mass appeal status and becoming the in thing—or by failing to thus "catch on." In the stock market, a high degree of trading activity calls attention to a stock. First, such a stock is listed in newspapers and screening databases as having very high or unusually high volume. But in addition, traders and to some degree even investors are prone to the power of suggestion created by the size of the crowd. In the absence of hard news, people will tend to suspect—and then believe and expect—major corporate news when a stock trades unusually heavily. "There must be something going on that somebody obviously knows about" is the driving thinking. Thus, at times buying and selling decisions are by-products of observations of unusually heavy volume itself.

Psychologists have shown in numerous experiments that humans rely more heavily than is objectively justifiable on whatever information they have most recently received. Likewise, most humans are seekers of authorities or leaders to guide them, especially in areas such as finance where they feel less than totally competent or self-confident. Finally, psychology has shown that we humans tend to act on (react to) vivid stimuli more than on routine or nonstartling information. This combination—namely, vivid news recently received from perceived authorities—is literally exciting to us in the behavioral sense. In the Internet age, that is even more true than earlier. When a piece of good or bad news is presented, Internet watchers are impressed not only by the fact itself but also by the immediate and substantial price reaction thereto—a reaction that of course is generated by unusually high trading volume. That combination of behavioral forces underlies a good deal of what was described in Chapter 9 in which we dissected the daily thinking and actions of market participants as they observed and then contributed to volume and price crescendos. Much of the same applies here, as we think now about volume spikes that drive large price changes in stocks.

Each of the dozen positive events listed early in this chapter involves one or more instances of "authorities" telling investors what is happening. At the least, there is an announcement by either the company or another recognized entity we view as authoritative—an industry "expert" called an *analyst,* employed by a major brokerage firm or mutual funds company. In addition, there may be validating authority or assurance granted by some other entity: a court, a government agency, another major company, or the board of directors. Thus, news carries in its very nature a degree of authority—a credibility that may dispose investors and, even more likely, traders to take action.

Prior to the Internet's ubiquitous presence in our daily (and specifically, our investing and trading) lives, news took a while to flow to investors and traders. Relatively seldom did the fact that a given analyst changed his or her opinion about a stock actually make news outside the brokerage firm in which he or she was employed. Corporate news itself was reported on news wires, and thereafter passed along by newspapers, TV, and radio to the public. Stockbrokers themselves spent a good deal of time calling their clients and relaying the news and its importance concerning current or proposed stockholding positions. When an analyst wrote a report urging purchase, the fact of issuance of the report was not usually news itself, and the report was mailed to investors large and small and digested at some leisure—and certainly on different days—by various market participants. Companies mailed out their quarterly and annual reports and duly filed 10-Q and 10-K and other required reports with the SEC. (Key information included in such sources was in time "discovered" by enterprising reporters and analysts and then reported to the investing public.)

Finally, the overwhelming majority of investors received stock quotation information only once daily, and even then that was well after the fact. Some big-city newspapers managed to get out evening editions with closing stock prices, and of course the morning papers contained all the details plus some analysis or at least commentary. In the world of investors, life proceeded at what today appears an incredibly slow pace—people actually *took days* to receive and digest investment-relevant information and then to decide on what if any action to take.

Our current era has telescoped all of what is described above from days to seconds. Corporate filings are broadly available in mere hours because the SEC now requires electronic filing of the content and because EDGAR disseminates the content immediately to anyone interested in looking. Not only do some investors look at their holdings nightly on home PCs, but millions tune in via the Internet to the market's live proceedings for at least some portion of the trading day. Some millions of others are watching, again live, on various financial-TV channels. The reaction to any substantive news has been speeded up immensely. So huge is the pressure to be constantly in touch and informed that various online brokerage firms and numerous telecommunications providers are now pushing wireless handheld terminals as a "necessity"—forbid the thought that you should be out of touch while in a car, a subway, on the sidewalk, at lunch, or in the shower! You are entitled to information now, and you are somewhat "expected" to take action as fast as the information reaches your brain. And you know with rising certainty that many others will take action immediately.

The above-described process of getting virtually everyone who cares informed immediately *and simultaneously* is contributing to an increase in market volatility. Whenever the Federal Reserve Board's Open Market Committee meets and releases its decisions on interest rates, stock prices and bond yields show minute-to-minute gyrations that look remarkably like the EKG of a person receiving external cardiac stimulation with high voltage (see figure 10–4). Another example of how rapidly and sharply prices move in response to news occurred just before Thanksgiving 2000 during the heated contest for Florida's electoral votes. The Miami-Dade County election supervisors voted on Tuesday morning to abandon their hand recount of ballots. In a flash—literally in minutes—the Dow Jones Industrials had jumped by more than 125 points ("the market" apparently favored an end to the uncertainty and/or a Bush victory). Then very shortly afterward came news that Mr. Gore's attorneys announced they would file suit to overturn that vote and force a resumption of recounting. You can readily locate the timing of those events on any historical intraday chart of the widely traded Diamonds. Thanksgiving Day brought a Florida Supreme Court decision not to grant the Democrats' lawyers' request, and stocks gapped higher at the opening in the lightly attended session on Friday after the holiday.

Turning back to individual stocks rather than general market averages, we have numerous instances when significant corporate news generates huge volume spikes that power price gaps and rapid runs. Leading types of causes were listed early in this chapter. It is important for us as market observers and students not merely to marvel at the volatility in price driven by these huge explosions of trading volume. More importantly, we will examine the mental processes—intellectual and emotional—that give rise to these phenomena duly recorded, instantaneously, in databases and price charts.

Internet speed, and a resulting concentration of trading activity, reflecting huge masses of investors acting all at the same time, produces a volume surge and that in turn drives major price change *because* there is a such an overwhelming imbalance, or preponderance, of buy orders when the news is good. The more surprising, the more extreme, and sometimes even more important the news item is, of course the greater the outpouring

FIGURE 10-4

Bank of America: Price and Volume Pulse (arrow) on News of Fed's Rate Cut (3-Day Chart).

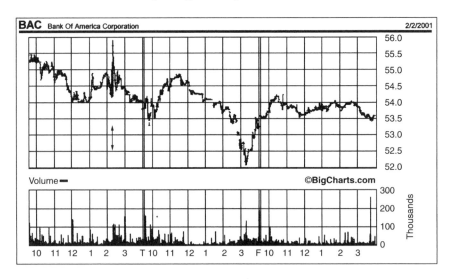

FIGURE 10-5

Single-Day Volume and Price Spike (Arrow) on Major Positive News

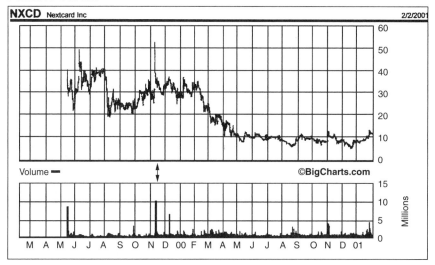

of buy orders. All of the investors who choose to trade in the direction of the (positive) news seem to believe they can be first to get onboard. Being first is assumed to provide a greater upside price ride since others who buy even moments or possibly hours or even days later will presumably pay higher prices than those first to act. This appears to be true at least in the very short term—increasingly a time frame measured in hours or less (Figure 10–5). A mass of investors receives positive information on a company at the same time. Many of them try to buy at the same time, and their actions in combination of course drive price higher very rapidly. Others who had not noticed the news, or who knew it but perhaps had hesitated to buy immediately without further research and reflection, see within minutes the steep price rise and find themselves possessed by an uncontrolled urge (dare we say greed?) to participate without further delay.

But something strange happens—strange or unexpected, that is, to all who look merely at the news and the tape action and do not peer ahead to the next few days. The fact that everyone who is in tune and online in real time is trying to elbow their way in line ahead of all the others makes the price rise very short in terms of time although for that very same reason extremely sharp in terms of points or percentage. The stock virtually explodes on the upside, and trading volume attests to how widespread the interest is. Herein lies the irony and the problem: The concentration of news reception and resulting buying power literally reflects virtually the entire crowd of those who might be moved to buy—all at once. The price explosion runs its course before the trading day is over. "Everyone" placing a buy order hoped and assumed they would get in before "everyone else" could. Very few turn out, on hindsight analysis available in fairly short order, to have been correct. Minutes become multiple points.

As huge volume drives the price skyward at a seemingly dreamlike pace, three things are happening. First, rising prices coax out from the woodwork more and more existing holders who are willing to cash in their happy windfalls—seemingly incredible one-day price gains they could not have imagined barely 24 hours earlier. Their selling begins to slow down the price rise by supplying increasingly large numbers of buyers with stock more readily than existed at the day's opening. Second, traders who are short the stock face the ugly reality of their misfortune, and, in panic, they contribute their buy-to-cover orders to the upside price and volume pressure. But once they have done so, they are no longer a factor helping to support the price rise. Finally, and by far most importantly, the buying crowd that all tried to get in at once is satisfied—they have finished their work!

Recent observation has increasingly confirmed that these explosions of volume and upside price moves more commonly run their course before a single trading day is over, rather than over a period of two or more sessions. Blame, or credit, the Internet and ubiquitous financial TV. No sooner is the huge price run being reported than it is in process of ending. Think about the psychology of the buying crowd. A huge percentage of those interested in the bullish side of the market—exactly the players most prone to being excited into taking action immediately—take action in a matter of a couple of hours or less. The cheering and the throwing of money has literally hit its greatest degree in a very short period of time. How is the stock to continue rising *from here?*

Stocks can rise strongly only if, and to the degree that, and as long as, a large and enthusiastic army of unsatisfied buyers continues to exist and takes action in greater numbers than those who might be coaxed to sell. We have described above how in fact the large majority of the most enthusiastic bulls has quickly done its buying. All you need to do is look at the trading volume to verify that, first, the buying response in the first hour or so was immense and, second and very important, that the degree of excitement has since cooled as documented by a decrease in trading frenzy. When volume falls off, price deceleration and reversal to the downside are quickly destined to follow. It takes a large mob of still-unsatisfied buyers to keep the stock rising; stocks do not levitate by magic! But, in very short order, the mob has completed its action.

Once the morning's fantastic price rise on equally stunning trading volume has exhausted itself by running its course, the remainder of the day will be spent in a tug of war between more evenly matched bull and bear camps. On the buying side will be a small contingent of late comers who for whatever reason (lack of immediate information or perhaps even failure to be present for the buying frenzy) now enter the market to buy despite already-elevated price quotations. They must be imagining the further spread of the news via evening TV broadcasts and next-day newspaper stories to other investors who will then buy and drive price even higher. (What they do not realize is that in the Internet-speed age, the largest proportion of the available and interested activist crowd has already taken action, so next-day buying will almost certainly not do the trick.) Other buyers late in the day and on subsequent days are of a longer-term, less immediately excitable nature. They see the stock's latest pullback as only a ripple against the tide (a tide they do not realize has already hit its high-water mark), and therefore they buy as relative bargain hunters. Ah, they think, see how smart I am not to have paid the highest prices on the first day. I'm a smarter fox than most others. My patience will be rewarded. Or so they think! They simply do not understand that most of the excitable buying crowd has already done its work and is satisfied. They are focusing on how good the story is rather than on the actual dynamics of supply and demand for the stock as clearly documented by volume. By ignoring volume, they are entirely missing the single most critical piece of information and therefore are making poorly timed, and thus poorly priced, purchase decisions. So much for the canard that timing the market is a useless and losing game.

DISSECTING THE AFTERMATH OF THE VOLUME-SPIKE DAY

On the day immediately after the one on which news caused the upside gap on huge volume, we begin to see a different mix of participants. Among the buyers are people who did not see the story at all on its first day and, despite (or because of) the first day's price jump are moved to buy the stock. In addition, there are some short sellers who either did not see the stock rocketing against them on the prior day or now are receiving margin calls from their brokers. They will be buyers out of some combination of panic and necessity. It is possible, but in recent experience not overly frequent, that the stock may make a new high price in the morning of the second day due to buying interest from such actors. More likely, the stock will trade on heavy volume (but not as huge as on the prior day, of course) and within a narrow price range somewhere near its prior-day close. The very fact that, after a huge run-up, it is not falling victim to rapid decline on heavy profit taking will encourage some buyers who see themselves as opportunist bargain hunters. They will form part of the demand for shares on this second day. Likewise, some first-day buyers who may now be a few points under water may choose to average down slightly with additional buys as they see their stock holding on to its huge initial gains well.

Sellers on this second day will include some owners who were unaware of the huge jump the prior day and now open their newspapers or get good-news calls from their brokers. There will also be a contingent of prior owners who watched the stock jump pleasantly on the first day and vowed to let it go as far as it wanted to before they would sell out. On this second day, the price jump has stabilized, and they therefore become sellers. A small number of traders who got in late (near the actual top) on the first day will now become concerned that there is apparently no worthwhile upside followthrough, and they will clip their losses by selling. Certainly any aggressive traders, once they either have losses or see the stock no longer rushing skyward on huge volume, will become early sellers. The day will produce a tug of war without an overwhelmingly clear victory for either the buying or selling camp. The mere passage of time, however, works against the bulls. The longer the stock continues to trade in heavy volume without making a higher high than on its upside-gap day, the less urgent is the emotional tug at potential buyers. Lack of excitement reduces their attraction to this situation, and that will be an ongoing process in subsequent days. Nearly always, the stock that gapped up and rocketed on day 1, on huge trading volume, will close just moderately higher or lower on day 2. Volume will almost never be higher on the second day. The most excitable members of the crowd all gathered and acted on day 1, mainly in the morning.

On the third and subsequent days, volume continues to recede as excitement subsides. The balance between buyers and sellers gradually but clearly shifts toward the bearish camp. Sure, there will be some "bargain hunting" by those who feel clever for not buying higher in day 1's rush. And a few early buyers, still loving the story, may average down by now adding to their positions at a lower price. But the excitement will be fading into the category of "old news" as days pass. Besides, some who might like the story will note that the stock has been unable to hold its first-day gain and therefore will wish to wait until it "finds support" before buying. Their potential purchase orders are therefore delayed, which means they are not helping to support the price as yet. Each day will bring its own new contingent of prior buyers who have seen their action result in paper losses. Seeing volume diminishing (the excitement of the situation clearly wearing off), they will conclude that an early and sharp rebound that could get them even is unlikely. So they become sellers—not in panic, but in a steady stream. Remember, there was tremendous buying on day 1 and, over time as the stock eases back down, more and more of those many buyers will become disappointed and will tend to become sellers either at market or on any rally that does not carry far. And rallies will *not* carry far because there is now such a huge amount of stock that was bought overhead, whose owners are now discouraged or bored or frustrated. Any tendency to rally will bring them out as suppliers of stock. They will say to themselves, "Well, at least I got out a few points better than at the worst of the decline." To use an old Wall Street cliché, the stock will be unable to get out of its own way. Literally.

Volume will decline in a gradually flattening curve, not necessarily perfectly each day but as a clear overall pattern. Price will be falling irregularly in the process, also generally at a decelerating pace. There will probably be one juncture at which both price and volume accelerate, however. If and when the price moves below the lowest level seen (probably at or near the opening) on day 1, two forces will join to accelerate the selling. First, absolutely everyone who bought on the gap-up day will now have a paper loss (some of them now quite large). Few will be willing to bargain hunt by averaging down. Instead, they will be much more likely to give up hope and sell. Downside acceleration in price now, accompanied by a notable volume increase, will further scare them into selling. Second, technicians almost universally believe that "gaps must be filled," and they will see that process now actually beginning. Those who hold will know they must sell, and those inclined to the short side will be sellers on upticks, adding downside pressure since the stock will be unable to rise much.

Depending on how truly important the original gap-triggering good news was, and somewhat depending on overall market sentiment, it may be that the stock will entirely close the gap before finding support and stabilizing. The generally decelerating downward move (in both volume and price) may take from several days to a few weeks to play out. A meaningful number of investors and traders will become interested in the stock once it does stabilize, especially if it indeed has entirely closed its gap. Those of a technical mindset will observe that the gap has been closed, so they will now feel free to cover their shorts and to buy. Those of a thrifty bent who favor the fundamental approach will reason that they can now get the stock back at its original pre-news price—quite a bargain! And they will see the height of the price flagpole on a chart and believe that therein lies their reasonable profit target, up a significant percentage. They are getting the assurance of the fundamental good news "free" and at a bargain price to boot, for their patience.

Thus the volume spike with upside price explosion plays out. It is visible over and over as one observes these events. One might describe its shape as an inverted V (if one mentally draws a dotted line from the pre-news price to the bottom of the first day's price range). You might also see it as a giant inverted check mark in which the tail is somewhat curved rather than perfectly straight. The reason for such commonality in shape is that the psychology of the situation plays itself out the same way each time, as described above. Once the price rise stops, which the shrinking of volume makes a certainty, the wearing-down process begins and proceeds. The company involved is different, the news is different, the exact price increase is different, but the psychological impact on participants is the same.

What would it take to interrupt the gradual eroding slide downward? General market strength will not be sufficient. A strong market rise will have traders seeking out stocks that are acting well, and this one will fail such a test. No, it will take nothing short of major, company-specific news to re-excite a large crowd of buyers to act simultaneously in such volume that they can overcome the downward pressure of the overhanging stock. You might say it will require a bigger piece of surprising and very favorable news than the original trigger. That is a tall order! As either a happy holder of the stock when the upside gap is in process, or an outside observer considering what if any action to take, you would do well to ask this seminal question: "How can the news get any better?" Seldom will you be able to state a specific additional piece of news that reasonably might be expected and that would "top" the excitement generated by the first trigger.

IMPLIED POST-SPIKE ACTIONS FOR TRADERS, AND FOR INVESTORS

The implication for action is clear when an upside price gap on huge volume occurs. Ideally, you must sell on the very first day. If you were absent from the action and become aware after the close, you must sell on the second day. It is possible but seldom a reality that the stock might trade higher in the morning of day 2. The volume dynamics of day 1 and the evolving change of buy-and-sell balance argue strongly against it. (Remember that in the Internet age, speed and efficiency of information and opinion transmission virtually assure that the buying crowd will maximize in 1 day or less.)

I would never hold out in hope of getting a higher price the second day since the odds are long against it. Emotionally, it is easier to sell a stock on the way up than later on the way down. On the way down, we are aware of exactly how much profit we have left on the table by not (with dumb luck) getting out at the exact high. On the way up, the potential for such regret is more imaginary since it cannot be quantified yet. As the former gap-up stock proceeds through its inevitable unwinding process as described above, regret will grow larger each day as the foregone paper profits become greater in points as well. Selling will become more difficult as the loss increases. That in itself should be enough reason to sell on day 1. The knowledge of how these inverted-V situations play out, almost always actually reaching a price peak on huge volume on their very first day, should be equally persuasive. The combination should give you a slam-dunk, open-and-shut case for selling on day 1.

"What about taxes?" I hear that predictable but tiring question from those who somehow believe they should be able to have profits without ever paying the federal piper. Get over it! You should be glad to have a large tax bill each year because that proves you were very successful in your investing and trading. Some of the upside gaps we have been describing are so sharp in percentage terms that the inevitable price downside from their tops will equal or exceed your tax cost of selling. Sell out and buy the stock back lower if you are hopelessly in love with it. In so doing, you will raise your cost basis and thereby reduce the tax-aversion rationalization's power in the future. The only ways you can ever escape paying taxes on your gains are to give the asset away or die with it. In either case, you will not enjoy the financial benefit of your gain. Pay your taxes and move on!

For traders who are so inclined, upside volume spikes driving price explosions provide fertile opportunities for short selling. I cannot and will not even attempt to argue the proposition that short sales provide comfortable positions for their owners. By nature the process has one always on edge. But I would say that shorting late on the upside-gap day or in the morning of day 2 offers a relatively lower-risk short position than many other situations can provide. If you understand the psychological interplay between bulls and bears that is set up once the buying mob has been satisfied in its first few hours, you realize that it will take tremendously favorable follow-on news to drive the stock higher in the short term. The waiting supply of overhanging stock is so huge (revisit the volume total of day 1 if you need convincing) that each rally attempt will labor and almost surely fail.

When a company has huge good news that causes a volume spike driving an upside gap—which will inevitably be followed by the wearing-off process described above—when and at what price does it make sense for investors who like the story for the longer term to become buyers? To state the answer very briefly, not in any hurry! Broadly speaking, you should expect such stocks to go through these stages:

1. A single-day upside gap and run on huge volume
2. A prolonged unwinding on declining volume and decelerating price erosion
3. Quite often, a complete closing of the upside price gap
4. A sideways base-building or horizontal-channel stage

In theory, one should wait at least until the average daily volume decreases enough to return to essentially its pre-news levels. This will show that the excitement factor has truly worn off. One might think in terms of an even longer wait. It will be necessary for a much larger percentage of the volume spike to be unwound in the form of disappointed selling—on top of the normal average volume for this stock. From a psychological and technical analysis viewpoint, there is really no hurry to buy. The unwinding stage must and will play out. To prove that this stage truly is completed, the stock must then be able to demonstrate its holding ability by not making new post-peak lows. That implies a sideways channel because on each rally there will be some discouraged holders who have not yet sold, and they will become sellers preventing the stock from rallying far. The highs they define then become the upside resistance points for future rallies. Therefore, one might say that there is no rush for an investor to buy these stocks until an upside breakout from the horizontal channel is accomplished (proving that the weight of selling is finally exhausted) or until a rising channel is in evidence. These signals will not occur many points above the absolute bottom after the unwinding phase, and in any event investors for the long term are not insistent on trying to enter at the absolute lows.

VOLUME SPIKES DRIVING PRICE COLLAPSES

As the next few pages will disclose, what happens following terrible company news precipitating a volume spike and price collapse is anything but a mirror image of those attractive upside cousins just discussed at length. In emotional terms, declines are much more than the opposite of advances, and losses are much more complex than the exact negative images of gains. Therefore, human behavior after a downside spike will be quite different than the simple reverse of what you've seen described and explained. And human behavior, remember always when viewing the market, is what drives purchase and sale orders to be entered, and those orders in quantity are the force that changes price.

Fear is a much stronger motivator of action than is enthusiasm, acquisitiveness, or greed—whatever it is that drives us to decide to buy stocks. That is why bear markets display steeper slopes than bull markets do. That is also why a given amount of bad news will provoke a much more severe downside price reaction—and on higher volume—than an equal measure of good news. Think about how stocks react when earnings are announced. If a company beats the analysts' all-important consensus guesstimate by 2 cents a share, its stock may rise a point or two. But woe to shareholders if a 2-cent shortfall against expectations should occur! You can count the point loss in major stocks in double digits, and the first-day percentage wealth destruction commonly runs in the 25 to 50 percent plus range. Absolutely vicious is the fury of selling on surprising bad news.

Not all corporate news events are predictable in terms of their timing. One fortunate exception is a company's cycle of quarterly and post-year-end earnings releases. For the reason described above, I strongly believe it is folly to own a heavily institutionally held stock through the date its earnings are to be reported. I virtually never do it. (Stop-loss orders cannot be of effective help because when your stock opens on an awful downside gap and triggers your stop, you are sold out not at your price but at the opening, which will often be substantially lower.) Before we explore in depth the anatomy and psychology of volume spikes driving price collapses, I offer a reminder about using a highly valuable information Web site that tracks the timing of earnings releases:

> http://biz.yahoo.com/research/earncal/20011126.html

The eight numeric digits represent a date in the YYYYMMDD format. In the version shown above, the date sought is November 26, 2001. Entering a similar line of code in your browser will produce a list of stocks expected to report on that particular day. You can also, perhaps more importantly, enter the ticker symbol of any stock you hold or are considering buying, and the Web site will display the date of its next expected report. The information table even tells you whether the release will occur before the opening, during trading hours, or after the close. If 50 percent or (in a good economy) even 60 percent of earnings reports are favorable surprises, the expected value of holding a stock through an earnings event is negative, when you multiply the probability times the extent of likely gain or loss. Taking care to avoid placing your money in the path of a possible disaster will help you experience a decreased number of the scary and wealth-destroying downside spikes we are about to describe. With commissions at under $10 per trade, you can make a roundtrip move on 200 shares for less than a dime a share. I find that cost to be extremely cheap insurance against statistically odds-on losses.

Unfortunately, timing-predictable quarterly earnings releases are not the only potential sources of bad news that can smash stock prices. So here we repeat the list of major types of bad news that can befall investors and traders.

- Earnings disappointments: either actual declines or shortfalls against analyst expectations
- Management warnings of future revenue and/or earnings declines or decelerations
- A divided cut by a company whose stock many investors count on for its income stream
- Announcement of revisions of past earnings statements or balance sheets
- Any hint of severe financial distress such as might lead to a bankruptcy filing
- One or more significant downgrades of analysts' opinions (sometimes with lowered price targets)
- Denial of a major patent previously expected to be granted
- Product-defect/liability litigation initiated against the company
- Dramatic explosion, fire, or similar event with loss of life and/or potential environmental liability
- Loss of a major contract or customer relationship
- Crippling strike against a company
- Large product recall
- Delays or early glitches associated with a widely anticipated new product that will impair earnings
- Unexpected death or voluntary resignation of a significant corporate leader (or more than one)
- Termination of a major corporate strategic alliance with a prominent partner
- Failure in trials of a major drug or medical device for treatment of a major desease
- Denial of FDA approval for a drug or device that is extremely important to a given company
- Loss in a major court or administrative proceeding, espescially if not reversible on appeal

- Termination of an agreement under which the company (or a major division) was to be acquired
- Withdrawal of needed financing (stock or bond sale; credit line)

These and similar events can trigger a huge volume spike that drives a downside price gap. Generally, the stronger the bullish consensus had been about a stock, and/or the larger the proportion of stock held by institutions, and/or the more tenuous the overall market mood, the greater will be the percentage price gap. For reasons discussed previously in this chapter, I believe that implementation of SEC Regulation FD in October 2000 has increased the frequency and size of potential news surprises. Thus the financial risks in holding stocks when news is forthcoming may be even larger than in prior years. I hope you will never actually experience a volume spike with downside price destruction; I wish I could believe you will be so fortunate. Being an equity investor or trader simply brings with it that risk. Our task in the next several pages is to dissect and thereby understand these spikes and their probable price aftermaths. It is not a pretty picture, and it definitely is not the mirror image of the inverted V formation we discovered in the case of surprising good news.

As noted earlier, fear is a much stronger driver to action than is enthusiasm or greed. That alone would be reason to expect that volume spikes driving price smashes will result in larger percentage declines than the price rises seen in upside spikes. But we must also add another extremely important factor, as elaborated on in Chapter 8: institutions. Unfortunately, many institutional money managers are judged on performance over fairly short time windows. Often this means as frequently as quarterly! For those of us individual mortals who own the stocks they do, their competitive professional treadmill means potential trouble at the slightest hint of disappointing news. Why? Each portfolio manager knows that if he or she holds a stock that has suffered a downside shock, he or she will probably underperform competing peers who sell out. Therefore, "everyone" except the most confirmed long-term value-style professional investor has an extra incentive for promptly joining in the selling frenzy when bad news strikes. Not to do so implies almost sure competitive disadvantage in the rankings derby when the next quarterly window closes. So the presence of institutional holders tends to aggravate the downside moves in stocks with bad news, because those holders' sales generally involve huge volume (Figure 10–6).

One example of this disturbing but familiar phenomenon was the September 2000 drubbing suffered by Intel (INTC) shares when the company issued a cautionary outlook for its upcoming quarter. Having closed at about $62, INTC opened at around 47, down nearly 25 percent (Figure 10–6). Trading volume on the first day, that of the volume spike itself, was an all-time record 308 million shares. Each of the next two

FIGURE 10-6

Intel: All-Time, All-Stocks One-Day Volume
Record on Earnings Warning

trading days saw volume still in excess of 100 million shares. That degree of bailing out simply was not primarily an avalanche of small orders, a few hundred shares each, from individual investors. As indicated in the graph, INTC suffered for nearly 4 weeks and eventually found support at 35, down well over 40 percent in trading that was continually well above average. This was institutional dumping of stock in one of the handful of building-block technology issues of our age. This and other technology leaders regularly go through such bloodletting for no better reason than the fact that brokerage "analyst" cheerleaders and institutional holders cannot seem to understand that complex companies are not automatic profit-generating machines that should be expected to grow at perfectly smooth and predictable rates every single quarter. There is no patience on Wall Street, as documented by the huge outpourings of sell orders that drive stocks down at the least hint of even short-term problems.

Day 1

Let us now look at the events and the emotions involved in a downside spike. As we do, keep in mind what a powerful force fear is in the minds of human beings. The bad news is announced, perhaps after the close yesterday or maybe before the market's opening today. You and thousands of others hold your breath, hoping against hope that somehow the stock will not be hurt too badly. Unless you have studied these things, you have only a vague general notion of how bad the gaps tend to be. In the late 1990s and year 2000, the preponderance of smashes ran in the 25 to 40 percent range on day 1. The carnage can be worse if there is any hint of matters that raise basic issues of trust and credibility. Misstated financials are deadly poison, for example. But run-of-the-mill bad quarters, or warnings about them, are worth the standard 25-to-40 as punishment. Single critical matters that can raise questions about corporate viability, or "soundness of the business plan" as the phrase has come to be used, usually drive day = 1 downward spike price declines starting at 50 percent. An example would be the delay or denial of approval of a single-concept biotechnology firm's drug in testing or up for FDA approval. By considering each of the kinds of bad news presented earlier, you can make some judgments as to how truly serious various sorts of events are.

Many institutional investors as well as individuals willingly line up to sell at the opening at whatever price that may provide. Their thinking is some combination of blind terror, not wanting to have to deal with the details as they unfold, and a foreboding sense that the first day of horrific price decline on extremely high volume will not be the end of the pain. An unpublished study I conducted for a university forum in 1998 found that, in that heady bull-market environment, almost 30 percent of downward spike situations found their price bottoms on the first day, and 91 percent did so within 5 trading days. Nevertheless, as in the case of the Intel smash discussed earlier, it appears that large numbers of shares are in the hands of holders who cannot stand the pain for as long as 5 days. If they could, they would hold for a bounce. On this first day, however, once the opening price is printed, those who still own the stock have a hold-or-sell decision to make. Some will conclude that the price cut has already been so deep that it cannot possibly go down any further, and they refuse to join the selling maelstrom. The stock is indeed all over the tape that morning as it tries to find buyers to grab at an apparent bargain who will, by doing so, support the price. Rallies are brief, however, as each is hit by new selling from holders relieved at the slightest bit of pain relief in knowing that at least they did not get the bottom price.

Shareholders who are not in touch with news media all the time, and who are not watching their stocks online, begin getting the bad news from their brokers. Some of them buckle at the knees and join the selling avalanche. Others vow to watch and see if the price will hold. The day of the spike very seldom ends with the price trading above its opening price. There is just so much stock that has been shaken out, and so much other stock in the hands of those who are ready to squeeze the selling trigger, that rallies seem unable to take hold for more than a few minutes. Tonight the nasty details will be broadcast on all the TV financial segments and will receive twice-hourly repetition on such media as CNBC and CNN headline news. The morning papers will inform any holders who have not previously been awakened to the depth of their injury.

Day 2
Day 2 starts with a brief tug-of-war at the opening bell. Some bargain hunters have appeared, and they face off against nervous or panicked hold-ers who have learned their financial fate since the prior close of business. A very key price level is the lowest price touched on day 1: If it fails, which will happen in 70 percent or more of cases, renewed selling ensues. Some is done on stop orders, and the rest comes in from those watching live with fingers crossed but still poised above the send-order key. Trading volume on day 2 is seldom as great as on day 1. Just as in the case of the upside price spikes described earlier, the largest part of the crowd that is excitable to action has done its work already. From now on, a contest between bargain hunters and worn-down and scared holders will be played out. Those institutional investors that make selling decisions pro-vide large blocks for sale, tilting the balance toward further price erosion. Those institutions that are attracted by the apparent bargain are most like-ly to scale into their desired positions gradually, rather than buying a mil-lion shares or more immediately. After all, they reason, why be heroes; this thing *could* keep going south. Day 2 ends with trading volume some-what below that on spike day, but still very much above average for this stock. Price most often will end lower since the odds and orders during the session were stacked somewhat in favor of the bears.

Day 3
Day 3 dawns, and the sense of panic has probably all but disappeared. There may be a few margin calls forcing some holders to sell out. Thank goodness that the Investment Company Act of 1940 all but prohibits mutual funds from using leverage (except in unusual and temporary cir-cumstances). Otherwise, in bull markets they would have built up margin-ed positions in their winners, and therefore their selling orders now would be even larger than we do see. The dreary sequence continues to play out, again with the stock's ability to somehow hold at previous low quotes con-tinuing to be a major factor all day. Each failure brings in more stop-order and live-participant selling as more and more people lose faith. Still, trad-ing will again typically be less heavy than on day 2, as the emotional

shock value becomes less severe each day. On day 3 or 4, perhaps depending on the trend and mood of the overall market itself, our stock might actually close higher by a small amount.

Day 4

The next morning might then bring in a few follow-up buyers willing to bet that a bottom has indeed been set. But at some point they will be outnumbered by a renewed wave of stock for sale by discouraged holders content to be out a few points or several percent better than the worst seen so far. A contest of strength is now going on between the tentative bulls and the army of still-discouraged and somewhat frightened (but no longer panicked) existing holders who could become sellers at any time. The entire capitalization is theoretically for sale on either rallies or failures to hold prior lows, while it would be difficult to conceive of ready and enthusiastic buyers whose buying power would even approach such size. As noted above, in a strongly bullish period, 5 days of this sort of action found price bottoms in just over 90 percent of cases. One must suspect that in a bear market, or even a sideways one such as seen in 1999 to early 2000, there is more discouragement and fear among holders. Implied in that observation is the likelihood that more than 5 days may be needed to bring any sort of lasting bottom. Trading volume continues to recede gradually, although not absolutely every day. We are still in a period of wound healing, and the cut has been deep. As more days pass and no hoped-for meaningful price bounce arrives, further numbers of holders will begin to see what appear to be more promising ways to use their money elsewhere. They are discouraged by the sense of "dead money here," and that perception feeds a continuing although hardly urgent flow of selling pressure over time.

Needless to say, the establishment and testing of a viable price bottom are possible only on the assumption that there is no further bad news forthcoming. The patience and trust of holders who have hung in, and likewise of many of the early bargain-hunting buyers, are of course pretty fragile. Another dose of bad news will be all it takes to turn them into sellers. If that occurs, a less dramatic repetition of the entire sequence will be required before the ship can hope to be righted for good. Assuming no such second shoe drops, after about five sessions or so the stock will have passed from its initial stage of critical condition into a more stable although still injured status. Assuming the overall market is not too bearish, and assuming no more bad news comes from the company, and assuming none of the companies in its obvious peer group issue parallel bad news, there is a reasonable chance the stock can pass into stage 3, which will be a lengthy period of tentative base building. The best possible good news is that the stock *may* have actually found its bottom. The bad news for hopeful holders can come in either of two forms. First, at any time an added adverse development can upset the whole fragile structure and re-ignite a degree of panicky and more urgent selling. A second scenario is that the stock will essentially go into a prolonged slumber. For starters, any rally of much extent will bring out sellers who have been waiting for a certain price, or for any chance to get out a few points better than in the beginning, saving face and a bit of money for their patience.

But a prolonged period of sideways net price movement, once the huge volume has quieted down, is almost certainly in prospect for our beleaguered stock. The previously displayed chart of Intel illustrates an almost inescapable price pattern among stocks that have suffered downside volume spikes. I refer to it as the lazy L shape. Mentally draw a dotted line straight downward, connecting the final price before the price gap and the lowest trading price on the volume spike day. That forms the vertical stroke of our capital L, and it is followed by a lengthy period of sideways consolidation in the stock, forming an elongated horizontal stroke making up the rest of the character L.

Why is this pattern so overwhelmingly "the best one can realistically expect" for a period of probably several months? Why does it seem that any attempted bounces turn out to be of that fabled dead-cat kind? Figure 10–7 looks at the thinking of holders and of potential buyers to find some answers.

As can be seen, the list of reasons to sell, either immediately or on any relatively minor price rebound, is considerably longer than that for buying. Reasons for holders to sell largely also weigh on the thinking of potential buyers and may deter them. Recalling that fear is a stronger motivator than enthusiasm, we can see that many of the reasons on the sellers' and avoiders' lists are fairly deep seated, having to do with the avoidance of loss, risk, shame, and pain. Many of the reasons on the buyers' list are rooted in hope or the need for hope. Especially in a bull market, when an investor or trader looks around at possible opportunities, it is reasonable that for all but the most confirmed bargain hunters and bottom fishers, a more upbeat and confident case can be made for any stock that has not suffered a downside spike than for one that recently has. In a bear market, fear rules the day, and therefore any stock that already carries a known taint of "bad news" is probably low on market participants' lists of favorites. High quality and dependability are the desired characteristics in such times.

FIGURE 10-7

Why Downside-Spiked Stocks Require Lengthy Recuperation

P I T

(P, portfolio managers;   I, individual investors;   T, traders)

Likely Reasons for Sale or Avoidance

P I T	Feeling betrayed by corporate management
P I T	Holding onto bad personal memories
P I	Awaiting some good actual news, typically at least next quarterly report
P	Avoiding showing the besmirched name on next report of holdings
I	Waiting out 31-day wash-sale-loss tax rule
P I T	Avoiding downside pressure of year-end tax selling, if event was in latter months
P	Feeling pressure of short-term performance-measurement competition
P I T	If held for a while, feeling bored and frustrated
P I T	Perceiving an opportunity cost of inertia and dead money
P I	Suspecting that further negatives will occur
P I	Waiting for opportunity for loss reduction on minor rallies
P T	Waiting for parallel events affecting stocks in same industry
P I T	Expecting downward revisions of revenue, EPS, and growth-rate
P I	Expecting a "piling on" of analyst downgrades
P I	Noting the absence of analysts courageous enough to sponsor or upgrade this stock
P I T	Noting the failure of stock's action to look strong, or even robust

Possible Reasons for Purchase

P I T	Bargain hunting
P I	Averaging down
P I	Doubling up temporarily, then selling high-cost block for tax loss after 31 days
P I	Believing the market is wrong (This will actually be the only bad news.)
P I	Taking fallen-angel vulture action
T	Buying because lows have been tested and held successfully

IMPLIED ACTIONS IN POST-SPIKE PRICE VICTIM STOCKS

Because of the numerous factors listed and discussed above, it should be quite obvious what you should do with stocks that have recently suffered a downside spike. Here is a summary:

- If they are not sold immediately on the first morning, hold for at least a week.
- Sell into any rallies after they run about 2 or 3 days.
- Fight the temptation to buy apparent bargains in any rush.
- Watch to see that the stock indeed holds its ground rather than sliding further.
- Definitely wait until trading volume returns to pre-spike normal levels, which indicates that the emotional aftershocks of the spike have finally been worked out.
- Because of repurchase-inhibiting effects of the wash-sale rules, wait at least 31 days from the spike, probably also from time lasting bottom was made.
- Wait until the next quarterly earnings report is released to see if health really is mending.

Great companies will from time to time suffer downside spikes on huge volume. This is almost inevitable in a bull market in which institutions buy and intend to hold favorites at almost any P/E multiple. Once their former idols fall, they become anathema, to be avoided. The higher they flew, the harder they will fall on any hint of bad news. The overhang of disappointed holders, including the early-stage bargain hunters as well, is so large that their available volume for future gradual sale will continue to exert suffocating pressure on a post-spike stock for a patience-testing length of time. And, in case it need be said, the old "cockroach theory" on Wall Street holds that pieces of bad news seldom are found alone—where there is one, there will likely be others soon to follow. That argument alone should prompt enough caution to make you wait for at least the next EPS report. In the vast majority of cases, you will find that stocks smashed in price on huge spikes in volume will not have run away while you were exercising patience and due caution.

One note of exception is worth mentioning: You will see upon glancing back that this entire discussion of stocks was based on the premise that the stock's precipitous fall was triggered by *company-specific news*. Every so often, we live through a market smash or a full-fledged crash. During such periods, virtually all stocks are thrown away mercilessly for one or several days. Quite often significant opening downside gaps occur, and trading volume on such occasions is usually above average (although not of truly spike-event proportions). In such cases, these stocks (indeed, most stocks!) were not gapping lower because of anything wrong with their underlying companies. They were merely among the innocent victims of millions of manic-depressive investors all acting out of blind fear at the same time. Once the market-wide crash is finished, innocent stocks are immediately eligible for purchase provided they were not tarnished, and especially provided that neither they nor their industry peers were the unfortunate news triggers for the final bash of selling anxiety. The reason such smashed stocks can be bought with greater assurance of early price recovery is that the overall market smash or crash was the problem, not the specific companies themselves. Once investors come to their senses in the rise after an overall market smash or crash, they will notice their cash positions are too high and will look for "good stocks" to buy. Even if they sold out and lost money in a particular stock during the selling melee of the mob, they will have few if any of the bad feelings usually associated with stocks that have undergone news-driven individual downward spikes. Stocks free of such taint and such specific bad memories and psychological and fundamental baggage will be OK to buy in the minds of millions of investors and traders. Therefore, do not apply the rules for spike-debilitated stocks to all stocks after a general market wipeout.

CHAPTER 11

Lower Volume at Later Price Extremes

Early in this book, I focused your attention on the importance of watching trading volume, which tells a story about the shifting forces of supply and demand. In general, and especially in Chapters 4 and 5, we documented the importance of watching price and volume combinations. A central message was that higher volume almost always (except when it is extremely huge) occurs on days when the market is moving in accord with its overall longer-term trend. Conversely, you were shown that days of lower volume are usually "resting" or consolidating times in which prices more often than not move against the prevailing trend. Stating the principle from a bull's view of the world, "up on higher volume and down on lower volume is good." In this chapter, we will develop the implications of lower volume in other than daily circumstances. We will look at situations in which subsequent wavelike moves to new (higher or lower) price extremes are accomplished without the accompaniment of commensurately higher volume. We will also examine circumstances in which a price move seemingly runs out of steam as it proceeds, as telegraphed by a gradual drying up of trading volume. Both such kinds of events usually signal a reversal in trend and therefore should not be ignored. We shall look at these declines in volume during both declining and rising markets since there are some differing psychological drivers at work, not all of which are mirror opposites of each other.

We begin with some qualifiers and caveats. First, trading volume is conventionally recorded in numbers of shares traded rather than in the dollar value of those transactions. As discussed briefly in Chapter 13, this reporting method can cause some significant distortions when we study different stocks in comparative terms. When we are looking at single stocks, denominating volume in shares rather than dollars seldom has serious negative consequences as long as we remember to adjust historical data for stock splits. There is imprecision in comparisons made in shares rather than dollars, but fortunately its effects are fairly mild. Our second note of caution is that trading-volume observations must always be placed in an appropriate context when market circumstances are clearly different. The most obvious example of this is when trading in the market overall is subdued due to pre- or post holiday circumstances. Such situations are common around holidays that traditionally involve vacationing and travel. For example, trading around Thanksgiving, Labor Day, and Christmas seems more severely decreased than that around Presidents' Day.

It is especially worth remembering that trading in the final several sessions of the year—between Christmas and New Year's Day—is usually quite slow by normal standards. For these sorts of reasons, one must be very careful in drawing conclusions from nominally lower volume at such times, as it may simply reflect the general market situation rather than a changed level of intensity of interest in a specific stock.

FADING VOLUME DURING AN ADVANCING WAVE

The first subject for volume-price examination is a price advance in which the latter portion continues despite clearly decreased trading volume. Here we are specifically thinking of a time frame covering not more than a few weeks, and we are watching trading volume on a daily basis as we observe its decline over time. There are several possible explanations for such behavior by a stock:

- The market as a whole has had a strong recent advance, and bulls have become more hesitant to keep buying at now-elevated price levels. This happened in mid-May 2001.

- The market as a whole has begun to decline, and potential buyers take note of this and therefore decide to delay further purchases in this favored stock.

- Those who have been driving the price of the specific stock higher have become cautious due to its own price climb and, one by one, are therefore stepping back.

- Those who have been driving the price of the specific stock higher have finished their accumulation work.
- Potential buyers observe that the stock has risen over a considerable percentage of days in recent weeks and know that "nothing goes straight up" or "nothing grows to the sky forever"—and so are not inclined to participate in the action at present.
- The stock's continued rise is being fueled less by true enthusiasts but now rather by come-lately momentum players and/or by now-scared short sellers who are buying to cover.

Two examples of rallies that failed to continue after their driving trading volume declined are provided within a relatively short time period by a single stock, retailer Kohl's Corp. (ticker, KSS). These are shown in Figure 11–1. In early November, the price rise that had begun in the final several days of October came to an end in the $57 to $58 range after several days of declining volume. These were interrupted by a single day (volume over 4 million) whose upside action was driven by favorable monthly retail sales statistics. Except for that day, in fact, nearly every day in the stock's 9-day rally from $49 was marked by decreasing trading volume, compared with the day before it. The second failed rally within a

FIGURE 11–1

Kohl's: Failing Up-and-Down Price Moves on Fading Volume.

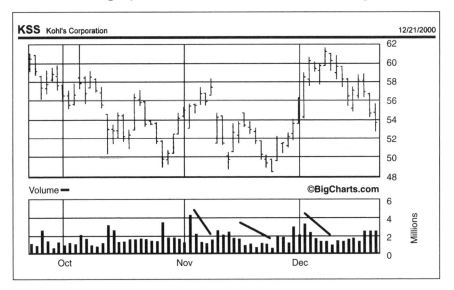

month has a more conventional look to it; this one began in late November at under $49 and reached to nearly $62 before playing itself out on waning buying interest on the sixth trading day in December. Through the second trading day in December, volume had been generally on the rise during that rally, but once the stock suddenly ran to over $58, succeeding days saw the price move higher on balance while volume declined by more than half. It is worth noting here that when we speak of a stock rising on declining volume, we should not require every single day to be one of net gains; the shape of the overall trend defines what is up or down.

FADING VOLUME DURING A DECLINING WAVE

This very same price chart also illustrates the process of volume declining as a downward price wave continues—a pattern that most often indicates that sellers have finished their work. Look again at the month of November where the stock drops from about $55 at midmonth to just a fraction above $48 a week later. One could readily interpret the 2 weeks from the earlier high at $58 as a single decline punctuated by some news-driven choppiness in its early phase (that was when the 2000 presidential election began its 5-week saga of extended uncertainty). Viewing the 2 weeks from $58 down to $48 as a decline, and examining the volume, we see that once again this stock had considerable volume early in its price move and then decreasing urgency by those driving its direction as the move lasted longer. In fact, the day KSS reached its low at just above $48 was the slowest trading session in the entire 3 months shown.

Putting aside the possibility that specific corporate news might be driving stock trading volume, what other causes might result in a pattern wherein the volume begins quite high but then declines on balance while the price continues to move lower?

- The market as a whole has had a considerable but not frightening recent drop, and therefore those who wanted to sell at higher prices either did so or have now pulled back for having "missed their chance"— they are not really panicky and therefore refuse to sell at the new lower price.

- The market as a whole had begun to decline while this potential stock was holding up; after a brief decline potential sellers note its relative strength and decide not to dump their shares so

volume becomes lighter. Buyers are too timid to step up in large
numbers, so the price drifts lower in quiet trading volume.

- At the top of the rally, many traders and investors choose to take
  profits from the recent upswing, while at the same time bullish
  momentum players are buying the stock in the (mistaken) belief
  it will keep rising. Their reaction accounts for heavy volume in
  the early stage.

- After the decline has gone on for some time, potential sellers
  who missed their chance to cash in at higher levels refuse to
  give their shares away at a bargain. Yet potentially interested
  bulls in large numbers remain on the sideline as they lack the
  courage to be the first to buy until they see the price decline
  actually stop. With both camps largely standing aside, volume
  keeps shrinking.

All of the above conditions require both that there is no negative news that
would drive a new wave of heavy selling *and* that the overall market and
the individual stock in question do not decline so long or so sharply as to
begin a panic stage when huge numbers of holders will all try to liquidate
at once. Either of these situations, of course, would drive volume higher
rather than allowing it to gradually abate.

Let us now look at the longer-term chart in Figure 11–2, in this case
a 24-month tracking of Winnebago Industries (ticker WGO). The patterns
we observed on the chart of Kohl's are *not* limited to short-term swings
measured in days. Winnebago's stock was hit hard in early October 1999
(just to the left of center on this chart) with bad news—corporate officials
projected a slowing of earnings due to rising interest rates. In a matter of
days, WGO collapsed from $24 to briefly just over $15. After a retracement
to nearly $22 at the end of February 2000, the stock was again battered on
above-average trading volume in early March and again cascaded down to
$15 before bouncing. A brief bounce found supply in the area around $18
until early to mid-April. What happened next was the tipoff that the decline
was ready to end. WGO shares declined gradually in late April and through
all of May on the slowest trading seen in more than a year. The stock slipped
quietly below the two-time bottoms at $15 in mid-May with no rise in trad-
ing volume at all. Normally, a decline to a new price low will bring out as
fresh sellers disappointed holders who are weary of their widening paper
losses and are refusing to take it any more. Here, there was no such cohort
of new sellers. What had happened in May was that those holders who had

FIGURE 11-2

Winnebago: Low Volume on Final October-November
Decline and Mid-January Advance.

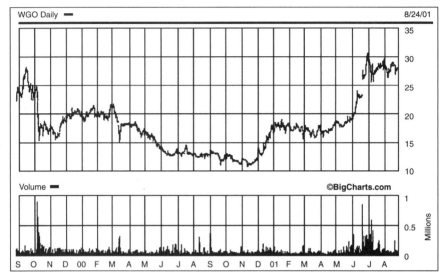

not been panicked out by the bad news and severe price declines the prior October and March apparently had decided the stock was now so cheap they would not sell even if it slipped to new lows.

Around June 10, trading actually picked up as the stock rallied about $2 to above $14. The renewed moderate decline in late July and early August—even though it resulted in a new appearance on the 52-week lows lists, came on extremely light trading. The 10 weeks from September 1 through mid-November were a period of sharp and widespread decline in the overall market, and yet while WGO did again move to slightly lower new lows, trading again was very slow overall. Sellers in any kind of numbers had virtually disappeared. Looking back over the stock's decline from $18 in early April to the bottom 7 months later, you can see that volume was low during declines and had actually started to perk up on temporary advances (late June, early September, late October). Clearly, the picture was one of incrementally slower volume during subsequent periods of decline—a sign of downside urgency disappearing.

The reason that a decline on volume fading away in its later stages usually results in a bottom is that it takes only a little positive news or concerted buying by bargain-hunters, or just one good strong day in the overall market, to bring out enough upside momentum to attract a rise in buyers. In other words, the stock had been declining into a relative vacuum of interest by both sides, and it takes little in renewed activity by the bulls to end the price drop.

LOWER VOLUME AT LATER PRICE-PEAK AREAS

While the graph of Kohl's in Figure 11–1 of illustrated declining volume as short-term price waves became older in number of days, our next case shows lower volume, not necessarily *during* each small rising wave but rather *at the end* of one price rise as compared with the next. Figure 11–3 is a chart of development-stage biotechnology company Maxim Pharmaceuticals, Inc. (MAXM), during the summer of 2000. For the first several bars on the chart (ending at June 30), the stock was rallying, culminating in a small crescendo and trading of about 800,000 shares as the price briefly scaled $54. MAXMthen underwent a correction that lasted less than 2 full days before renewing its price rise. This time, the stock

FIGURE 11–3

Maxim Pharmaceuticals: Rally Failure After Lower Volumes at Price Peaks–June30, July 10, and July 17.

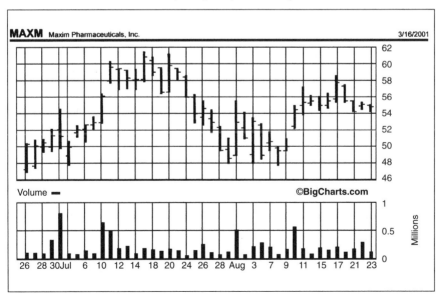

actually made two very short term higher-wave highs before finally failing and declining by over 20 percent in the second half of July. The first rise was completed on July 10 and 11 with volume each day at or above half a million shares but still below the level of interest on June 30. After 3 days of resting in the 57 to 59 range, It again made new highs on its next wave. Whether one measures that as ending on July 15 or July 20, either time above $61, trading volume has declined substantially at the later price peak. A very similar volume-and-price pattern can be observed in early to mid-August: The first up-thrust culminated with high volume on August 10; after a rest of several days a new short upward price wave carried the price to over $58 on August 17, but volume was less than half what it had been a week earlier. How can we interpret such action, and why is it indicative of a likely move to the downside?

- In much the same way that declining volume *during* a wave indicates decreased bullishness as price rises or as buyers apparently have done their accumulating, subsequent price peaks accompanied by lower numbers of shares traded indicate waned interest by the bulls. Since this pattern takes more time to develop, it encompasses more thinking and emotional energy by all involved and therefore probably has more serious price implications on the downside.

- The overall market may have lost its upside zip, so fewer traders are driven to continue their urgent buying on successive rallies. Volume at the end of each wave is smaller.

- As price goes higher each time, fewer potential buyers and fewer momentum chasing traders see the stock as a worthwhile bargain.

- With the size and urgency of the buying cohort smaller than at past price highs, it takes a relatively smaller amount of overall market weakness or specific-stock inclination to initiate profit taking to stop the later advance. The lower volume on that advance proved that it was a weaker one from a technical viewpoint even though it actually moved the price higher.

- The final price high may be driven less by aggressive bullish buyers in large numbers and more by the urgent covering of scared or margin-called shorts.

- A first upside price wave may have been driven by a "buy" recommendation by a major brokerage analyst. A second brokerage house may drive the later wave, but as price goes higher, fewer clients can be convinced there remains a bargain, so trading on the later wave is slower.

- In similar fashion, several institutions may be the prime buyers in the first wave. After a pause for digestion, they and/or others resume buying, but as the price goes higher, some drop out of the bidding and volume decreases.

- Finally, there exist some number of volume-savvy technical analysis-driven investors and traders. For them, the fact that lower volume drives subsequent peaks is a warning, and they will withdraw their buying interest. Yes, technical analysis does to some degree feed upon itself.

VOLUME LOWER AT SUBSEQUENT PRICE BOTTOMS

A useful sign that an existing downtrend in price may be about to come to an end is the observation that the stock's more recent declines to lower lows on subsequent waves have no longer been driven by levels of trading volume as active as in the past. You should remember, however, that the end of a decline in price does not necessarily signal an automatic immediate rise in price; often a stock must spend a fairly extended time period in "base building" before it is able to rally significantly. But the patient investor who is interested in a stock should note signals that a protracted decline is about to terminate. He or she can then do more intensive work (technical and/or fundamental) to help decide whether entry is justified without delay. At a minimum the stock can be watched more frequently so as to detect any tendencies to actually begin rising. Time, of course, *is* money!

Two stocks, coincidentally both involved in the food chain, nicely illustrate the importance of reduced volume at subsequently lower price extremes. Sara Lee (ticker SLE) actually did so twice in a 12-month period from early 1999 through early 2000 (see Figure 11–4). This, it should be noted, is not a very volatile stock. It made a price low just under $22 in late April 1999 (very near the start from left to right on the chart), with daily volume once hitting 10 million but consistently reaching the 4- to 5-million range in late April. After a 10 percent plus rally in price, a renewed erosion began in mid-May. SLE made new lows below $22 twice in August but trading volume was never above 2 million shares per day. This indicated that sellers were somewhat exhausted; no new panic occurred when the lows of late April were taken out. A worthwhile rally of over 25 per-

FIGURE 11-4

Sara Lee: Lows in May, July, August 1999
Occurred on Lower Peak Volumes.

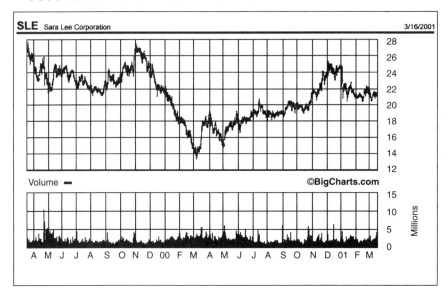

cent extended to late October. The stock failed to hold its August lows in
January 2000, and volume began rising. However, even though price eroded
to below $14 by early March, you can see that trading was consistently in the
2- to 3-million area daily, or well below the levels of about 5 million that had
created the Spring 1999 lows at about $22. Below 14 proved to be the low.
At under 10 times trailing earnings, apparently the stock seemed such a bargain to owners that they stopped selling.

Another illustration of reduced selling at subsequent price waves'
lows can be seen on the chart of Winn-Dixie, the southeastern U.S. gro-
cers (Figure 11–5). When WIN made its low at about $33 in May 1999, a
modest peak in daily volume was responsible. A piece of adverse news in
early October triggered a few days when trading topped half a million
shares. Subsequent price lows in early December, and again in late
February 2000, did not occur on higher trading than had been seen in
October. Late February was a decent signal that the decline was basically
over. Perhaps it was still early to buy, but urgency on the part of sellers had
clearly waned. The stock subsequently settled into a pattern of very gradual price erosion from May through September. The two slight selling climaxes in early and late August saw nowhere nearly as much selling as that

in late February. While the fundamentals remained quite unattractive, sellers were done marking the stock down, as shown by the lower trading activity at subsequent price lows. Late January 2001 shows a breakout (rather than culminating) volume crescendo.

APPLICATIONS FOR SHORT-TERM TRADING

While the primary purpose of this book is not to encourage short-term or day trading, it would be a gross omission not to mention here that the patterns of declining volume *during* a price advance and *during* a price decline can be applied on an intraday basis. Various charting services available over the Internet (such as BigCharts.com) allow users to display trading in 1- or 5-minute intervals. Displaying a chart of 1 or 2 days' price and volume action can be very instructive if you are considering buying or selling, because short-term patterns on charts look very much like longer-term patterns. Quite often, you will note that a stock that is rallying will display considerable volume in the morning's first trading hour or so, followed by a decline in trading activity whose chart looks like a gradually flattening ski slope. (This is quite similar in shape to the time-decayed volume patterns over several or more days in cases after

FIGURE 11-5

Winn-Dixie Stores: Lower Volume on Downward
Price Waves, Summer 2000.

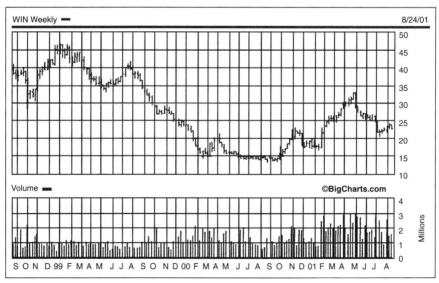

stocks have reacted to major price-moving news on huge volume as in Chapter 9.) The price may continue to move slightly higher as intraday volume decays later in the morning. A stock in such a condition is highly vulnerable to price decline since the most keenly interested buyers apparently have already done their work for the day. Short-term traders, including but not only day traders, tend to be very momentum conscious, looking for action and departing when it stops. Such participants are likely to note the flattening of the price increase that is caused by the lessening of buying pressure. Unless the overall trend of the full market is decidedly bullish, individual stocks that have seen concentrated buying early in the session followed by a considerable decrease in trading activity are likely to decline later on in the day as profit takers note that they have peaked in price—and there is a lack of urgent buyers to support the higher quotations. Some traders refer to the process of trading this pattern as "fading the opening."

Likewise, the concept of decreased trading volume at subsequent highs of price waves also works well as one watches a stock rally on a 10-day intraday chart (such as can be found at BigCharts.com). Typically, the first hour (or even 90 minutes) of the trading day produces above-average volume. If one observes several consecutive days of rising price on strong volume and then sees a morning in which the stock continues to trade higher but on notably lower volume in the early hours volume, it is a strong candidate for sale on a trading basis. Whatever was prompting numerous bulls to place buying orders overnight and into the first hour or so of trading in prior days is now clearly no longer providing that impetus, or at best it is driving a smaller cohort of bulls to remain as active buyers than had been the case on previous days. Something has changed (deteriorated) in the psychology of the crowd that had been pushing the stock up. Stocks require active buying interest to push them higher (especially after recent advances have already occurred); the cooling of overnight buying pressure as compared with that on earlier recent days is a highly meaningful signal.

ANALYSIS

When examining trading volume, either during price moves or at the ends of price waves, you should think in terms of the emotions of people who own or are considering the stock. People's thinking about stocks must become intense enough so that they are moved to take action. If they are not moved to action, they do not place buy or sell orders. When a greater number of people are moved to action, we as students of behavioral finance say that a crowd has formed. It is important for us to observe the size of the current crowd and to compare that with the size of crowds that got excited at prior times. When we are looking at the gradual trailing off of volume as a price move continues, we are seeing that fewer people are moved to action as the price move becomes more extended or severe. Our logical conclusion is that the excitement is waning. That excitement to action may be in the form of enthusiasm on the part of buyers (on a rising price wave) or some combination of disappointment and panic on the part of holders (on a decline in price). When less excitement (or incitement) to action is occurring in one camp, it takes only a moderate change in the number of participants with the other camp's opinion to tip the balance and reverse the direction of prices. That is why a feathering out of volume during a price move is a warning of a price reversal to come.

Times of sharp price movement that culminates a previously existing price move are virtually always created by the gathering of a significantly larger-than-normal crowd. When a price rally has been going on, an increased number of traders and/or investors has taken note. In a concentrated period of a few days, they individually conclude they no longer can go on without owning the stock in question. The acceleration of price itself helps stimulate their desire to buy, so they will no longer miss the exciting upside price action. When counted from a distance by means of tallying their trading volume, these buyers constitute a small crowd or mob of buyers whose decisions to buy are clustered in a brief time period. The stock "blows off" on high volume. After the temporary excitement has peaked, the stock naturally declines or consolidates. The next rally, if it runs to a higher price level than its predecessor, ought to also attract and incite to action a larger crowd. If it does not do so, we as observers of crowd action conclude that excitement *at later highs* is smaller than it was earlier at then-exciting peaks. This tells us the bull market in this stock has become extended and tired. We are sellers because the crowds are no longer as big as they were before. It is like the start of the decline in popularity of a rock group, whose most recent new album sells fewer copies than the prior one did. Their star has reached its highest point and is now in decline.

Sharp price decline, of course, elicits a very different emotional response than does a pleasantly sharp rise in price. Sharp decline, whether driven by specific news or not, results in more than just a lack of buying interest (the exact opposite of widespread buying excitement at a sharp price peak). No, a sharp price decline produces first discouragement and then finally some degree of panic among owners. We can measure the collective amount of such psychological pain by noting the trading volume that occurs during a price collapse. That volume is actually *causing* the price collapse, of course. And the price collapse at some point causes rising panic among holders who sell *because they are scared by the price drop itself.* When such sellers have been flushed out, the decline is over. Now, if the stock rallies and subsequently drops again, such that it reaches an even lower price level than during the first little panic, it is very important to compare the size of the panicky crowd the second time around. If it is still large, the price may yet go lower if another selling wave comes on later. But if the size of the selling crowd is smaller at the new price low, we can conclude that the decline in price is largely complete.

What has happened psychologically is this: First, so many people panicked at the earlier time of price collapse that fewer such weak-willed holders are left to be shaken out this time. Second, the new lower price lows are probably making more traders dig in and refuse to take their larger paper losses. This involves denial. Third, the new lows may be causing the stock to appear quite cheap to old holders, who simply decide they cannot be parted from their shares because the now-lower prices represent such a huge bargain. These factors together mean that the pool of ready sellers is smaller than at a prior low. The stage is set for an end to the decline. A stock that has hurt and disappointed a lot of holders usually does not immediately have a large and enthused audience once it starts to rally. Each rally brings out some sellers who are relieved to have gotten a few dollars more than earlier low quotes. Time is required for turning the ship around from a southbound to a northbound course. So the end of a decline in an individual stock (absent a major crash in the overall market, which cleans out all sellers) should not be taken as a signal that a large rally is an immediate prospect. That positive change will take some combination of time to heal wounds—plus actual improving news to attract a large number of buyers. Few except the truly patient vulture contrarian value players are willing to buy recently damaged goods at the early bottom. Others want to wait for more evidence. Thus a bottom in an individual stock does not mean an immediate major rally or bull market. Think always in terms of the mental states of people who have been or might now become involved with the stock. They must be moved in considerable numbers in order to mount a new uptrend.

SUMMARY

In this chapter we have examined in some detail the fading of volume during price trends, both upward and downward. We have also looked closely at the failure of volume to reach higher levels when price peaks or price lows are more extreme than prior ones. Both of these kinds of conditions are "lower volume." They must not be confused with dull, ongoing, listless trading, which often occurs in extended bear market times. That is the subject of our next brief chapter.

CHAPTER 12

Cautions about Misinterpreting Low Volume

Throughout this book, you have seen a theme develop: Not only is trading volume a centrally important part of the technical information we must know about stocks, but higher versus lower volume has great importance. The latter point was a major basis of the approaches and tracking techniques discussed in Chapters 4 through 7 and again in Chapter 11. With the exceptions of extremely high (climaxing and therefore reversing) volumes driven by the factors discussed in Chapters 9 through 11, an underlying theme is that high or higher volume marks the primary price direction while low or lower volume occurs when a stock is consolidating or correcting against the primary price trend. Now, however, we must raise as cautions several situations in which you should not automatically interpret low, quiet trading volume as implying an imminent price reversal from the prevailing direction. As an overall summary, we might say that low volume as a persistent condition has considerably less technical-analysis predictive power than low volume interspersed with and in contrast to higher volume.

PRICE: A BY-PRODUCT OF TRADING ACTION

As background for what follows, we should go back to some of the very basic concepts introduced in Chapter 1. Price change does not happen in a vacuum, or by magic, or randomly. Price change is the effect of trading.

People are moved, by any of a long list of possible drivers, to place buying or selling orders that result in demand for, and supply of, shares of a given stock. If no one decides to take action on a given trading day, there will be no transactions and volume will be zero. The stock in question will not appear in the following day's newspaper listings. Simply stated, investors and traders must make and implement decisions to buy and sell a stock in order for it to trade. The balance of urgency about buying versus selling, expressed in the numbers of shares offered and bid for, and the kinds orders used (market, stop, stop-limit, and limit) will determine what direction price takes. Price is a by-product of trading action.

It is nearly impossible to imagine such as situation in this age, when daily trading on the New York Stock Exchange has been as high as 2 billion shares in a day (equal, incredible as it may seem, to total *annual* trading as recently as 1979!), and reported trading in a day on NASDAQ has topped 3 billion, that a stock literally might not trade on some given day.* "The stock exchange" does not make a stock trade on a given day. It requires one or more orders from the public for a trade to occur. One at-market order from the public to buy, for example, will cause the specialist to supply shares at a price fairly near the prior level, and thus volume will be recorded and price may move moderately.

So, while trading actually starts the day with no guarantee of occurring, let us look similarly at influences on price direction. It turns out that there actually exists a bias in the direction of more selling than buying, although admittedly the amount of volume involved is not very significant. For most exchange-listed stocks, somewhere from about a million and on upward to several hundred million or even a few billion shares already are in the hands of investors. The latter range from day traders, and institutional holders who typically have annual turnover patterns of 75 percent or higher, to employees of the listed companies, to utility shareowners who hold long term primarily for dividend income, to inactive elderly investors and even the estates of deceased persons. Shares are held by these owners and theoretically could come up for sale on any given day—even regardless of specific price and especially without any trigger such as corporate news, or even anyone's emotional reaction to recent

---

*We know that in fact this does occur, and we can verify it simply by checking the published daily tallies of stocks rising, declining, or closing unchanged from one trading session to the next. At the time this was written, about 3,300 to 3,400 stocks per day were being traded on the NYSE, and sometimes the daily totals varied by as much as 30 stocks or so; on the American Stock Exchange, typical trading encompassed about 800 issues, and daily variation was sometimes about 20 stocks, or over 2 percent.

price trends. An estate is finally being settled, and a stock held is liqui-dated for cash to pay taxes. College tuition is due, and those shares that grandmother gave the new baby 18 or 20 years ago must be liquidated. Someone becomes unemployed and has to meet the monthly bills. A retiree sells a bit since he cannot live on income alone and so must occa-·sionally dip into principal. Some number of shares of each stock exists, and any of those could become available for sale on any given day. There is supply and, theoretically at least, virtually no structural source of demand. (Three potential kinds of special buyers exist, although not in every case and usually not involving large numbers of shares: corporate buyback programs, market-purchase dividend-reinvestment programs, and short sellers who may need or choose to cover are those sources of potential buying in a news-free market.) On balance, except at certain times in the dividend-reinvestment cycle or at very cheap valuations, it is fair to say that a nonvolatile stock probably begins each day theoretically in a slight net supply situation rather than one of net demand: someone somewhere has an estate or an unexpected dentist bill to settle, or one of the other sources above may want to sell 100 shares or more.

Thus we can see that in the case of most stocks there is likely to be at least some trading on a given day, even absent a news trigger or any other source of emotional stimulation that would cause buying or selling. In earlier chapters we mentioned that very high trading volume, in itself, acts as a trigger for some investors and particularly for traders to join in the action. Excitement breeds additional activity, so to speak. It can equal-ly be said that to a certain extent very light activity and boredom in a stock can become self-extending. Except for the relatively few stocks bought for their dividend streams, investors and traders alike seem to prefer to "go where the action is" rather than shop around where there is little or no action. And, certainly, as a practical matter, investors of any size, from the wealthy individual to the professional portfolio manager, must confine their study and action to stocks that trade in sufficient volume to accom-modate their buying and selling. Thus indeed, light volume in a given stock can tend to drive away some potential participants, and therefore light volume might tend to continue.

It is for that reason that we cannot necessarily say that low trading activity forecasts an imminent change in price direction. As discussed in Chapter 11, lower trading volume while a price advance continues is an unsustainable condition and warns of a reversal to lower prices in short order. It would be highly unlikely for a stock that has a large number of shares outstanding and in the floating supply to be able to rise in price on a sustained basis on the basis of persistently low trading volume. First, as a stock rises in price, it becomes ever more fundamentally overvalued. That condition would prompt increasing numbers of holders to sell out, which would both increase the trading volume and turn the price downward. Second, widespread computerized tracking via commercial technical analysis software and numerous free Internet charting and database packages would very soon call attention to the above-average price performance of an issue rising persistently. That added attention would attract momentum-based traders, again with the result that volume would cease to remain very low.

The possibility that a stock could continue to trade sideways or lower on persistently light volume, however, is much more realistic. In theory, if a stock descended to very low fundamental valuation levels, it should attract a rising level of buying interest among value-oriented and contrarian investors. In actual practice, however, contrarians and value investors are a relatively small minority—or at least came to be so in the prolonged bull market of the years 1982 through early 2000. As long as *some* stocks and groups are showing positive action, there is a fairly strong tendency among those with bullish leanings to concentrate their activity where some visible price action already exists. That preference in itself tends to draw potential attention away from dormant or persistent quietly declining stocks. There is also a natural psychological and sociological tendency for people to suspect and fear stocks that are going down. Our seemingly instinctive reaction is to believe that other investors and traders in large numbers "must know something" about such stocks or else their prices would not be acting the way they do. Therefore, we reason, why bother to spend any effort researching those issues? If there were an interesting story, or when at some point there actually starts to be one, we will know it from the change in price action and can then become buyers.

The line of thinking described above might be summarized in the sometimes-noted axiom that it takes buying power to put a stock up, but a stock can decline simply of its own weight. That truth is well to be remembered when you are looking at a stock that declines or moves sideways persistently on routinely low volume. It is important for each of us to remember that we are much smaller than the overall market and therefore should not expect to be able to impose our wills upon it. We might be correct in that a given stock is vastly overpriced or severely undervalued on its fundamentals. But that does not mean that the millions of other investors who make up "the market" each day it is open for business must immediately come to share our wisdom and therefore move the price of the stock to a level we consider proper. It will take buying in some size to push the price up. The strongest evidence of what the majority of market participants believe is the price they will pay and the amount of trading volume that is occurring to discover and sustain that price level. Mind you, the mere opinion of the large majority does not make them correct in a factual (value) sense; but in an operational (price) sense, for the present, their collective opinion is making their judgment prevail. Their collective opinion, whose strength is evident in the very amount of stock that is changing hands at and around a current price level, will keep ruling the day until or unless some item(s) of news become widely known to change the prevailing valuation paradigm. Our contrary opinion, whether it be more bullish or more bearish than what prevails in the meantime, will remain a minority view. Unless you or I decide to bring a large enough block of capital to bear, such that our persistent buying or short selling of the stock can actually change the balance of supply and demand, our view is not yet ready to prevail. It will indeed take volume buying to put the price up.

It is because of the prevailing of collective majority opinion, in the form of sufficiently balanced bids and offers to keep a stock around some price level or in some price trend, that a price formation can continue—most readily on the downside or in a sideways direction—even on persistently relatively low trading volume. For that reason, seemingly habitually light trading is not necessarily a sufficient sign that price is about to reverse to the upside.

DOCUMENTING HISTORICAL VOLUME LEVELS

We have been discussing trading volume and in the process have almost casually applied labels such as "slow" and "light" and "low"; there are of course much more precise ways to document what a stock's historical average or typical or normal volume actually is. For that dwindling minority of market followers who are not electronically connected to the data world via the Internet, I would strongly suggest saving the annual stock tables published by *The Wall Street Journal* and by many local newspapers on or around the first weekend of the new calendar year. These contain not only the year's price quotations (high, low, last, and net change) but also the all-important total of share trading for the past year. Even without a calculator, you can fairly easily ascertain what mean daily volume in a stock was: Multiply the year's total volume shown by 4, and then delete the final three places in the resulting figure. This is, of course, dividing by 250, which is almost exactly the number of trading sessions in a typical calendar year. You can then compare recent daily volumes in the stock you are studying to the prior year's daily average level. Another way to find past volume data is to look at *Daily Graphs* charts, which many public libraries carry. There, you can visually note what average volume levels tend to be in a given stock.

Other readily available methods of judging whether current volume is low or average involve Internet access. Here are three URL addresses that will readily answer the question. I would suggest you bookmark one or more of them according to your preferences.

> http://chart.yahoo.com/t?a=09&b=18&c=00&d=09&e=22&f=00&g=d&s=intc

At this address, you can set any time range from one date to another and then acquire the daily trading-volume data via download to a spreadsheet. There, you can quickly take an average and median. If you gather the data in weekly or monthly aggregates to save spreadsheet space, note that the volume shown for each period is already the average daily volume and *not the total* volume for that period.

The Yahoo! financial Web site pages also provide (in text boxes below the chart) volume data at this address:

> quote.yahoo.com   (and insert ticker symbol and choose "chart" before clicking to get data)

However, the average shown is not labeled so as to indicate what time length it covers. By experimenting with recent new issues, I have determined that the average is for more than 6 but fewer than 12 months, but it is not for 200 trading days (a popular measure for moving price averages). While it provides a quick reference if you are examining a Yahoo! chart, the lack of information on the nature of the average may be a considerable drawback. If you wish to follow a number of stocks in a reusable single list rather than flipping from one chart to another, this additional facility provided by Yahoo! can be of use; you need to set the columns to include both current intraday and average (again, of undefined window length) volume:

> http://finance.yahoo.com/p?v&k=pf_2

If you would prefer to know the exact length of the window for which "average volume" is shown, try

> www.bigcharts.com

and choose the chart length you wish to view from the drop-down menu. Below the chart itself you will see an invitation to access a "printer-friendly version." If you click on those words, you will find a two-page display. That

version, unlike the first graph you viewed in color, will contain some interesting data, including average daily volumes for two periods: both 50 and
200 days (plus total shares outstanding, market capitalization in dollars, and
short position—the last updated monthly). If you prefer to save the entire
detailed URL so you can go there directly, it follows here:

> www.bigcharts.com/print/print.asp?frames=0&symb=itx&unused=0&o_   ⸜
> symb=itx&freq=1&time=8&style=320&default=true&backurl
> (change ticker symbol)

In addition, of course, you also can simply resort to casual visual inspection of any online price chart of a year or more in length. Usually you will
be able to tell by that means whether volume has been declining and currently is below "average." However, in some cases a temporary cluster of
high volume some time ago may be difficult to smooth out mentally, so
the hard numbers produced by the above-cited sources will serve to render a precise verdict. Of the three approaches, I prefer that from BigCharts
because it is so readily available while one is looking at the volume and
price chart itself.

There are, of course, some potential traps in labeling as "low" a given
current amount of volume for an individual stock. These derive from overall market conditions. Days preceding stock market holidays, the days
before and after Thanksgiving, and the period from about December 20
through December 31 are notorious for below-average volume. Many professionals take the day off, or if they do commute to work, they refrain
from trading because markets are quite illiquid at such times. Low volume
at those dates thus has become somewhat self-perpetuating. Among official
holidays, Memorial Day, July 4, and Labor Day are most notable for providing excuses for long weekends and therefore slow trading volumes. It
should also be noted that on occasion a severe weather condition (major
snow or a hurricane) has been seen to decrease market volume deeply. The
bottom line is that you cannot "count" such days as very low volume situations for a stock since they are created not by specific lack of interest in
the stock itself but rather by semiholiday conditions for the market overall.

TWO CLASSIC DECLINING-VOLUME
TYPES OF STOCK

Two types of stocks that may produce extended periods of very low volume
are worth special mention. These are troubled companies and less-than-
successful post-IPO situations. Let us explore these on a psychological
basis, so you understand what is behind the (lack of) action.

The Troubled Company

While a lot of stock trading is emotion based and therefore not financially wise, what people typically do is a fact of life and therefore is relevant to understanding how the market works in volume (and resulting price) terms. First, we know that most people generally do not have the courage (or interest) to attempt "bottom-fishing." That implies that a gradually and persistently declining price will tend to repel potential buyers; they will wait for price to start rising or for some dramatic news to kindle their interest in bargain hunting before they actually move in to buy. Thus, it is normal for a persistently declining stock to exhibit fairly consistently low volume; in effect, it gradually falls into a deepening slumber. Now, consider the owners of such a stock. They are disappointed, to say the least. We know that investors have a terrible time coming to grips with losses: Closing out a losing position is an act of final closure that prevents recouping the loss; taking a loss means admitting "I made a mistake," and we do not like feeling dumb. As a stock declines, then, holders become progressively less inclined to want to sell. This is especially true if the stock sinks slowly without any highly emotionally stimulating news crises that would scare holders into bailing out in panic. Thus, we see that a stock that declines gradually but persistently tends to make both the potential buyers and the potential sellers relatively disinclined to take action: Volume declines with price.

Figure 12–1 charts the oldest U.S. commercial airline, TWA , which entered its third and final bankruptcy in early 2001 before having its assets bought by American Airlines. This chart illustrates this very typical pattern. After a brief run to the upside in both volume and price ending in early February 1999, TWA settled into a prolonged slumber that ran through about September or October. After a very similar appearing and temporary volume and price jump that ended in late May 2000, the volume again dropped off to a very low level for several months.

What about the occasional sudden jumps in volume? Why did they not signify an end to TWA shares' price decline? Knowing, as we now do, the eventual fate of the company, one could reasonably surmise on a fundamental basis that most investors sensed impending doom, as the company kept losing money during an economic boom while competitors flourished. But that fundamental conclusion of course drove potential bargain hunters to avoid the stock no matter how low its price. Therefore, no buying buildup. The occasional jumps in price and volume were driven by temporary good news. When you, as an investor or trader, are trying to use a change in persistent low volume as a signal to buy a depressed stock,

FIGURE 12–1

Trans World Airlines: Nonclimaxing Low Volume with Persistently Eroding Prices Starting February 1999.

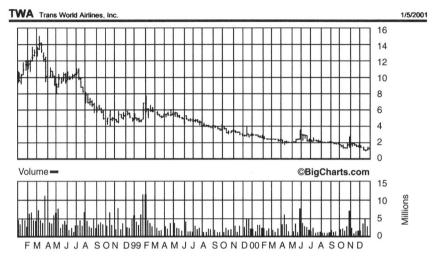

TWA Trans World Airlines, Inc.   1/5/2001

you must be very careful to note the cause of a rise in volume. Generally, unless some positive news (which indeed will cause a temporary jump in volume and therefore in price) is truly sensational in its implications, you will find that such a jump is a false and costly signal to follow. True, some speculative buyers will be hooked by whatever the good news is. Some faithful owners will probably also decide to average down on good news, in hopes that their ordeal will now end. And some short sellers may cover their profitable positions when they see good news and upside volume and price action. That will quickly pass, however! When other holders see that the price improvement is starting to slip away, they will come in as sellers and thereby drop the price back. Then the dreary process of declining price, lack of interest, and low volume will resume.

The Post-IPO Issue

A second sort of stock deserving specific mention is the post-IPO issue. As this was written in early 2001, the IPO market had become much slower than in the sizzling years of 1998 to early 2000. But when IPOs are red or white hot, a very consistent pattern of price and volume is observed. Typically the newly public company's stock begins trading far above the IPO price—perhaps up 100 percent or even 200 percent—as the overly enthusiastic and naive public rushes to "buy at market" while some of the lucky holders who got in at the issue price immediately flip their shares out for huge gains. What has happened is that a huge amount of trading has occurred at severely elevated quotations on the very first day.

Sometimes on the second day there may be some follow-through on the upside, and again volume will be huge. What is key to remember is that for every wonderfully satisfied seller there is a new buyer who has paid a high price. In classic fashion, once the crowd's demand has been satisfied, volume starts to cool down and predictably price falls with it. A few traders sense that the stock is no longer hot, and they manage to sell for small losses. People and especially institutions blessed with cheap stock at the issue price now also see the price beginning to fade, and they start to feed a stream of selling orders, further pressuring the price lower. The psychological dynamics are very much like those in upside spikes, as described in Chapter 10.

The process begins to feed on itself. All the while, however, volume is trailing lower. The reasons are twofold: First, those who were inclined to jump out quickly with either a fast huge gain or a small quick loss have already done so in fair numbers as each day passes, so their activity is now history. Second, however, we have the large cohort of public buyers who, sheeplike, bought in the first few hours at way above the issue price. They all have paper losses. Probably most of them have faith in the concept behind the company or the industry, or were specifically attracted to the stock for some personal reason (employer, neighbor, broker advice, etc.). While a few become scared enough quickly enough to get out in the early days, most keep their faith. After all, they think to themselves, the stock traded as high as $130 once, so it can easily go there and higher again. They conveniently block out of their minds that the issue price was $25 and that the company has no significant revenues yet. Those owners have ensnared themselves in a downward spiral that has only just begun.

As the price wends its way progressively lower in coming weeks, a few give up hope and bail out. But most cannot bear the thought of accepting the folly of their first-day action and stubbornly dig in their heels. Every time the stock rallies for a day or two, a bit of hope is rekindled, making the likelihood they will soon sell even more remote. Whether fortunately or otherwise, IPOs are not eligible for purchase on margin for the first 30 days of their lives. Were that not the case, many buyers would more quickly be forced, by receiving margin calls, to think hard about selling out or putting up more cash. Therefore, the classically shaped tail of post-IPO prices is rather lengthy, more so than is the pattern of decline for a long-existing stock that experiences a sudden but temporary burst in price on huge volume.

The charts of two stocks, as shown in Figures 12–2 and 12–4, plotted from the dates of their respective IPOs, will illustrate what was described above. First, we examine the price and trading-volume history of TheStreet.com, Inc. (TSCM), a financial news and commentary Web site provider that came public on May 14, 1999. In classic fashion, TSCM rocketed from its offering price of $19 per share, opening above $60 and trading briefly above $70 on its first day. Alas, that was the end of its bull market. In under 2 weeks, trading had shriveled from about 13 million shares (twice the total IPO offering!) to under 1 million per day. Volume increased somewhat late in the year when the stock held and then rallied about $15 a share, but from February through November 2000, trading generally lightened as the price melted into the lower single digits. (December 2000 saw a predictable rise in volume with no meaningful price rally as tax selling took hold.) We are providing both a daily and a monthly basis chart (Figure 12–3) so you can see the volume trend more clearly in summary form.

Not only the companies that go public and then fail to make it in the business world tend to exhibit such chart patterns. Fortunately, stocks of companies that have established businesses before becoming publicly traded tend not to decline so severely or for such long times. UPS, the well-known delivery company, went public in November 1999. Its shares jumped less spectacularly but nevertheless handsomely by the second day from their issue price of $48 to $77 (see Figure 12–4). At that level, their

FIGURE 12–2

TheStreet.com: Daily-Basis Volume History,
Peak Excitement at IPO.

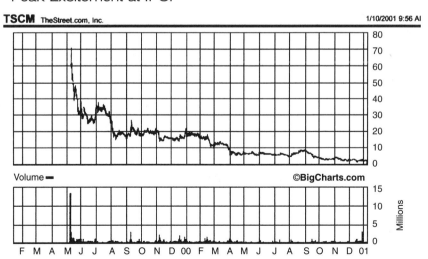

FIGURE 12-3

TheStreet.com: Monthly-Basis Volume History, Peak
Excitement at IPO.

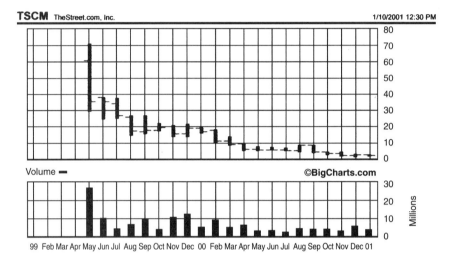

P/E was about four times that of comparable rival FedEx, but some justified that because UPS was argubly an "Internet company" due to its contract with Amazon.com. Note the smoothly and sharply declining volume
pattern that continued through just before the start of February 2000:
Through that time the stock had stabilized in the 63 to 70 range, so relatively few holders had major losses as the high had been only about 77.
Therefore, few saw any reason to sell out to heal their financial and psychological wounds. However, when the price broke at the end of January
2000, an increase in volume occurred as greater concern and urgency
asserted themselves. You can see on the volume portion of the chart that
until the panicky general market mindset took over in September and
October 2000, volume again trailed off over time.

Only after that emotional cleanout did the stock begin to exhibit meaningful and sustained increases and then ebbs and flows of volume. *Not driven by news or by new price collapses, those changes in trading volume
were meaningful.* They signaled a shift in the prevailing psychology surrounding UPS stock. The stock had come out from under the shadow of its
own IPO and had begun to trade like a seasoned issue. If you are watching
a stock with a prolonged period of gradually declining volume, you should
wait for it to display that sort of behavior. Shortly, you will learn a system
for following daily action that will alert you as a stock changes its trading
personality in this way. First, however, some mental pitfalls to avoid.

FIGURE 12-4

United Parcel Services: Sharp and Smooth
Post-IPO Volume Decline

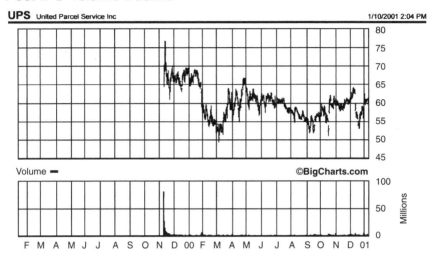

FLEETING SOURCES OF VOLUME INCREASES

December will predictably bring a rise in volume, although not necessarily any corresponding improvement in stock price. Many shareholders in declining stocks who have been unable to accept their financial fates all year will now respond to the tax subsidy by actually realizing their losses (which, of course, had already been available all year long). Investors who use full-service brokers will receive telephone reminders that tax-selling season has arrived and that they really should clean out some painful old laggards. Self-starting investors will also note the calendar and take available losses to reduce net taxable gains for the year. Some investors, knowing that such tax selling will put pressure on a stock's price, may sell to avoid further wealth erosion, and short sellers may also try taking advantage of the temporary seasonal swoon. All of these actions of course increase trading volume. Those reasons for selling go away for certain when the calendar turns, and in some years the selling pressure abates as early as December 15 to 20. So volume will calm back down. Price will obey the January Effect rules and rise for some part of the new month, providing holders and clever traders with favorable exit opportunities. But the entire phenomenon of rising volume will have been an artificial episode driven by the calendar rather than by truly rebuilt interest in the stock. You must ask whether there is anything of lasting importance that has prompted rising volume with rising price. If you see no such factors, conclude that the long and mournful price decline may resume.

Other fleeting causes of rising volume must also be screened out if you are to avoid buying a previously somnolent stock too early. News is an obvious factor, and it is easily noted by watching for headlines with your favorite online chart package. Even if that Web site does not pick up a story, you might find a news item by checking national and especially headquarters-local newspapers (online, of course) for mentions of the company name. Such sites allow free text searching, so use it. Also, you should surf your way into chat rooms that discuss the stock. Be careful because the air is thick with hype and strong opinion. Read the postings only for the purpose of seeing if there is some *news* being cited and commented on. Finally, you may occasionally find that a brokerage firm has issued a favorable report (although this is fairly rare in depressed stocks since most analysts, too, are momentum influenced if not driven, and they prefer to stay where the action is). A good and well-updated source for listings and brief summaries of brokerage analysts' reports (action advice) is as follows:

X

http://biz.yahoo.com/z/a/h.html

Another source for such information is also very comprehensive:

bigcharts.multexinvestor.com

Here, you can quickly note whether a new report has been issued; in most cases, however, viewing the contents involves paying a fee.

Some other possible causes for a nonsustainable uptick in volume might include significant news (possibly an acquisition) involving another company in the same industry as the stock you are watching; an appearance at a trade show; a management interview or analyst comment on some financial TV program or on a Web site you did not notice; a press release that did not get picked up by the online charting utility you monitor; or a change in technical price chart formation such as described above in the UPS example. If you cannot discern any reason for the greater activity, it will do no harm to phone the investor relations department at the company and ask if they know of any reason for heightened trading in their stock. Phone numbers are easily found at the end of earlier company press releases you can find, or in corporate profiles provided by Hoover's. Try to reach corporate headquarters rather than any outside financial PR agency since the latter will not say anything without first receiving clearance to do so by the company!

Your task is to discern whether the pickup in volume was event driven or otherwise. If you can find no specific evidence, you may well assume it was not an event unless you see a volume pattern such as is characteristic of a volume spike as described in Chapter 10. Remember, you need not note an actual upside price gap or spike to detect such a situation: Even a small positive stimulus can cause a minor volume spike in a long-depressed stock. If no such volume pattern exists and the price has risen, you may reasonably conclude that there is buying pressure gathering for non-news-triggered reasons. *That* is the kind of change in psychological milieu that you want as a signal to buy following persistent low volume.

A VOLUME/PRICE SYSTEM FOR NOTING SHIFTS IN BEHAVIOR

Chapter 5 spoke of the importance of noting daily-basis price/volume combinations. Those can be especially important here, when examining long-depressed and quietly trading issues. You will recall that the days in which heavier trading takes place represent the dominant price direction while days of lower activity are resting, consolidating, countertrend days in terms of price direction. Stating the case from a bull's perspective, up on higher volume and down on lower volume is positive for price.

You may be looking at quite a number of stocks at a given time, and you may not necessarily be in touch with the market every day to exactly the same extent. In any case, it can quickly become an overwhelming mental task to keep all your past volume/price observations in your head. You also want to avoid time spent redoing previous thinking. The system of volume/price tracking presented here should solve those problems. Each trading day, you want to notice whether the stock rises or falls and the direction of the volume. I have found that not only a comparison of closing prices (net change as shown in the newspapers) but also separate comparisons of lows and of highs will be useful in absorbing an accurate sense of a stock's technical strength or weakness. Thus, three combinations need to be observed for each trading session:

High versus prior-day high, against comparative volume

Close versus prior-day close, against comparative volume

Low versus prior-day low, against comparative volume

A simple system of symbols, as shown below, will enable you to quickly record and later review these combinations of volume and price dynamics:

	While Volume Is...	
	Up	**Down**
Price is higher.	+	/
Price is lower.	−	\

To make them stand out sharply, you should encircle the plus and minus signs since they occur on days with higher volume. The slash marks should stand alone as such; they represent price movement taking place in lower-volume trading sessions. The system works visually because the circled marks are more important and the weaker, uncircled slashes are less crucial. In a stock that is gently but persistently trending lower on generally lackluster volume, the majority of your marks over time will be slashes, and especially backslashes (\) representing lower price on lower volume.

A stock becomes interesting from a bullish viewpoint only when you start to see a shift toward those two circled symbols, the plus and minus signs, and of course especially circled plus signs since they represent higher price on higher volume (again, discount any news-triggered action). The presence of more circled symbols over a period of perhaps 2 weeks or so indicates that for some reason (again, excluding news) a larger amount of attention is being directed to the stock. Interest has perked up. The prevailing psychology is shifting from defensive and bored to more active and interested.

I learned several decades ago to plot the three daily representations of high, close, and low prices in a vertical set with high represented at the top and close in the middle. Thus, for example, a stack of three plus signs means that volume for the day expanded and the high, close, and low were all at higher prices than on the previous day. Three minus signs means that volume expanded and all three price comparisons were lower. Of course, you can get various combinations of plus and minus signs on a given day, or of upward and downward slashes (but no other combinations since the volume characterization of the day governs!). Remember, all three comparative price markers (high, close, and low) may not be the same on a given day. For example, price range (both high and low) might be lower on Tuesday than on Monday, but a late rally on Tuesday might push the net change for that day higher. This would be shown in the coding system as a vertical −, +, − if volume were higher or as a vertical stack of \, /, and \ if volume were lower.

Perhaps a few examples will make this more concrete. Here are the symbols for a neatly behaving stock that marches evenly higher for 4 days on alternating higher- and lower-volume activity:

High	+	/	+	/
Close	+	/	+	/
Low	+	/	+	/
Day no.	1	2	3	4

For simplicity's sake, conveniently again having all its measures moving in sync, on days 5 through 7, it begins declining on alternately higher and then lower volume:

High	+	/	+	/	−	\	−
Close	+	/	+	/	−	\	−
Low	+	/	+	/	−	\	−
Day no.	1	2	3	4	5	6	7

Aside from wanting to see a predominance of circled plus signs, you will particularly hope to note two combinations, which my long experience has shown can indicate price reversals:

+\
−\
+\

This pattern is bearish, showing a high-volume downside reversal on the first day and a decline on lower volume (the buyers have departed) on the second day. Conversely,

\+
/+
\+

is a bullish pattern. The first day saw an intraday upside price reversal on relatively light volume, which was followed the next session by a price jump on higher volume. Buyers have become involved.

For those readers who are more easily stimulated by color or perhaps are of a more artistic mind, here is a second way of coding the daily volume/price combinations. This set of symbols, which you can accomplish with three pencils, substitutes on a one-for-one basis for the mathematical symbols and slashes described and used above.

	While Volume Is...	
	Up	**Down**
Price is higher.	Green button	Black X
Price is lower.	Red button	Black button

Reading from top to bottom and one day at a time, the important reversal combinations described just above would be as follows:

Green	Black		Black	Green
Red	Black		X	Green
Green	Black (bearish)		Black	Green (bullish)
1	2		1	2

After a few days of practice (perhaps over a weekend using several different stocks' recent historical price/volume charts), you will rapidly get a feel for reading these codes and making price predictions with them. Again, the higher-volume signals become more prevalent over time after a prolonged listless period when the slashes or black marks dominate.

SUMMARY

This chapter has focused on how to analyze stocks that have settled into prolonged periods of low-volume action, generally associated with gradually eroding prices. Once a bear market (overall, or in a stock or group) takes hold, people tend to lose interest because the vast majority of participants prefer and exclusively use the long side of the market. Declines are discouraging or at least boring, while rallies are exciting and rewarding. We explored the thinking and emotions that occur when stocks are acting in this way, so you now understand the psychological dynamics ruling the trading environment. An important market dictum—namely, that it takes volume to push a stock high but it can decline of its own weight without much trading—was introduced and explored for its implications. We concluded by introducing a set of symbols with which you can quickly record daily comparative (high, closing, and low) price and volume combinations, and we explained what sorts of symbols and patterns to watch for when hoping to note changes in prevailing levels of trading interest and bullish/bearish swings in the crowd's thinking. Knowing all this, you should now be equipped to deal skillfully with stocks that persistently trade on low or declining volumes.

PART FOUR

PRACTICAL APPLICATIONS OF YOUR NEW VOLUME KNOWLEDGE

CHAPTER 13

Using Information from the Most-Actives Lists

Most newspapers that carry the daily stock tables (some actually have abandoned the stock listings and provide only mutual funds' quotations!) are providing a service they probably did not intend when deciding to publish information on the most actively traded stocks. If you study the patterns, over time you will be able to discern shifts in market mood and changes in leadership. That use of this information will involve some investment of time and effort; a less intense but still valuable way of using most-actives data is a simple daily examination so you know exactly what is hot and what is not. This chapter will explore both the more rudimentary conclusions as well as the more subtle nuances to be gleaned by watching this fascinating collection of useful information.

STOCK INCLUSION BIAS

At the outset, I must state one caveat: There is a certain degree of bias in the information that the most-actives lists can convey. To some degree, it is valid to observe that really only certain stocks are in any practical sense able to land on the lists of 10 or 15 most-active issues that newspapers typically print. Companies with huge numbers of shares outstanding are simply more likely to have more shares traded than are other firms with more limited capitalizations. As of this writing, ExxonMobil had 3.47 billion shares available for trading, while Phillips Petroleum had 255 million. If on a typical day the 15th most-active NYSE-traded stock has turnover of, let us imagine, 20 million shares, it is simply many more times likely that XOM will reach the actives list than that P will do so. It would take about $^2/_3$ of 1 percent of XOM's shares to equal 20 million traded, while nearly 8 percent of Phillips' shares would need to change hands to reach that same threshold. Many smaller-capitalization issues effectively have no chance to reach the most-actives listings since it would take an unlikely 100 percent-plus turnover in a single day for them to reach the list. Another bias that should be noted is this: The lists are compiled in terms of numbers of shares rather than dollar value. Therefore, if a reasonably active stock should be split three for one, it would thereafter have a greater chance of reaching the list—and yet the value of shares traded would likely be little changed. Fortunately, some years ago the major exchanges imposed a minimum-price rule on what stocks they would list as most actively traded. Generally, an issue below $2 is not shown on such lists any longer. However, in the current age of heavy institutional domination of overall trading activity, extremely low priced issues might miss the cutoff anyway since the likes of Microsoft, Intel, Cisco, ExxonMobil, and General Electric are so heavily owned and actively traded by their large holders.

It would be helpful if, rather than basing listings of top traded stocks on share counts, the exchanges would supply the media with lists sorted by trading as a percentage of outstanding shares. One major newspaper that does provide a useful special list is *Investors' Business Daily,* which notes what stocks have traded at unusually high multiples of their average daily share volumes. That newspaper also runs a daily column called "The Real Most Actives" near its table called "Where the Big Money's Flowing"—both in the A Section. You can reasonably easily discover how active the latest day was as compared with average activity via this Internet address:

> http://quote.yahoo.com/q?s=xom&d=t

You would then enter the stock symbol of interest and choose "Detailed" for the type of report requested. The display will compare current versus average (period not disclosed) volume, and you can use its data to calculate number of shares outstanding by dividing total capitalization by current price.

EXCHANGE-TRADED FUNDS AND OTHER STOCKS

One unique feature of the most-actives lists provided by the American Stock Exchange is available only on its own Web site. While the exchange supplies the 10 most active stocks to the media for newspaper publication, on its own Web site it provides two lists of 5 each: exchange-traded funds (ETFs) (see Chapter 14 for much more discussion of these) and other stocks. It seems likely that over time the AmEx may need to provide dual lists for the media because the ETFs are gradually taking over the top 10 spots among all issues traded there. In 1998, typically 4 or 5 of the 10 ten heaviest-traded issues were ETFs, and by early 2001 that had risen to 6 or 7 each day, with SPY and QQQ usually in the lead positions. If you wish to see the 5 most active non-ETF stocks on the AmEx, go to this address:

    http://www.amex.com/

    Looking at the actives lists on the NYSE and NASDAQ can actually be more instructive since they tend to provide more variation in daily content than does the AmEx list. I find four major uses for most-actives data:

- Noting any industries in which heavy activity is clustering
- Noting whether gainers or losers predominate
- Looking for high-volume intraday price reversals
- Seeing whether huge trading in one or two issues has affected an exchange's overall total

    In making such observations, you may find it necessary to mentally exclude some stocks that seemingly land on the actives list almost every day. In addition, you might need to exclude stocks whose very high trading activity was obviously driven by news. These are usually easy to spot by looking at the price changes involved: large-percentage price losses— in the range of 20 percent or more—almost invariably will reflect negative corporate news surprises of some sort, as were discussed at some length on Chapter 10. Significant-percentage price gains probably also reflect news, although it is worth checking whether the news was fresh that day or has been getting an ongoing positive response for several days (see Chapter 9 regarding volume crescendos).

CLUSTERS BY INDUSTRY

What will be truly interesting, because they are indicative of overall market interest, are stocks that are very active without benefit of some major current news item. Suppose you noted among the top 10 or 15 about three stocks in the oil industry, none of which was affected directly by same-day corporate news. That might indicate that the oil group was worth further investigation because of a notable concentration of volume action. You would want to examine the individual stock charts of those three stocks, probably beginning with either a 12- or 24-month version. That view would quickly allow you to put the present day's volume level into an extremely important context: Was it one of the handful of greatest daily volumes in a year or two? If so, and if there were no major new news, you are seeing a significant phenomenon. The nature of that heavy action must then be noted in relation to stock price behavior. You need to ascertain whether the high trading volume was occurring at the start of a price move in one direction or the other, or if perhaps the stock had already moved a good deal and the latest day's high volume is an indication of a crowd getting excited (late) and jumping onboard. The latter situation would make you most cautious about taking action in the price direction you observed. You would not want to buy when a huge crowd is now doing so *after* a considerable price run-up had already taken place, for example. In fact, if you were a holder, such an observation should drive you to sell, and if you are an aggressive trader, you might well consider a short sale in anticipation of the buying crowd spending its money and energy—and the predictable unwinding of the stock price thereafter.

You would make such an examination independently for each of the several stocks in one industry, and you would be especially struck if you found non-news-driven, heavy-volume patterns in the same price direction affecting a few stocks in the same field in a similar way. Are they all breaking out from recent congestion (either upward or downward)? Are they all reaching a climax or exhaustion by running in their well-established price direction on now-extreme volume? Such patterns, if noted, would call for possible portfolio action. That would be especially true if, for example, you saw a market-leading group displaying upside exhaustion behavior. Think back to 1999 and 2000 and recall how, for a very long period of time, the technology stocks were an accurate mood indicator for the overall market's tone and direction. If an upside-leading group is running out of gas by exhausting itself on high volume, a downturn on the market is very likely an immediate prospect.

Not only reversals but also very small price changes on heavy volume would be of interest. You might note two or more stocks in the same industry or sector that were very active but made little net price move in either direction. In the spirit of Equivolume charting as described in Chapter 7, you might be observing the formation of either a supply or a support area for such stocks. In any case, the high volume functions as the tipoff that further analysis is called for because high volume (especially in the absence of major new news) signifies intense crowd emotion that has driven a large number of investors and/or traders to action. Your interpretation of that action can provide a profitable opportunity if you begin with a volume-sniffing detective's perspective.

The identities of individual high-volume stocks can provide you with much useful information. And the volume data might actually provide useful information about fundamental changes in an industry or the overall economy. For this type of analytical use, you do not want to ignore those individual stocks that made huge-percentage price moves on extremely heavy volume. They may be giving you a valuable piece of information about changes in the economy. In this connection, for example, think back to October and November of 2000. Gasoline prices had shot up and the stock market's leading group, technology issues, had been declining for 6 months. Retailers and producers of big-ticket consumer goods started issuing negative alerts about their sales, margins, and profit trends. The most-actives lists included stocks not very frequently seen there such as Gateway, Best Buy, and Circuit City. Their stocks cratered in huge trading volume on company warnings that sales had turned decidedly flat.

That was my personal first clear warning that the U.S. economy had very likely entered a consumer recession. I had fretted for some while about the usual cyclical expansion of consumer credit in relation to incomes. I had imagined that, while most stock market declines are caused by recessions, it was quite possible that an unwinding of the very positive 1998 to 1999 "wealth effect" would mean that *a decline in stocks might cause the next recession.* And here we had sharp evidence that suddenly all was not well in retail-land. Those high-volume declines in key stocks were the source of a clear message that then began to play out in wider circles on the fundamental side. Wal-Mart said traffic was flat; Maytag and Whirlpool said appliance sales were down; UPS and FedEx both said business was off their growth trends; even the relatively small retailer Michael's Stores (crafts and related goods) said store traffic was down because customers were making fewer trips due to high gasoline prices.

In early December, cold weather highlighted some news from the utility industry: A power shortage in California was threatening lifestyles and therefore consumer confidence, and skyrocketing natural gas prices were jumping residential gas and electric bills by 75 to 100 percent across the nation. A retail-sales decline was the result. All of these were individual bits of news that one could cluster into a fundamental-news theory because of *an early alert provided by high-volume action* in just a few important stocks. Once again, watching volume per se proved a useful pursuit for the curious and observant investor.

Another way to use the active-stock lists for industry analysis focuses on the AmEx itself. That is because well over half its trading as of early

2001—and that percentage was rising—consisted of action in the various exchange-traded funds (EFTs). You can usually count on the NASDAQ QQQ and the S&P 500 SPY as being the two most heavily traded items on the AmEx. What is perhaps more useful to watch will be what *other* ETFs make their way onto the actives list. These may be industry or sector ETFs representing energy, technology, health care, the Internet, and so on (see Chapter 14 for a longer list). They may also include small-cap or mid-cap baskets, whose appearance would indicate strong taste (if the price is up) or distaste (price down) for such stocks relative to large-cap stocks such as the S&P 500 or Dow 30 represent. As in our earlier discussion of the industry identity of non-news active individual stocks, here again the appearance of particular ETFs on occasion might very well mark a significant turning point for stocks of their particular type. You can fairly easily discover what is going on by examining a 12- or 24-month chart of the active ETF itself. The key points to note are how extreme the present day's activity is in historic terms, and then whether the price move represents a breakout (the start of a trend, either upward or downward) or a culmination and psychological exhaustion move (high volume plus continuing price change in the well-established prior direction). The implications for buying or selling that ETF, or stocks of the type it represents, are clear.

DOMINANCE BY GAINERS VERSUS LOSERS

Here again, it will be very important initially to screen out those companies whose stocks have been driven to high trading volume by current news. Such issues can be excused from your further consideration since they do not represent the general mood of the investment community: They are reacting to company-specific news developments. Having done that, you will be left with a collection of stocks trading actively without immediate news prompts. Which way they are going can be a useful fact to observe over time. One way to do that is to construct a percentage-gainers index.

After excluding those stocks obviously driven to huge trading volume by current news, you can count the rest into two groups: price gainers and price losers for the day (ignore any that may have finished unchanged). Calculate the percentage of gainers as part of the sum of gainers and losers. I would do this in one of the following two ways.

First, even though the numbers of shares that cut off the bottom of the three lists are of course different, I would suggest that you *combine* all the (non-news) stocks on the NYSE, AmEx, and NASDAQ into a single population and compute the percentage of gainers. That percentage should then be compared to the overall number of gainers and losers on the three exchanges combined. The two numbers should be plotted on a graph over time and trends observed. On extremely one-sided market days (large gains or awful losses in major averages) obviously you will find very high or very low percentage readings for both the broad list and the most actives alone. On more "normal" market days, differences between the actives and the general body of stocks can be important. If, for example, 60 percent of all stocks (excluding those finishing unchanged) are up but only 40 of non-news-driven very actives are up, you may be seeing an erosion of leadership in large stocks, which would undermine the general confidence of investors and traders. Conversely, on occasion you might note a few days when the overall advance/decline balance is fairly negative or even roughly neutral but the list of non-news actives has a more positive cast to it. That could indicate the start of some big-money interest in accumulating stocks, which in turn would probably presage a rally. Leadership is important psychologically, and the actives lists often reveal the character of leadership. To reiterate: It is very important to note carefully whether individual highly active stocks got that way because of news reactions. Those must be excluded from your "ups" and "downs" counts to get an unbiased view of the market mood as reflected by leading stocks. Otherwise, your calculated percentage of active gainers will be flawed for analysis purposes. (The analysis just described bears some resemblance to the philosophy underlying the TRIN calculation discussed in Chapter 6. Both approaches seek to discover change in market direction by noting changes in the behavior of big money.)

Second, I would *separately* compute the percentages of gainers among gainers-plus-losers for the NYSE and NASDAQ. (Here I exclude the AmEx because of its trading being dominated by ETFs rather than individual stocks, which leaves only a small number out of the 10 top traders that can possibly represent non-news-driven opinion indicators.) The NASDAQ is generally known as the more volatile, the more "new economy," the more younger-company, and the more speculative market as compared with the NYSE. If you compute and plot daily percentages of non-news-driven active stocks that are up on NASDAQ versus on the NYSE, you will be constructing an index of speculative interest.* It tends to move to extremes at market turning points, and any sustained divergence of the two exchanges' percentages tips you off to a shift in the

---

*In a similar spirit, *Investors' Business Daily* includes as one of nine components in its
   "Psychological Market Indicator" the ratio of total NASDAQ to NYSE trading volume.

nature of market leadership. An excellent example of the latter occurred in the late winter/early spring of 2000, when NASDAQ (led by technology and e-commerce stocks) was making a major top. Leadership there was deteriorating in percent-up terms as compared with the numbers on the NYSE.

PRICE REVERSALS ON HIGH VOLUME

A number of technical analysis systems take special notice when stocks reverse course during a trading day; those that include attention to volume give this kind of observation even greater importance. Before thinking about this phenomenon further, two important exceptions must be stated:

- A stock affected by intraday fundamental news does not count for our purposes.
- When the overall market makes a major turn on high volume during the session, whether driven by major external news or not, again the significance of an individual stock doing the same is discounted. One example was the mid-day bottom of March 22, 2001.

Imposing those two exceptions, what we are going to find are stocks that, for no readily apparent reason, turned around during the session on high volume. That represents a demonstrated major change in crowd psychology *because* the volume was unusually high. Such action usually has very short-term profit implications for traders, and it can often have longer-term (trend reversal) informational value for investors not focused on the short term. Japanese candlestick charts will display important types of sticks on such days; Equivolume charts will be marked by over-square days; divergence students will often note such stocks being at extremes; users of weighted moving averages will soon thereafter see price crossovers. For our purposes, the central and telling issue is that very heavy volume marked a change in sentiment for the stock in the minds of a large number of active participants. Once again, volume tells the tale in timely fashion.

It is important to view the information before your eyes in the widest possible context rather than as an isolated single fact. Suppose one semiconductor stock makes a high-volume reversal during the day without apparent news, and it lands on the actives list so it gains your attention. First, of course, you would want to check charting sites that also attach news items (the My Yahoo! tickers list feature does this, as does BigCharts.com) to be sure that no news drove the move. Then, think more broadly: If Intel acted this way, it would make a great deal of sense to look right away at

AMD, National Semi, Cypress, Micron Technology, Texas Instruments, and any others you might be aware of. If the Intel intraday reversal was mirrored by similar patterns in some of the other names in its industry, you might be on to something very useful. Again, check the charting sites' news postings (and maybe even the company Web sites and the chat room postings) on the other companies to be sure you are not missing a news cause for the price reversals on high volume that you have observed. The more reversals in a related cluster of stocks, in an absence of big news on them, the greater is the likelihood that you have noticed a major reversal of crowd opinion regarding an industry group. Having done so, you have two advantages over the person who merely noted the one reversal in Intel: You have further confirmation across the industry group (stronger basis for action), and you will also have looked at a number of companies' charts and fundamentals and can be in position to choose the one to trade that looks best—not by default, simply the first single stock you noticed.

EXCLUDING SINGLE-STOCK DATA FROM EXCHANGE TOTALS

Occasionally it is necessary to mentally adjust volume totals from the major exchanges because of unusually high volume in individual stocks. Such events occur in one of two scenarios: Sometimes an IPO comes to market and is very actively traded the first day, but more frequently extremely high volume in an individual stock is caused by corporate news (usually negative, since fear generates more action than does greed). In such cases, when the trading is extremely heavy, the activity in that single stock can have the effect of skewing total volume on its exchange to the upside. If the trading is considerable, it can have the effect of misleading students of trading action who are using relative volume data to form opinions about overall crowd behavior in the market. Such erroneous "readings" can arise in either of two ways:

- Total turnover of the exchange itself can look extraordinarily high, perhaps prompting a conclusion that a high-volume (crowd action) extreme is being recorded at the end of a price move.
- Total turnover on the affected exchange, when compared with its equivalent on another exchange, can provide a misleading ratio reading, again possibly falsely indicating an extremely high and therefore emotion-laden situation.

Since the above description may seem a bit theoretical, let us take an actual example. On September 22, 2000, Intel Corporation revised downward its forecast of business activity and therefore profits for the balance of 2000 and into early 2001. For our purposes here, the exact details do not matter—and of course by the time you read this, they will have become ancient business history anyway. As you can readily observe from the graph in Figure 13–1, the news was taken very badly by investors and traders: Price dropped 22 percent on the first day and trading volume was 308 million shares—the all-time greatest single-day, single-stock volume on any exchange at that time.

Let us now look at the degree to which this huge volume in one stock would have misled you about overall market conditions if you had not mentally adjusted total-exchange trading figures to account for it. Total NASDAQ trading on September 22 was 2.163 billion shares—of course including the total for Intel itself. Thus, without Intel, the total NASDAQ volume would have been only 1.854 billion shares; the one-company event at Intel directly increased total trading on that exchange by one sixth. On the same trading day, volume over on the NYSE was some 1.181 billion shares. If you included Intel's record-setting volume in NASDAQ's total, the raw ratio of NASDAQ to NYSE volume was recorded as 1.83:1—the highest since September 5 and possibly indicating an overall-market selling climax (since it was a down day and a high ratio indicates above-normal emotional activity driving the market). By eliminating

FIGURE   13–1

Intel: Example of Huge Single-Stock Volume Biasing Exchange's Total

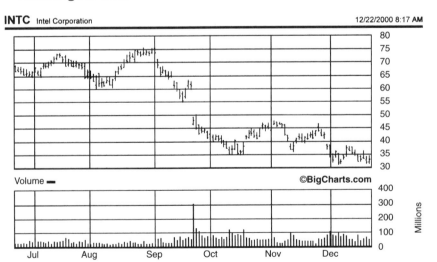

Intel's volume, you would have calculated a NASDAQ/NYSE volume ratio of 1.57:1—considerably more normal and probably not one to make you think a significant market turning point had been reached on the basis of volume studies.

It would, of course, be more fair and accurate to *normalize* Intel's volume rather than totally subtract it. You could choose any reasonable time window for calculating average volume, but if you selected 21 trading days (a calendar month), you would see that average daily Intel volume had been 42.5 million shares, or far short of the 308 million now seen. If you substituted that average-volume data item for Intel on September 22, adjusted NASDAQ volume would have been 1.897 billion shares, and the ratio of NASDAQ to NYSE volume would become 1.61:1. (All of the above calculations arbitrarily assume that the Intel news did not affect other stocks. It indeed did, as the technology sector in general took a nosedive, but we have no way to calculate exactly how much extra trading occurred on either NASDAQ or the NYSE in other stocks because of the Intel news.

Figures 13–2 and 13–3 provide details on trading in Intel's stock and volumes on the two exchanges. There is of course no scientific way to assign an appropriate threshold of trading in a single stock that should act as a trigger for such adjustments to your data tracking. Perhaps 10 percent of the volume on one exchange or the other being generated in a single stock might be appropriate. It would be especially important to take note of such circumstances when an individual issue *on the NYSE* trades in huge volume. That is because NYSE daily volume lately has been running at a lower level than that on NASDAQ; as a mathematical result, a change of 10 percent or more in the magnitude of a denominator has moderately more effect on a ratio greater than 1 than does a 10 percent adjustment in the numerator.

SUMMARY

In this relatively brief chapter, we have explored a number of ways in which you as a student of trading volume and its implications can make in-depth use of information presented in the major stock exchanges' most-actives listings. You have learned, first, that it is important to filter out those extremely high volume stocks whose presence on the lists has been driven by corporate news when analyzing the actives lists for an overall bias in terms of advancing versus declining stocks. That balance can be useful when it diverges from exchange-wide totals. You have also been shown that clustering of non-news-driven, high-volume stocks in one

FIGURE 13-2

Intel, NASDAQ, and NYSE Trading Volumes,
August–September 2000

Date	Intel Vol Mill Shs	NASDAQ Vol: Mill Shs	NYSE Vol Mill Shs
8/23/00	36.2	1460	871
8/24/00	23.4	1545	837
8/25/00	20.8	1285	686
8/28/00	42.8	1371	734
8/29/00	23.0	1488	796
8/30/00	21.8	1535	818
8/31/00	28.5	1901	1072
9/1/00	18.3	1471	768
9/5/00	58.4	1666	848
9/6/00	62.3	1756	998
9/7/00	34.7	1633	985
9/8/00	29.7	1506	967
9/11/00	30.5	1481	899
9/12/00	29.0	1594	991
9/13/00	70.1	1654	1068
9/14/00	50.5	1698	1014
9/15/00	75.7	1775	1268
9/18/00	50.8	1612	962
9/19/00	58.9	1706	1025
9/20/00	70.3	1801	1104
9/21/00	57.1	1615	1089
9/22/00	308.7	2163	1181
9/25/00	130.2	1772	982

industry can indicate something important in terms of either a change in fundamentals or a signal of shifting overall market psychology about leadership. We noted that it is important to look beyond the individual stocks on those actives lists and to look at industry peers as well. Important issues to check include whether the extremely high volume coincided with price breakouts from congestion areas, or by contrast exhaustion price moves that extended a well-established price trend (up or down).

Watching for clusters of highly active stocks in a specific industry or sector was shown to be useful in identifying breakouts and exhaustion conditions (indicating importantly changing psychology by traders and investors as evidenced by very heavy volume). In addition, you saw that occasional

FIGURE 13–3

Illustration of Normalizing Total NASDAQ Volume to Exclude Intel Volume Event

Date	NASDAQ Vol: Mill Shs	NASDAQ Vol with Intel Normalized	Vol Ratio: Actual NASDAQ to NYSE	Volume Ratio After Normalizing
8/23/00	1459.6	1459.6	1.68	1.68
8/24/00	1544.9	1544.9	1.85	1.85
8/25/00	1284.9	1284.9	1.87	1.87
8/28/00	1371.3	1371.3	1.87	1.87
8/29/00	1487.9	1487.9	1.87	1.87
8/30/00	1535.1	1535.1	1.88	1.88
8/31/00	1900.9	1900.9	1.77	1.77
9/1/00	1471.3	1471.3	1.92	1.92
9/5/00	1666.1	1666.1	1.97	1.97
9/6/00	1756.3	1756.3	1.76	1.76
9/7/00	1632.8	1632.8	1.66	1.66
9/8/00	1506.3	1506.3	1.56	1.56
9/11/00	1481.4	1481.4	1.65	1.65
9/12/00	1594.0	1594.0	1.61	1.61
9/13/00	1653.5	1653.5	1.55	1.55
9/14/00	1697.7	1697.7	1.67	1.67
9/15/00	1775.4	1775.4	1.40	1.40
9/18/00	1611.9	1611.9	1.67	1.67
9/19/00	1705.9	1705.9	1.66	1.66
9/20/00	1800.7	1800.7	1.63	1.63
9/21/00	1614.6	1614.6	1.48	1.48
9/22/00	2162.9	1896.6	1.83	1.61
9/25/00	1771.7	1641.5	1.80	1.67

high-volume intraday reversals in price, under specifically defined limited circumstances, can be of high informational value. Finally, we explored occasions on which it might be appropriate to modify your observations about total trading on one exchange or another because of extremely high activity in one stock on a given day. In all these circumstances, you have seen once again that volume always tells a meaningful story.

Chapter 14

Mutual Funds and Exchange-Traded Funds: Volume and Price Signals for Action

In Chapter 9 we explored the psychological, and therefore, *price,* implications of crescendos in volume. Likewise, in Chapter 10 we focused on the predictive importance of volume spikes. Here, we will discuss the application of those insights in conjunction with the occasionally extreme price patterns of mutual funds and the volume-and-price patterns of exchange-traded funds (ETFs). Most investors involved with individual stocks would never think to seek technical-analysis insights about stocks from the world of funds. There is, however, a good deal to be gained by adding that body of data to your intellectual arsenal, so I hope that if you are basically a "stocks person" rather than a funds owner, you will overcome the temptation to skip beyond the next several pages. Your forbearance will be duly rewarded!

VOLUME CRESCENDOS AND SPIKES

Crescendos in volume, exactly because they document the formation and mounting size of a trading crowd, cannot occur without predictably parallel simultaneous crescendos in price. Crescendos in volume can and do coincide with parabolic-like moves of price in both directions: up and down. As you will recall, we explained in Chapter 9 that a volume crescendo corresponding with a downward sweep in prices *marks the end* rather than the beginning of a price decline. Beginnings of price declines accompanied by high volume are virtually always driven by adverse news, which by its nature causes an immediate widespread reaction and therefore a sudden spike in volume rather than a gradual build-up of trading activity.

Likewise, volume crescendos accompanying (and of course, actually driving) upside price crescendos are much more likely to mark the conclusions of price advances than their instigations. Again, startling positive news spurs a price and volume spike. Volume and upward-price crescendos reflect the capitulation of previous doubters who finally conclude they absolutely "must buy," as and after the climate of information and opinion has become extremely widely known and very bullish and excited.

NET ASSET VALUE

The reason we have reviewed here the circumstances and implications of price crescendos is that they are readily observable in the values of mutual funds (and the recently highly popular new exchange-traded funds, on which more will be said later). Every mutual fund publishes its net asset value (NAV) per share on a daily basis. In accounting terms, this amount is the equivalent of an operating corporation's book value per share—except that the underlying individual assets' values are much more precisely known and, conveniently, change daily as the stock or bond market moves. One of the great informational values that a mutual fund's NAVs convey is the overall *shape* of price movements actually shown by the fund's underlying portfolio securities. The combined chart patterns of dozens or even hundreds of stocks are distilled into the elegantly sharp single data point called NAV; over a period of time these NAVs form patterns that reveal what is going on in the underlying securities. The most common conventional analytical use of NAVs of mutual funds is the computation of performance for comparison and marketing purposes.

TRENDS IN SINGLE-SECTOR, OR ONE-INDUSTRY, FUNDS AND SINGLE-COUNTRY FUNDS

Here, however, we are not interested in that facet of NAV history. Instead, we see very useful informational value in the trends of NAVs over time. For purposes of our discussion here, we will now focus attention and analysis on single-sector, or one-industry, funds, as well as on single-country funds. These are of special interest because their NAV patterns reflect on a smoothed and combined basis the movements of multiple stocks all revealing investors' collective understanding, beliefs, hopes, and fears about a particular kind of stocks (and of course, first, about the companies represented by those stocks). For example, a technology-sector fund will own perhaps a hundred or more individual high-tech companies' shares. On any given day, a few might move contrary to the general trend, but when all are combined into a single NAV, the result is that the change in NAV reflects that day's movement in investor expectations ("psychology," if you will) of the technology sector, as well as of the airlines, utilities, consumer services, or energy stocks, and a decent-length list of other kinds of sector funds.

In an exactly parallel fashion, single-country funds reflect quite accurately the changing optimism and pessimism of investors in, say, Germany or Korea toward their national economies and future outlooks. [It is important to note here that because a mutual fund available in the United States to American investors is quoted in U.S. dollars, changes in country and region/world funds not only reflect movements in the underlying indigenous securities markets also but include the overlay of any change in currency value against the dollar. Therefore, changes in the NAVs of such funds reflect shifting expectations about both equities (or bonds) and currency values (a mixture of inputs).]

NAV PATTERNS IN MUTUAL FUND PRICES

What you want to look carefully for, and act promptly upon seeing, is the tracing of a crescendo-shaped pattern of daily NAVs in these sector and country funds. Noting the occurrence of such events will be useful in any of several ways:

- It could help you time entry or exit (on a contrarian basis of course) in that fund itself.
- It will provide, by implication, an alert about diversified funds known to be heavily weighted in the sector or country fund's focus.
- It will alert you to the formation of a crowd in underlying stocks of that fund's type.
- It will help you time entries and exits (and perhaps alert you to avoid mistaken actions) in individual stocks that make up the industry in which that fund invests.

If you see a sector or country fund whose daily NAVs are arching skyward at a dizzying, accelerating rate, what conclusions can you draw? It is not that the portfolio manager is a genius who is having a great run for the past week or so. Rather, it means that the underlying kind of asset (e.g., real estate stocks or British stocks) is forming an upward price crescendo, almost certainly driven by a volume crescendo. That telltale chart formation signals the formation of a crowd that will soon reach maximum size and as a result will no longer be able to push price up for an unending string of trading days. Once the crowd's size has peaked, remember, the excitement is over and some of the crowd members will take their money elsewhere as soon as *and precisely because* the excitement is over. The inescapable result is the end of the price rise, followed by a downside reversal and retracement, in the underlying stocks.

Downside price crescendos in mutual funds, when noted on funds' NAV price charts, imply the imminent likelihood of an end to the scary and climactic price damage. A rally of unknown duration and extent is very probably about to begin quite shortly in the particular type of stocks that fund holds. Let us examine the crowd dynamics underlying that confident assertion. As noted above, a downside price crescendo (as contrasted with a sudden spike) represents growing panic on the part of an increasingly large crowd of investors. As described in detail in Chapter 9, four factors combine to increase, and then eventually diminish and end the panicked selling: a diminishing pool of sellers as they in fact take action; the numbing effect of the decline itself; margin calls made and acted on; and finally bargain hunting that halts the price slide. When this combination of motivations plays itself out in the crowd of would-be and actual sellers over a string of days, the downside price crescendo is formed and brings about its own ending. The mutual fund's melting NAV, traced out visually on a chart, is a motion picture of crowd opinion and action in the specific kind of stocks held by that sector or country fund. While fear is stronger than greed and so downside crescendos can last a bit longer than upside ones, the intensity of the crowd's emotion is quite soon dissipated, and the selling climax is completed—usually in the range of 4 to 7 trading days.

Therefore, we can summarize the highly useful information potential of mutual funds' NAV patterns by saying this:

While we are unable to see daily purchase and redemption activity ("volume") in mutual funds, when their prices form upward or downward crescendos we can be very confident that their underlying stocks are experiencing crowd-behavior volume climax patterns. A reversal of price direction is imminent and should not be ignored. Precisely because they represent a nondiversified collection of portfolio securities, sector and country funds accurately portray climaxes in crowd opinion regarding specific types of stocks.

SOURCES OF INFORMATION ABOUT MUTUAL FUNDS AND EFTs

Where can you access funds' charts, and more important, first, where can you discover which particular funds to use as emotional indicators of their underlying markets? Fortunately, the Internet age has given us easily available and free information choices in quantity. In years past, you would need to go to the library and pore over past newspaper issues to accumulate a history of each fund's past daily NAVs and then plot them by hand on graph paper. Having done that homework, you would still need to maintain your charts on a real-time basis each morning. While there is some benefit to such activity in terms of the rich and intense impressions you acquire in the process of personally hand plotting such charts, the tradeoff today is a vastly increased array of information instantly available at your fingertips' command.

While there are numerous Internet charting facilities available, the two I like best are BigCharts and Yahoo! For looking at the NAV trends of mutual funds, the latter serves most readily because of its symbol-lookup features. As an example, you can look up a fund either by submitting its five-digit ticker symbol or by selecting the "symbol lookup" feature and then typing the start of its name into the box provided.

http:quote.yahoo.com/t?s=TAVFX&d=c

That would provide you with a chart (365 days is the default, but you have other choices) for the Third Avenue Value Fund. My mentioning it is definitely not a recommendation, but looking at its chart will quickly give you a sense of how the value-versus-growth tug-of-war has been going. This is because the chart of each fund can show that specific choice against the Vanguard Index 500, which is more growth than safety oriented in my opinion.

The URLs for the Yahoo! and BigCharts sites are, respectively, as follows:

- finance.yahoo.com/
- www.bigcharts.com

While I am very happy with the BigCharts site as my primary charting package for stocks, as noted above it is not my first choice for fund studies. Here is the reason: Its default chart style is the vertical bar chart *with volume* (great for stocks but not applicable to funds), whereas the other site named uses the simple line plot from close to close as its default, which is good for funds analyses. Also, as mentioned earlier, the Yahoo! facility provides easy symbol lookups.

Whatever charts you choose, remember that what you are looking for is a crescendo-shaped pattern—like a waterfall in a downside price move, or roughly the opposite shape of curve for upside accelerations. For reasons discussed earlier in this chapter, you can be quite well assured of the meaning of an uninterrupted crescendo of accelerating price change in one direction for approximately four to seven trading sessions: that trading volume in that fund's stocks has been accelerating, reflecting the formation of a crowd whose concentrated and accelerating selling or buying activity is temporarily pushing stock prices in a climactic fashion. One important note to remember late each year: These charting facilities do not adjust for sometimes-large annual capital gains distributions that usually occur (for technical tax reasons) most often in October or especially December. So you must visually forgive a large one-day vertical drop at those times and not interpret it as a climactic selling crescendo. If you are unsure whether a fund's nasty 1-day price decline represents bad performance or an ex-dividend event, check out the fund's history for the month in question by using this URL:

http://chart.yahoo.com/t?a=09&b=18&c=00&d=09&e=22&f=00&g=d&s=bebax

Set the radio button to "dividends," and insert the ticker symbol of your fund of interest.

In Figure 14–1 is a list of symbols of some sector and geographic mutual funds. This should give you a good working list as a start. Fund families with considerable numbers of sector funds include Fidelity, INVESCO, Rydex, and ICON. You can easily find the full current listings by visiting their Web sites. These and other sector funds' symbols should serve you well as rapid references to the emotional conditions of various kinds of stocks. That information is important whether you are thinking of buying or selling either stocks or funds. Remember, the telltale crescendo-like shape of a specialty fund's NAV plot will tip you off to the high likelihood that a volume crescendo is occurring in those kinds of stocks.

FIGURE 14–1

Symbols of Some Sector and Geographic Mutual Funds

Europe	FEURX	Natural Gas	FSNGX	Real Estate	CSRSX	Housing	FSHOX
Asia	IVAGX	Airlines	FSAIX	Consumer	ICCCX	Biotech	FBIOX
Japan	WPJGX	Leisure	FLISX	Health Care	FHLSX	Gold	FSAGX
Latin Am.	FLATX	Energy	ICENX	Technology	FTCHX	Retail	FSRPX

While you are not seeing actual volume plotted on a fund's chart, you are viewing big price footprints, implying what kind of volume activity is going on.

Besides symbol lookup, the Stockmaster site is helpful for a special list it provides on an updated basis every trading day. The URL for that display is as follows:

http://stockmaster.com/exe/sm/topfunds?UPT=8791

This page is a listing of the 40 funds whose data or charts have been requested *the most times* in the Stockmaster site since midnight on the day you are inquiring. Therein is yet another, and very useful albeit short-term, indicator of what the crowd is thinking. Remember, when the crowd does extreme things, the crowd can be expected to be wrong. A clarification is crucial at this point. My preceding statement about crowds should *not* be interpreted as meaning that the funds listed are bad funds. What I would look for instead, in using this list, is any clustering of *particular types of funds* because that will mean those are the ones the public is either in a bullish lather over, or is scared about. Examples would be a large clustering of energy funds, technology funds, health and biotech funds, or funds investing in one country.

Noting such a cluster would be a useful signal of intense crowd attention—and you will know whether it is bullish or bearish by the day's market trend. When this chapter was written, not one of the 60 largest-assets funds was a sector or country fund—and only 5 of the top 100 were: 4 in technology and 1 in health sciences. (Bear in mind a statistical truth about this daily list: It is naturally biased in favor of very large funds since those have the most shareholders, so any random tally of daily inquiries will reflect that skewing.) Here, then, you have another perhaps-unexpected tool from the land of mutual funds. Even though trading volume in funds is not available to the public, you can use the listing of what kinds of funds people are *looking at* as an indicator of crowd intensity.

Yet a third information tool from the mutual funds world is also of use. The previous discussion focused on fairly short term trends in crowd interest, but this next information source contains aggregated data covering longer periods; it is updated only once monthly and even then nearly 30 days in arrears. The Investment Company Institute, based in Washington, D.C., is the official political representation and research organization of the U.S. mutual funds industry. The ICI, as it is popularly known, conducts fine research on various important aspects of the funds business, such as assets and flows of money. While most ICI-collected data are available only to its member companies, some summary statistics of interest are posted on its Web site. Here is the URL for a monthly updated release on flows of money:

➔   http://www.ici.org/facts_figures/trends_0601.html

Those four numeric digits near the end represent the calendar month and year for which fund inflows and outflows are tallied (in this case, June 2001). Each page shows data for the listed month and its immediately prior month, plus year-to-date and prior-year numbers. You can readily change the month/year setting to view older releases, back as far as January and February 1998, in the 0298.html release. One unfortunate shortcoming of the ICI data is that they are presented only at a very high level of aggregation rather than by detailed type of fund (such as technology or energy). Nevertheless, interesting and often-useful information is provided there if you will put it into recent and historical context. Here, as mentioned above, you are looking not for very short term hints on what the crowd is doing, but instead for bigger-picture trends and *especially exceptions to trends.* As of early 2001, when this was written, there were about 85 million mutual fund holders in the United States, so data on fund flows represent the collective decisions of a *very* large crowd. While you cannot see "trading volume" in the sense of what daily stock tables and real-time graphs provide, the net purchases and sales of mutual funds, running in the tens of billions of dollars monthly, clearly do represent quantifiable activity on the part of the crowd, which is definitely valid as an indicator of volume.

INSIGHT GAINED FROM TRACKING MUTUAL FUNDS

In general, it is very accurate to say that the mutual fund buying public consistently and dependably does a bad job of market timing. If you have any doubt about that, or believe I am too cynical, review the numbers in Figure 14–2, showing the annual average prices at which investors bought and sold the two largest equity mutual funds. If you graph the net aggregate inflow into equity funds over time, you will find that times when the market goes down hard or makes a low are exactly when the public either reduces its net purchases of funds (small inflow) or actually pulls money out (net outflow). Conversely, and not at all surprisingly, when the market is boiling hot and probably forming what will later be seen as a temporary high area, net public purchases (what the industry and ICI call "sales," less

FIGURE 14-2

Poor Buy/Sell Timing by Fund Investors

	Average Prices per Year		
	Buy	Sell	52-Week Average
Fidelity Magellan Years end March 31			
1994	69.67	67.55	67.59
1995	88.56	81.39	86.27
1996	81.43	78.76	79.06
1997	98.75	94.06	95.32
1998	116.16	111.05	111.34
1999	112.78	111.05	99.52
2000	130.26	**130.37**	123.49
Vanguard 500 Index			
1994	35.34	32.06	34.40
1995	51.51	50.97	51.00
1996	62.45	**62.94**	62.98
1997	80.46	**81.03**	81.48
1998	101.00	100.25	101.52
1999	122.19	**122.71**	122.41
2000	131.27	129.21	131.40

Note: Figures in bold indicate selling above buying price.
SOURCE: Lipper Inc.

redemptions) of mutual funds are very high. In Figure 14-3, look at the early months of 1999 for such a period. That was when the Dow Jones Industrial Average was first scaling the 11,000 level.

The monthly data must be interpreted after mental allowances for some seasonal trends. For example, January is usually a very strong month for net inflows because many employees receive and invest year-end bonuses then. Likewise, while many 401(k) plans send employee and company contributions to the funds every month, there are many retirement plans that make only quarterly contributions, and those tend to cluster in January, April, July, and October. So inflows gain a bit of extra strength then. Likewise, many people wait until March or April to make their prior-year contributions to IRA and Keogh/SEP plans, so April is usually a strong month for equity funds' inflows.

For these reasons, I suggest you follow the ICI flows numbers on a 12-month running-total basis. As the graph in Figure 14–3 shows in vertical-bar form, each month's net flow is plotted in billions of dollars, and run as a line through those bars is the trailing 12-month average. Here is what you want to note: When fund flows in a single month, or maybe two consecutively, run very far above or below the 12-month moving average, it is a strong sign that the public is acting as a huge, emotionally driven crowd. When they do so, they will shortly be proven wrong. A period like early 1999 was a clear warning sign of a high market, while the occasional short positive bars and certainly the relatively rare net-outflow bars mark bottoms. Observe September/October 1998, for instance.

I would track only the data for stock mutual funds, as the ICI calls them, which appear as "Net new cash flow" at the bottom line of Figure 14–4. The data on bond funds represent a mixing of investor motivations: Some people are moving in or out of bonds/bond funds because of relative interest rates, their expectations about interest rates, or in a few cases as a safer haven when they fear stocks. Likewise, I would be especially cautious about trends in money-market funds (Figure 14–5). These are a catch-all or default that reflects the opposite of investor decisions about stock *and* bond funds, and individual stocks. But money funds also are the modern replacement for savings and checking accounts, so seasonal savings flows are reflected there, too. You can virtually count on soft money-market net flows in April (tax time) and in the summer (vacations) and December/January (holiday shopping and subsequent bills). But if stocks have been weak late in one year, as they were in 2000, January (as it did in 2001) may show strong money-fund net inflows as investors park year-end bonus money instead of going on to equity funds,

FIGURE 14–3

ICI Flows, on 12-Month Running-Total Basis

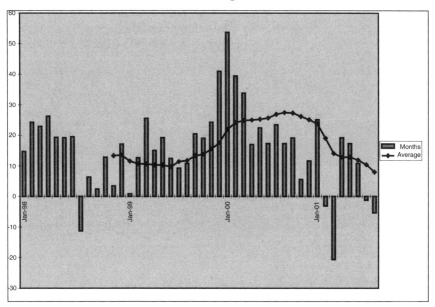

FIGURE 14–4

Net New Cash Flow of Long-Term Funds, Millions of Dollars, Stock Mutual Funds

	Aug 2000	July 2000	YTD 2000	YTD 1999
New sales	102,063.6	93,957.1R	949,118.8	591,592.6R
Redemptions	−82,066.9	−77,653.1R	−726,632.5	−482,890.6R
Net exchanges	3,436.9	1,038.7R	33,020.4	3,341.3R
Net new cash flow	23,433.6	17,342.8R	255,506.7	112,043.3R

Note: R = revised data.

Courtesy of Investment Company Institute

until a higher market restores their courage (belatedly). Equity fund flows, however, speak volumes as to investor moods without any need for adjustment other than seasonal.

ICI flows data are published on the final or penultimate business day each month, thus imposing a 1-month lag on the information's availability. If you are hoping to anticipate the numbers as confirmation of your

FIGURE 14-5

Net New Cash Flow of Money-Market Funds,
Millions of Dollars

	Aug 2000	July 2000	YTD 2000	YTD 1999
Net new cash flow	22,122.5	33,346.1R	67,393.4	91,096.6

Note: *R* = revised data.

Courtesy of Investment Company Institute

thinking about what the crowd probably is doing, you may find some
value in watching *The Wall Street Journal* each Friday, since it publishes
net-flows information on money funds. High money-funds inflows, as an
example, might confirm your suspicion that the public is panicking out of
stocks and stock funds. Interim estimates of equity-fund flows are posted
every several days at www.trimtabs.com.

EXCHANGE-TRADED FUNDS

To this point, we have focused on the implications of short-term price
trends in mutual funds' NAVs, and on a Web site tally of investors' same-
day interest in given kinds of funds, and on ICI funds-industry data on net
money flows, as evidence of the size and intensity of the crowd's activity
in the market. Whether the signals be short or longer term, the patterns
reveal the equivalent of volume. When crescendos occur, a change in price
direction is imminent.

Now we will examine a relatively recent but virtually exploding
investment vehicle class that can give direct evidence of volume activity.
This collection of traded items has come to be called *exchange-traded
funds,* or ETFs for short. Because these instruments are relatively new on
the Wall Street scene, we will begin by providing a brief description and
explanation of them; those readers not requiring such a tutorial should
skip ahead to the next headline in the chapter.

An ETF is a trading vehicle that represents a defined basket of stocks
of a given type. Some ETFs follow well-known securities indices or averages, such as the S&P 500 (ticker SPY), the Dow Jones Industrials (DIA),
or the NASDAQ 100 (QQQ). Others represent custom-made collections
of securities making up a single investment sector, such as pharmaceuticals stocks (ticker PPH). In technical or legal form, ETFs can be mutual
funds, unit investment trusts, or even depository receipts. Like conven-

tional index funds, because they are not actively managed, they impose very low expense ratios as compared with actively managed funds that are trying to beat the market. Regardless of their form or exact expense ratios, ETFs possess two crucial common elements:

- They trade all during the market session, as a stock does, rather than being priced only after the close, as a traditional mutual fund is, once daily.

- Unlike closed-end funds, ETFs have special structural features that virtually totally ensure that they will trade at no more than extremely small premiums or discounts to their true underlying values.

One added feature of ETFs must be noted, for those not already familiar with them: They can be shorted instantly, even in a declining market, since they are exempt from the uptick rule imposed on normal stocks. If you want more detailed information about the nature of ETFs, and perhaps want to read a prospectus, consult the Web sites that are named below, or respond to the advertisements placed in major financial magazines and newspapers. These are *very* intriguing investment vehicles that can allow you to take a long or short position in a whole part of the market, eliminating single-stock selection risk (e.g., you buy IBM and Hewlett Packard goes up instead). As an indication of how big the interest in ETFs has become, their total net assets reached about $80 billion in early 2001; that was well over half the size of Fidelity Magellan. Our purpose here is not to extol the virtues of ETFs as trading and investment vehicles but instead to show how they efficiently represent the opinions of many thousands of active investors about whole economic sectors. As such, they may be viewed as single-symbol indicators of the sort of volume dynamics we are interested in using to understand the crowd's position on market sectors and/or individual stocks.

HOW TO USE ETFs TO DETECT IMPORTANT VOLUME PATTERNS

When this was being written in early 2001, nearly 100 ETFs had been invented, and all but one were listed on the American Stock Exchange. The oldest is SPY, referred to commonly as the "spider" for the S&P 500 Index. It was introduced in 1993 but did not immediately become a major phenomenon. The major period of heavy new introductions was from late 1999 through the fall of 2000. Indicating the stature of these recent offerings, the major sponsoring organizations include Morgan Stanley, State Street Bank & Trust, Merrill Lynch, Barclays Global Advisors, Vanguard, and Nuveen. Major equity indices and static specialty sector baskets were the early offerings, while late 2001 was to bring the first ETF based on a bond index, and cloaked promises were being made about intraday trading in perhaps half a dozen actively managed mutual funds' ETF share classes. All of this is to say that a wide variety of types of investing and trading concepts are covered by ETFs, so you as a detective of volume patterns have a rich field to explore and use in your research work. *The Wall Street Journal* in May 2001 began a useful new practice: It now removes ETFs from the stock tables of these listing exchanges and presents their quotations in a single, separate daily table.

I have little doubt that additional ETFs will come to market subsequent to this volume's going to press. So I urge you to consult the Web sites listed below for updated lists of available items and their ticker symbols, as well as commentary and explanation:

- **www.NASDAQ.com**   (click on "Exchange-Traded Funds" near upper-right corner)
- **www.amex.com**   The American Stock Exchange
- **www.iShares.com**   Barclays Global's Web site, featuring its numerous iShares
- **www.holdrs.com**   The Merrill Lynch-maintained site focusing on its special ETF offerings called HOLDRS Trusts. These are publicly traded on the AmEx, and you need *not* be a Merrill Lynch customer to trade in them.
- **www.IndexFunds.com**   This site expanded in October 2000 by creating an "ETFzone" with extensive information on the subject.

Here is how to use ETF information as an important intellectual weapon in your detective work about market trends using volume data: An ETF is a single stock that embodies the perceptions of the trading public about a certain, well-defined kind of stocks. The HOLDRS Trust for pharmaceutical stocks (ticker PPH), the iShares for Germany's stock market (EWG), and the S&P Sector Spider ETFs for technology or energy stocks (XLK or XLE) are examples. If you detect a volume crescendo or a volume spike in these ETFs, you are noting a significant signal about a large crowd's emotional thinking regarding a whole segment of the market. This is bigger information than a volume event in an individual stock, which might be caused by narrow, firm-specific news (officer resignation, new product, lawsuit). Volume action in a sector or country ETF reveals that tens of thousands of investors are concurrently taking the same kind of buying or selling action, and that means that a huge crowd's opinion has suddenly reached an emotional extreme, a maximum, about that kind of stock.

You can use volume dynamics you detect in ETFs in three major ways:

- Buying or selling (including shorting) that ETF itself
- Buying or selling individual stocks in the same part of the market that an ETF represents
- Buying or selling mutual funds of similar investment objectives

Here are just two examples, beyond the obvious idea of trading in the ETFs themselves: Suppose you have warmed up to the idea of buying an oil stock or a brokerage or money-management firm's shares. You check out the chart (which of course includes volume since an ETF is a stock!) of the XLE (energy) or XLF (financial services) Sector Spider. You see that right now it is experiencing a volume crescendo or a volume spike to the upside. That tells you immediately that in buying, you would be joining the crowd in the peak of its frenzy, that is, buying late and therefore high. You postpone pressing the "enter order" key on that buy trade. Or, suppose by contrast you are feeling pretty uncomfortable about that sinking technology stock you own, and you are thinking of heading for the emotional safe harbor of cash for a while. There's nothing especially wrong in the company's own news, but technology stocks have just been in the doghouse lately.

What to do? Well, you consult the volume and price pattern on the chart of XLK (technology) or perhaps TTH (telecommunications) or even HHH (Internet)—whatever applies most directly to your personal stock position. If you discover that a price gap with a volume smash or spike on the downside, or perhaps a volume crescendo in a selling climax, has just occurred or is presently in process, you know that the presently intense pain is about to end as the whole group has been cleaned out and a rally can now begin. Conversely, if there is no sign of any emotional selling— lack of any sort of volume buildup while the ETF declines in price—you can expect your stock to remain under pressure with the group, which has yet to reach its emotional nadir on extremely high volume. You would then either sell at market, perhaps try for a sale on a slight rally, or put in a stop-loss order to limit future capital exposure.

For quick but only partial reference, Figure 14–6 is a list of some of the major ETF tickers of value for watching key sectors of the market.

FIGURE 14-6

 Some of the Major Sector and Style ETF Tickers

Mid-cap stocks	MDY
Small caps	IJR
Value style	IVE
Growth style	IVW
Technology	XLK
Financial services	XLF
Energy	XLE
Utilities	XLU
Semiconductors	SMH
Health care	IYH
Biotechnology	BBH
Pharmaceuticals	PPH
Chemicals	IYD
REITs	IYR
Consumer services	XLV
Consumer staples	XLP
Internet	HHH
Telecomm	TTH

Many more can be found by going to the Web sites named above. Mentioned only briefly in passing above was a country fund. Actually, 17 of the longest-existing ETFs are single-country baskets. They were originally jointly created and introduced by Morgan Stanley (before it temporarily added Dean Witter to its moniker) and Barclays Global in March 1996. (The original name for these vehicles was WEBS, standing for World Equity Benchmark Shares; it was changed in mid-2000 to "iShares," a brand name that now represents a wider array than country funds only.) A handful of additional countries were added in the summer of 2000, along with several regional vehicles. While I urge you to consult the iShares URL listed earlier for a complete and probably expanded listing, Figure 14–7 lists some of the major and more interesting country markets you can monitor and trade or invest in via iShares.

While our focus here is on the psychological tales that trading volume tells about stocks and sectors of the market, it is worth also noting that ETFs offer a unique advantage over individual stocks when the decision you make is not only to avoid or sell but actually to go short. These

FIGURE 14-7

Some Major Country Markets for Investing via iShares

Germany	EWG	Japan	EWJ	United Kingdom	EWU
Mexico	EWW	France	EWQ	Italy	EWI
Switzerland	EWL	Brazil	EWZ	Canada	EWC
Spain	EWP	Taiwan	EWT	South Korea	EWY

can be shorted without waiting for an uptick, while individual stocks cannot. Suppose, for example, that a volume climax on the upside has gripped the Brazilian market, and you now believe a decline is in the offing for technical or fundamental or news reasons. If the price collapse is already in process, you may not be able to short Telebras before it careens several points lower, but you can indeed immediately short the EWZ iShares to establish your bearish position.

How big a phenomenon have ETFs become, and therefore how apparently dependable are these vehicles as volume-dynamics indicators? Consider these facts:

- By early 2001, ETFs trading represented about two thirds of daily total AmEx volume, and it was rising.

- Where ETFs and single-country closed-end funds exist for the same countries, in about 80 percent of cases the ETFs trade more actively, and in some instances by many times more.

- On virtually any trading day, as of early 2001, the AmEx's list of the 10 most active stocks was populated with either 5 or 6 ETFs.

- On the American Stock Exchange's own Internet Web site, it posts *separate* most-actives listings for ETFs and "all other issues."

- A number of prominent brokerage firms have changed the titles of their closed-end funds analysts to "ETFs and closed-end funds analysts."

Thus, whether you choose to trade in them or not, you can add ETFs to your arsenal of detective tools when watching for volume crescendos and spikes—surefire signals of imminent price reversal. These are now on your list as well as some (at first glance) unlikely information sources such as mutual funds' price trends and monthly flows data in mutual funds from the Investment Company Institute (ICI). Thus, you are equipped with broader context about the crowd's emotional state than is provided by the volume data of single stocks alone. Figure 14-8 is adapted from the actual ICI data tables of interest, as numbered on its Web Site (Figure 14–8).

FIGURE 14–8

Four Selected Important Mutual-Fund Money Flows Tables from ICI*†

Table 2. New net cash flow of long-term stock mutual funds, millions of dollars

Dates	New Sales	Redemptions	Net Exchanges	Net New Cash Flow
Mar 2001	84,163	-93,548	-11,215	-20,600
Feb 2001	80,685R	-77,673	-6,311R	-3,298R
YTD 2001	280,605	-263,035	-16,359	1,211
YTD 2000	429,140R	-309,412R	20,650R	140,378R

Table 3. Net new cash flow of money market funds, millions of dollars

Dates	Cash Flow Net New
Mar 2001	13,467
Feb 2001	58,026R
YTD 2001	174,997
YTD 2000	69,255

Table 5. Annualized rate of redemptions from stock funds

Dates	Percent of Ave Net Assets
Mar 2001	25.4%
Feb 2001	25.9%
Mar 2000	22.8%

Table 6. Annualized rate of redemption and redemption exchanges from stock funds

Dates	Percent of Ave Net Assets
Mar 2001	9.3%
Feb 2001	40.5%
Mar 2000	37.8%

* Ave = Average; R = revised data; YTD = year to date.
† Tables furnished courtesy of Investment Company Institute, Washington, D.C.

CHAPTER 15

Profiting from Year-End Phenomena

This chapter covers several price and volume phenomena that occur at or before the end of each year. The term *year end* is truly accurate since one of those situations we shall describe takes place in October, which is the *tax* year end for many mutual funds. Much of what will be discussed here is indeed tax related, although the holidays themselves also play a role. We will proceed chronologically. Although the early part of the discussion seems hardly related to trading volume, the connection will become apparent later.

WHAT TO WATCH FOR, AND DO, IN OCTOBER

A bit of background in taxation and investment regulations will serve well as a context for what happens in October—a pattern that is often visible in the trading-volume behavior of individual stocks. Mutual funds and closed-end funds are Registered Investment Companies under the Investment Company Act of 1940 (commonly referred to as "the '40 Act"). They are therefore subject to regulation by the U.S. Securities and Exchange Commission (SEC). In addition, because they are afforded special *conduit,* or *pass-through,* status under the tax laws, they are governed by certain special provisions of the Internal Revenue Code. For purposes of discussion in this chapter, the central regulatory and tax items of interest are the requirements that funds pay out certain minimum percentages of their net realized long-term capital gains on or before certain dates. They must pay to shareholders (which since the tax "reform" act of 1986 means that they must declare dividends to shareholders of record by the final day of their fiscal year) at least 95 percent of such gains.* If funds fail to pay distributions as prescribed in the regulations, they lose their legal status as Registered Investment Companies; it would then be illegal for them to continue selling shares to investors. Not at all surprisingly, compliance is universal.

For purposes of computing their net realized long-term capital gains, funds have the option of adopting either the calendar year *or* a fiscal year beginning November 1 and ending on October 31. A considerable number adopt the October 31 convention, and this gives rise to not one but actually two tax-selling-season cycles each calendar year—one in late October plus the better-known one in December. We as individual investors have a notable aversion to paying taxes—in fact, one so strong that it often interferes with our making rational investment decisions. But that is a topic for discussion elsewhere.† Mutual funds, as pass-through entities, are entitled to avoid paying any federal income taxes at the corporate level if they comply with the interlocking rules of the SEC and the IRS. Rather than avoiding taxes as an emotional mantra, the funds have a different incentive—to retain assets and indeed to gather assets more successfully—which underlies some of their tax-driven behavior. We will examine those two issues briefly.

Mutual funds and closed-end funds pay their advisors—companies that make the investment decisions—an annual fee that is computed as a percentage of average assets in the fund, usually calculated on a daily basis. Not only does this provide the management company an incentive to perform well, through increasing the value of the portfolio, but it also exerts some influence on tax-oriented behavior. Each year the tax laws require that the fund must pay out 95 percent of the net realized long-term gains it takes. Investors as stockholders of the fund will normally not reinvest all of their realized gains distributions, at least in part because they plan to use some of that cash to pay their own taxes on the fund's gains. Suppose a fund has taken some fairly large net profits during the year. The end of the year approaches, and it faces paying out a fairly large percent-

---

*Actually, funds do have a seldom-used option to retain such gains and pay the tax thereon at the corporate tax rate, which was 35 percent at the time of this writing. That causes taxpayers confusion and fund managements extra telephone traffic and is generally used only rarely, and almost exclusively in the case of closed-end funds that have generated very large realized gains in proportion to their overall asset bases.
†See *It's When You Sell that Counts,* by the author, McGraw-Hill, New York.

age of its assets in cash as a capital-gains distribution, knowing that not all of that amount will be reinvested back into new shares. Its portfolio manager faces the need to raise cash to enable payment of the required distribution, and she sees that as a disruption to portfolio strategy. And of course, if things have gone well and the market has risen, selling securities to raise cash will itself trigger more gains on which to calculate the distribution required.

Therefore, there is a clear incentive for funds to sell off some of their positions that involve paper losses. Every capital loss realized before the end of the tax year offsets on a dollar-for-dollar basis a part of the gains previously taken, thereby reducing required distributions. (It might be argued that such tax-loss selling is mainly in the interests of the management company since it will help preserve its fee base; the portfolio manager can legitimately claim that predictable selling *by others* in depressed stocks the fund owns implies it is prudent to sell those same issues to avoid losses deepened by such selling pressure.) We thus see there is a setup for a tax-selling season created by funds' activity. Because the funds have a choice of fiscal years for distribution-computation purposes, two seasons exist: one in October and a second in December.

Aside from the asset-retention incentive described above, which can be served by taking available offsetting losses, the fund industry knows that the media and the public have increasingly come to focus on so-called tax efficiency of mutual funds. Accordingly, funds are described as having well—or badly—held down current tax liabilities for their taxable-account investors by minimizing net realized gains as a percentage of overall total return, with zero the ideal and 100 percent viewed as most inefficient. Chicago-based Morningstar in particular has seized upon this concept as a near crusade. (What is ironic is that the formula it has adopted to express tax efficiency produces a meaningless, negative number in years, such as 2000 for many funds, when total return is negative.) In any event, the widespread media repetition of the tax-efficiency drumbeat— with index funds featured as the poster children—has raised fund investors' awareness of the taxwise behavior of fund managers. Several dozen actively managed funds have come to market in recent years that manage their portfolios with a strong eye on current tax minimization. Investors in some unknown numbers are indeed making or weighting their decisions at least in part on the tax efficiency of funds' past records. The new 2001 rule by the SEC that funds be required to disclose after-tax as well as pretax returns in their prospectuses and annual reports both reflects and will further heighten this consciousness. In all, investors' behavior regarding funds' demonstrated tax efficiency clearly represents a (growing) reason for portfolio managers to take some available losses late in each tax year. (There is, of course, no particular reason to postpone the realization of losses until the end of each year, but human nature is such that we tend to deny our problems and remain hopeful that our underperformers will vindicate our judgment by becoming winners if we hold on longer.) It should also be mentioned that in those occasional years when federal tax rates are to be cut, funds do their owners a small tax-saving favor by reducing recorded gains in the old year.

Yet a third aspect of taking losses acts as a subtle prompt for ridding a fund's portfolio of its embarrassing components: Funds are required to publish full holdings in their annual (and semiannual) reports to shareholders, and a collection of unfortunate choices still showing among the listed positions makes for unappealing publicity and unhappy holders. Jettisoning the poorer actors before the reporting period ends makes sense as well, then, from this added viewpoint. It is called window dressing.

You can fairly readily identify individual stocks, and industry groups, that are being affected by this tax-driven behavior, both in the latter part of October and again in December. Most investors are quite aware of what the winning and losing parts of the market have been over the course of that latest year or so. If there is any need for documentation, several quick references are available:

- Various stock screeners, such as that by Yahoo!, can rank by year-to-date performance.
- A look at the lists of new 52-week lows on the major exchanges will highlight beleaguered groups.
- Checking the YTD or 12-month performance columns in newspaper funds listings is an easy approach; see the ICON, INVESCO, Rydex, and Fidelity Select sector funds in particular.
- As a supplement to the above, use tickers of the exchange-traded funds discussed in Chapter 14.

If you own, or are considering making bargain-hunting purchases of, these laggard stocks, you should do some more checking before diving in immediately at any time during the fourth calendar quarter. Special care is due in the second half of October and again from about November 15 onward, as these have become the traditional tax-selling periods. Watching for this price-and-volume action is especially important in years when the market has done well because it is then that the funds have the greatest incentive to prune their losers. You should not be surprised to know that *volume tells the tale!* A look at the *Standard & Poor's Monthly Stock Guide* (or any of several other hard-copy and online reference sources) will quickly tell you what percent of a stock is held by institutions. The greater that percentage, the more likely a stock is to come under high-volume tax-selling pressure in late October and again toward year's end. Obviously, individual daily volumes may fluctuate up and down, but on the whole you can readily spot concentrated trading volume at the bottom of any daily-basis bar chart such as those by BigCharts and others. An example, in this case of AT&T Corp, is provided in Figure 15–1. Note the heavy solid black appearance of the volume plots in October, preceded and followed by lighter volume in the immediately surrounding months.

How do you use this information as a trader or a bargain-hunting investor? First, you need to discern when the tax-selling pressure actually abates. That is fairly easily noted in two ways. First, if you watch an assortment of depressed and highly institutionally held stocks, you will see a concurrent reduction of volume in virtually all of them within a day or two when the actual selling abates. (It is important to inspect a dozen or so issues in different industries so you are not misled by particular action in one part of the market.) If the overall market is weak, it is likely that tax selling will crescendo and then decline before the month of October is complete—as the crowd will be anxious to finish its disposals before prices go even lower—and as early selling that drives prices lower encourages even more money managers to take action promptly (the

FIGURE 15–1

Mutual Funds at Work: October Tax-Selling Buildup in Widely Held Depressed Stock

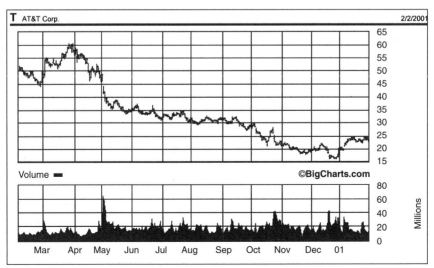

formation of a minicrowd!). If the market happens to be performing well in October, expect that tax selling will be less severe early but then very sharp in the final few days or a week as portfolio managers hold on in hope of partial improvement courtesy of that rising price trend. In either case, the volume will tell the tale. Another information source worth watching is *The Wall Street Journal's* "Abreast of the Market" column on page C-2, which will typically comment on the coming and passing of tax-selling pressure and will often quote various major money managers nearly daily on the phenomenon's progress. Yet another useful gauge is the daily number of new 52-week lows, especially if it declines for a few days when the market overall is not especially strong. That combination tells you the big selling has abated in severely depressed stocks.

Armed with this volume-verified evidence of when tax selling hits its maximum and then recedes, you can implement some tactics successfully:

- First, understand the climate. The stronger the market has been in the past year or longer (as in late 1998 and late 1999), the more pressure (volume and price) you should expect the gain-offsetting selling to put on depressed stocks, especially those widely owned by institutions. In "down" years, the pattern will be much weaker, unless gains were strong early, leaving losses still needing to be found, as was the case in 2000.

- If you are comfortable on both sides of the market rather than only as a long investor, sell short volatile and depressed stocks in early October, and cover in late October when selling volume in such issues as a whole begins to taper off for a few days. Follow your shorted stocks' prices down with protective buy stops so you will be taken out if a sudden updraft in prices occurs.

- Hold off on any buying of depressed stocks, even if they seemingly scream "bargain" on their fundamentals, until the final part of October, when you finally do see that overall tax-selling pressure, as documented by trading volume, is actually subsiding.

- If you do buy such stocks at that time, be cautious and nimble. Caution should require that you look up the analysts' consensus earnings for the next quarter to be reported, and satisfy yourself that the company is not undergoing continuing business stress. Avoid companies that have only recently started to have bad earnings comparisons, as they are statistically likely to have more.

- Being nimble means that you should be positioning these bargain buys for a trade of about 5 or 6 weeks only. Why? Some buyers will come back to repurchase their discards after their 31-day wash-sale-rule period has passed. That implies some buying pressure—perhaps on a visible volume pickup—in late November to the first week of December. But then you must sell out because after the buying crowd does its work, these still-depressed stocks will next feel a second round of tax-driven selling in December. You want to be out of the way for that episode and thus able to make a clear-minded decision on whether to repurchase such stocks, lower, around Christmastime.

DECEMBER: REPEAT OCTOBER'S PROCESS, BUT WITH REFINEMENTS

Virtually all of what has just been said about late October as a tax-selling season is applicable again at the end of each calendar year. Two significant differences apply in this second round, however: The second tax season is more lengthy, and it applies especially to certain additional types of stocks. As recently as a few decades ago, when institutional ownership and trading were a smaller proportion of the overall market action, year-end tax selling was usually confined to about the final 10 calendar days of December. As the pattern became more broadly noted, however, and as the volume of selling to be done by institutions rose, the season came to begin progressively earlier. Participants have now realized that they must beat others to the punch, so the process simply begins earlier. (This is rather like retailers' putting out their Valentine's Day merchandise on January 2, in hopes of beating each other.) Tax-selling season in recent years seems to have begun most commonly around November 15. Again as in October, the market's late-year trend has some effect: In a strong year there may be more holders waiting for hoped-for price recovery, but in weak years there seems less reason, and potentially more price disappointment, in holding on to proven laggards.

Once again, you should check the listings of new lows on the major exchanges, look at the one-year or longer charts of various ETFs, and consult the lists of ICON, INVESCO, Rydex, and Fidelity Select industry-focused funds for the worst-performing areas of the market. You should again exercise caution about fundamentals, as described above. But you should also be disciplined in avoiding any temptation to jump in too soon on the buying (or short-covering) side. December's tax-selling process will take a while longer than that of October. Once again, watch the volume plots on charts of key stocks, and also be sure to watch a dozen or so stocks spanning a broad cross section of industries rather than one or two, so you get a signal based on the overall pattern rather than perhaps on some suddenly changing, industry-specific or single-company news. The trading volume will become heavy and then will subside. The earlier the selling starts (perhaps as of mid-November), the greater the chance it may end as early as about December 15. The later it starts, and the better the overall market has acted during the latest year or two, the greater the chances that tax selling will continue for longer toward the year's actual end. Figure 15-2 shows a stock reversing on December 29.

The volume action, read along with price change, will tell you a clear story. You should have chosen *in advance* your list of buyable bargain names. Once the volume action tells you that the selling season is finished, you will need to act rapidly to get the best prices because many others will be buying their lists too and the sellers will have finished their work. It will take too much time to compile your list, or you will be pressured into doing a sloppy research job, if you start only after the volume signal is given. Expect it, and be prepared to pull the buying trigger; that volume signal *will* come.

The December tax-selling season takes on some added aspects not evident in October because the mix of sellers is different. Retail (individual) investors join the institutions in December, and these investors hold some kinds of stocks that the mutual funds and pension funds and insurance companies tend not to own. Low-priced stocks in general fall into that category of holdings. So names trading below $10 and especially below $5 are prime

FIGURE 15–2

Rite Aid: Tax Selling Ends When Volume Abates
(December 2000)

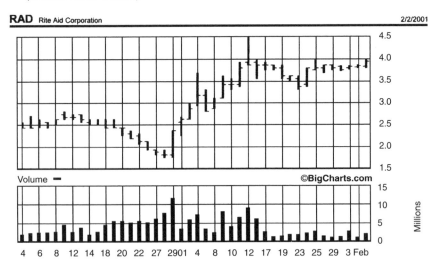

candidates for tax-selling pressure. And remember, if such stocks are long-downtrodden companies' shares, there will be little institutional interest in either buying or selling them, so you should not expect to see a huge amount of trading volume. You will, of course, see a clear increase in share volume, but do not expect it to get into the millions daily per stock as would be the case with widely institutionally held stocks.

CLOSED-END FUNDS

Closed-end funds are a particular addition to the list of December-effect candidates. There are two reasons for this. First, closed-end funds are almost entirely shunned by institutions (because of a bias against "layering of fees" in the form of one fund's paying management expenses for another fund and because most are microcap in size). Therefore, only the December season applies, as that is when individuals do their portfolio tidying and tax adjusting. Second, closed-end funds, like mutual funds, face the requirement to pay capital-gains distributions. Savvy investors in this specialized area (representing only about 2 percent of total fund assets) know that discounts to net asset value widen in December until after funds trade ex-dividend. Then, patient buyers jump in to buy their targets after avoiding a tax liability. Many funds go "of record" ex on the very last trading day or two of the year (and by exchange rules therefore will trade "ex" the amount of the distribution 2 trading days earlier, so the net selling pressure on their prices tends to be stretched out to nearly the end of the trading year). When thinking of closed-end funds, do not exclude the many bond funds that actually dominate that investment realm (about 75 percent by both count and assets). If stocks have been up and bonds flat or lower for the year, you can expect heavy selling in closed-end bond funds as individual investors look for whatever available tax-saving losses they can harvest before December 31. Municipal bond funds in particular have a strong seasonal tendency to trade to their deepest average discounts in late December and then snap back by several percent in January. Those not presently aware of the closed-end funds world should check out the weekly listings, arranged by investment objective, that are provided each Monday in Section C of *The Wall Street Journal* and daily on the Internet at the following URL:

interactive.wsj.com/edition/resources/documents/CEFmain.html

This listing is a part of the *WSJ Interactive Edition,* available at $29 per year to hard-copy subscribers and at $49 to those who do not buy the paper edition. In the spring of 2001, *The Wall Street Journal* started listing closed-end funds in a separate alphabetical table daily, and removed them from the various exchanges' stock tables.

Of particular interest from the viewpoint of buying closed-end funds for a December-January bounce are those issues that have been brought to market in the latest calendar year. Their shareholder families have not yet settled down to a longer-term and more satisfied mindset, so if such funds have not done well early in life, they are major targets for December tax selling. Be patient even if a deepening discount to NAV seems to be enticing: *Let the trading volume tell you* when the pressure has finally abated. It is quite easy to discover which closed-end funds are the newest. Consult the weekly listings in the statistical pages of *Barron's*. Look in the rightmost column, where the 12-month market performance is shown for equity funds and where the 12-month yield is displayed for bond funds. If those are shown as "N/A" and a market price is quoted, indicating a market-traded closed-end fund, you are looking at a fund less than a year old. An extreme example, shown in Figure 15–3, was meVC Fisher Draper Jurvetson, ticker MVC, a venture-capital closed-end fund that conducted its IPO in late March 2000, just as the NASDAQ market started its year-2000 meltdown of over 50 percent. MVC traded to a discount of over 45 percent late in the year, giving first-year investors a paper loss of 50 percent as the stock dropped from its IPO price of $20 to slightly under $10. The shares showed a volume-driven period of tax selling in December, and then snapped back smartly in January 2001 (Figure 15-3).

Yet another group of stocks, not quite as easy to identify comprehensively as are the closed-end funds, makes a fine target for tax-season moves and of course can be timed equally well by examining trading volume. These are common and preferred stocks that have been newly issued in the past year and therefore do not yet have a seasoned shareholder family. Included here would be not only IPOs but also any corporate spinoffs, if they have performed negatively in price terms. They will be strong targets for tax selling by individual investors.

An ideal opportunity occurs occasionally at the end of years when interest rates have risen. In these situations, preferred stocks as well as utilities and REITs show up in large numbers on the new-lows lists in early December. The end of year 1999 provided an excellent example, when a number of REITs had sold preferred shares in late 1998 or early 1999, and these had gone to discounts from issue price due to rising interest rates. They provided high yields beyond what was appropriate to their quality ratings, and also offered January-bounce capital gains opportunities following intense, volume-documented, December tax selling. The

FIGURE 15-3

December Tax-Selling Buildup in Depressed First-Year
Closed-End Fund.

MVC Mevc Draper Fisher Jurvet Fd I   2/2/2001

chart in Figure 15–4 for Mid-America Apartment Communities Preferred
C is a very typical example. There is a particular added pressure on such
income-oriented stocks since their holders are by nature risk averse.
Declining prices and /or broker prodding can readily scare such owners
into tax-oriented sales of losers in December. You can pick up the bargains
at just the right time, once the average daily trading volume begins to trail
off. This pattern is also shown in a municipal-bond fund two years in a
row (Figure 15–5).

Closed-end funds also provide an inverse December/January price
move when they have performed exceedingly *well*. Curiously, this phenomenon is tipped off by *low* volume of trading in December. Recall that
we pointed out the low institutional and very high individual ownership of
closed-end funds' shares. This implies that shareholders are very tax conscious. While holders of stocks that have done badly tend to sell in
December, holders of stocks that have done very well take a converse, but
delayed, tax-conscious approach: They postpone selling from December
into the next January in order to nail down profits but also postpone paying taxes on their gains. (While this phenomenon is quite pronounced in
closed-end funds, it also occurs to some degree in small-capitalization
stocks for which the public is the primary holder and institutions are largely absent.) Among closed-end funds, one easy way to spot the potential for
such December/January reversals is to look for funds trading at premiums

FIGURE 15-4

December Tax-Selling Volume Climax in Recently Issued Preferred Stock. Two Years Running.

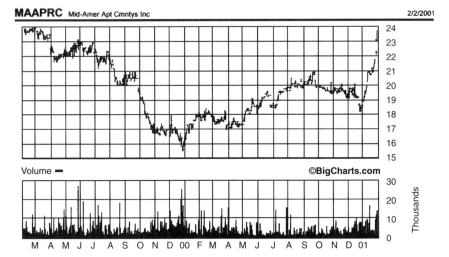

MAAPRC Mid-Amer Apt Cmntys Inc   2/2/2001

late in the calendar year, and whose total returns for the year are well above average. Again, the Internet Web site named and weekly listings by *The Wall Street Journal* and by *Barron's* are of use for creating a starting list of candidates.

The accompanying charts of John Hancock Bank & Thrift Opportunity Fund (BTO) and of The Turkish Investment Fund (TKF) show this remarkable year-end phenomenon very well—and twice each in a period of a very few years (Figures 15–6 and 15–7). The former performed as we have described above at the ends of both 1996 and 1997, trading on considerably reduced volume in December both years after large percentage price gains, and then seeing higher volume and selling in January. Likewise, TKF showed the same patterns after considerable 1-year price advances in December 1993 and again in December 1999. Not only are such patterns logical when considered in light of the tax-timing circumstances, they also fall into the proper theoretical model as described in Chapter 11: Higher price levels on receding volume are always to be considered suspect.

THE HOLIDAY-WEEK LULL

Much of Wall Street takes off most or all of the final several trading days of each calendar year. This period corresponds roughly with the last 1 or

FIGURE 15-5

Two Years of January Price Runs Following December Tax Selling on High Volume

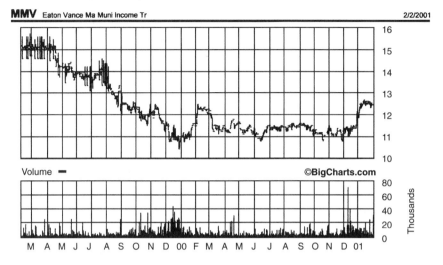

FIGURE 15-6

Note Downside Reversals Early in Both 1997 and 1998

BTO John Hancock Bank and Thrift Opportunity Fund   12/15/2000 2:31 PM

NAV:	Change:	Offer:	Yield:
	⬇ –0.0625	8.375	n/a
8.3125	Percent Change:		52 Week Range:
	–0.75%		6.00 to 8.69

FIGURE 15−7

January Price Collapses on High Volume following
December Rallies on Light Volume

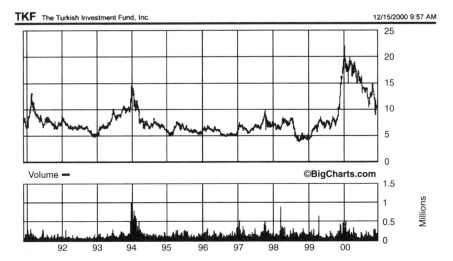

2 days before Hanukkah and Christmas—and right through the end of the year, depending on how the holidays fall on particular days of the week. Is this because the Street is disproportionately populated by extremely religious people? Not really. Rather, it is a combination of realities: Much of the investing public tends to be fairly uninterested in the investing world during that period—perhaps because they are home for the holidays and have wrapped up their year-end tax-oriented moves. And for many of the professionals on the Street, it can be use-or-lose time: After a high-pressured year, they are faced with taking their remaining allotted vacation days or being unable to carry them forward. Since business is likely to be slack anyway, what better time to take a few days away from the action? For such reasons, you will almost never see a major acquisition announced in this period, so therein is yet another reason for the pros to stay home: lack of action. Further, in most years official Washington is likewise shut down for the duration, so little if any important news that would affect the markets is to be expected.

All of this has some definite implications for those who do remain present in the last week or so of December, and the telltale signs are there for the viewing in the form of trading-volume data. Basically, you can often expect to see a reversal of price direction from the last week of the old year to at least the first few trading days of the new. If you see that as a very short period of time, admittedly you are correct. But even if one is not intent on being a short-term swing trader, such information can be genuinely valuable to the longer-term investor who wants to make some moves and would be happy to pocket a few extra percents in return for knowing the inside game and playing according to its rules. Good timing is better than bad timing or random timing.

Think about the sequence of events. The professionals, knowing they will be taking off a week or more, adjust their positions according to prices and prospects as they see them, and pack it in by a couple of days before Christmas. During the period from then until January 2, as any examination of volume data will readily attest, the game is left to the smaller players and in particular the individual investor. If the balance of opinion among such traders should push the market decidedly in one direction during the year's final week, it will almost surely do so on light trading volume—because the professionals are on the sidelines. Now let us look at what will probably happen on the first trading day of the new year. The professionals are back. They look closely at the new prices of stocks in which they are interested. If those have moved much from the levels at which these very same pros were content to leave them before Christmas, they will take corrective action. If stocks have fallen on light volume for no specific corporate reason, the professionals will use this turn of events as an opportunity to pick up bargains. Conversely, if those movers of large amounts of capital had left prices at one level before their extended holiday week and now find them considerably higher, they are likely to snicker a bit about the bullishness of the "little guys" and will take profits—again reversing the price trend seen in the old year's final week. In any case, the action will definitely fall into the category of low-volume moves being contrary to the trend, at least in the short term.

Figure 15–8 summarizes the commonplace thinking of big-money stock market professionals and the impacts they may have on market prices over the first few days of a new trading year. In each case you will note that the likely direction in the new week, when all the big players are back and trading volume is heavier again, tends to be opposite what the "little guys" established as a trend or level *on low volume* in the interhol-idays time span. Therefore, it makes sense for the savvy—and especially the volume-aware—individual investor to close positions that went well during the final week and to establish long or short positions on the final trading day that will benefit from a reversal in the starting days of January. One small exception to that micro level timing advice exists: If the old year was strong and the final week was also quite strong, the predictable plethora of year-end magazine and newspaper and Internet Web site arti-cles will say the new year's trend will be extremely bullish. That should

FIGURE   15 – 8

Influence of Market Professionals on Market Prices in
First Few Days of a New Trading Year

Old-Year Market	Final-Week Market	Professionals' Attitude upon Return	Resulting Price Action: Early Days
Bullish	Up	Take trading gains; lock in old profits not taken in December due to tax delaying.	Down
Bullish	Down	Still bullish so shop among bargains created last week.	Up
Bearish	Down	End of tax pressure; new year seen as "fresh start"; buy bargains.	Up
Bearish	Up	If still holding a bearish mindset, "Sell that rally!"	Down

result in a fair amount of buying by the public that will carry the market higher for at least the morning of the first trading session after New Year's Day. In this case one would not want to sell or go short on December's final trading day but instead would postpone such actions at least until midday into the new year's first session.

It should be mentioned in closing this chapter that elements of such patterns as described above also tend to occur around other long holiday weekends: Reversals afterward are more common than not. However, in those cases price differences tend to be smaller since not as much time has passed during the absence of the dominant institutional investors and because of the lack of overlaid tax-year reversal timing strategies, which obviously exist only at the turning of each year. Regardless of the particular season, one need not be a trader to take advantage of short-term phenomena to gain an extra percent or several when entering or exiting positions. And in the circumstances described here, as usual, we can say with some assurance: Volume does tell the tale.

CHAPTER 16

Short-Term Applications

I have not aimed this book specifically to traders. Nor have I tried to convert anyone into a trader, whether of the swing or the intraday variety. That said, however, one cannot deny a major reality of today's stock market: Things move fast. Unless one is a zealot buy-and-hold investor (and it seems doubtful that many of that group will still be reading as they reach this late chapter!), one must be realistic and prompt about taking what opportunities the market provides. Those who would hold passively for the long term predestine their returns to being no better than the long-term average for the market (about 11 percent per year, mean). Everyone else, because they expend more energy in study and execution, must seek higher returns as compensation for that added effort and risk taking (risk in the sense of unknown return and not simply downside exposure). The only way to achieve something other than the start-to-end average return is to buy and sell more than once; that is a mathematical truth. Call that market timing, call it responsive gain realizing, call it opportunistic responsiveness, or whatever else you wish. Sometimes it involves acting quickly when mob action (read: high volume) signals a turning point. Sometimes it may include selling something fairly shortly after buying it—sooner than intended—if financial advantage is provided. For those of a more aggressive bent, it may include using the short as well as the long side of the market.

In this chapter we will explore some information that the market provides us during the trading session. This breaks into two major areas: overall market volume and its implications, and individual-stock information. Again, my intention is not specifically to encourage day trading;

rather I want to inform and enlighten you about this useful, detailed, short-term information so that you can use it when appropriate, rather than be unaware of it and forfeit such opportunities by default.

DAILY AND MORNING VOLUME PATTERNS

Each day of the week tends to be slightly different on average. Not only are there fairly well-established patterns of which days tend to provide rises or declines more often than the others, but—not at all surprisingly—trading volume also tends to exhibit small biases over time.* If you set an "average" day on the New York Stock Exchange in terms of trading volume as equal to an index of 100, Figure 16–1 shows how the daily patterns of average volume have looked in recent years.

In making these calculations, I have purposely made an adjustment for Fridays. Each third calendar month of the quarter contains a trading session commonly referred to as a "triple-witching Friday" because on that day CBOE stock options, index options, and futures all expire. This is the Friday preceding the third Saturday of the month. Needless to say, traders who have positions in any of those instruments must close out their positions, and in many cases they will roll them over to a later expiration month. This process generates a noticeable increase in trading volume in individual optionable stocks and in stocks included in major indices such as the S&P 100 and S&P 500. Therefore, I have excluded these Fridays—1 out of each 13—from my calculation of an "average"

FIGURE 16–1

Daily Patterns of Average Volume

Mondays	92
Tuesdays	101
Wednesdays	104
Thursdays	105
Fridays	99

---

* See the very useful and historically fascinating annual deskbook called *The Stock Traders'*
   Almanac by Yale Hirsh (Old Tappan, NJ: The Hirsh Organization).

Friday's volume (inclusion raises the overall average by about 10 percent but that higher figure is misleading for 12 weeks out of 13). One might reasonably argue that some other adjustments are warranted. For example, the Friday after Thanksgiving is traditionally a very slow trading day. So are days on the weekend side of July 4. And there is often a half-day session just before Christmas Day. However, these each occur only once per year and therefore might affect averages by only about 1 percent if trading is literally half of normal on these special days. So I have left them in when doing my calculations.

Why is it important to note overall trading volume, and when is it possibly misleading? As developed throughout this book, trading volume reflects the size and interest and fervor or urgency of the crowd. Occasions when volume becomes unusually high—without the trigger of major news—tend to mark a peaking-out of sentiment. On the downside these are referred to as *selling climaxes* while on the upside the term is *blow-offs*. Comparisons of current-day overall trading volume tend to be misleading at and around holidays and long weekends, and of course on option-expiration days, as well as when major news drives traders to take action. "Major news" as used here can include threatening geopolitical developments including OPEC production and price decisions, significant economic indicators released, actions by the Federal Open Market Committee, and unfortunately an occasional assassination (or its attempt) of a world leader. But significant corporate news can often act as a major stimulus to overall market trading activity when the specific news is interpreted as having wider implications for the economy and therefore the stock market. Examples of this might include the following:

- Surprising revenue projections or reports are released by industry leaders such as IBM, AT&T, Microsoft, or Intel.
- Major companies announce layoffs, which is especially significant if the layoffs are not explained by normal consolidation after a major recent acquisition.
- There is major patent or technology news having implications beyond a particular company (the FDA approves or disapproves a key drug or testing protocol, changing the rules, or a patent or copyright is denied or affirmed, affecting the basics of intellectual-property law).
- The government starts or drops a major antitrust prosecution, contradicting expectations.
- One or more major banks (Bank of America, e.g.) announce

increased reserves for nonperforming loans, indicating that the economy is affecting debt repayments.

■ A crisis affecting one company is seen as having wider implications. A recent example was the California electricity shortages that began in winter of 2000 to 2001. Fixing that problem was seen as implying a ripple of higher costs throughout the economy; utility bankruptcies threatened to cripple small businesses as suppliers.

What you should be looking for are increases in daily trading volume that are *not* associated with such news triggers. Especially notable are occasional series of days in which trading increases consecutively while prices move sharply up or down, without a specific news trigger. These incidents indicate formation of a crowd mentality about the overall market—either very bullish or scared and bearish. As discussed in Chapter 9—and in Chapter 14 regarding ETFs—such crescendos represent exhaustion of the previously prevailing opinion and therefore imply an imminent price reversal.

Probably the easiest way to watch for such changes in daily overall volume is to observe the graph of recent months' daily volume that accompanies the start of the New York Stock Exchange stock tables in *The Wall Street Journal,* usually on page C-2 or C-4. A daily or weekly quick inspection will indicate whether trading volume has lately been unusual, and your memory will serve well concerning corporate or world news if there has been such a trigger. Otherwise, a volume increase is notable. You can know approximate total daily trading volume only near the very end of a session or the exact number after the market has closed for the day. The latter may prove a bit late if you sense an implied need to buy or sell because of unusual crowd activity.

However, you can get a meaningful sense of the level of total NYSE trading in real time by watching first-hour and even first-half-hour data. (In doing so, be sure to check the most-actives list to make sure that extraordinary action in one stock is not influencing the total.) Early-morning trading data are indicative of any overnight buildup of strong opinion by the crowd. Data for recent years show that there is a fairly symmetrical intraday pattern displayed by half-hourly volume. The first and final half hours typically feature the heaviest volume, and a plotting of the 30-minute totals is shaped like an elongated letter U with the low occurring in the 12:30 to 2:00 p.m. time range (lunchtime on the East Coast). You can find the record of the specific totals for the last 2 trading days and the week-ago-day's comparison in the lower-right corner of the "Abreast of the Market" page of *The Wall Street Journal* (and at www.WSJ.com); 5 days of data are printed in the *Barron's* "Market Laboratory, Stocks," section. However, if you are concerned that something psychologically important is occurring in real time as you watch, you will very likely find that referring to the printed data a day or a week later is inadequate for decision and action purposes. Therefore, I offer for your consideration the following observation on early-morning trading.

Overall market trading activity in the first half hour of each session is considerably heavier than would be the case if volume were spread evenly throughout the day. There are 6.5 trading hours daily, so a perfectly even distribution of volume would imply about 7.7 percent of volume (one thirteenth) should occur by 10:00 a.m. ET. In actuality, trading in the first 30 minutes typically runs at nearly double that rate, or 13.0 percent, on average (and about 13.8 percent on triple-witching Fridays). Of course, it is impossible to know at 10:00 a.m. today what percentage of *today's* eventual overall total volume has been traded since most of the day still lies ahead. Fortunately, there is a good alternative that you can use as a gauge in real time: Simply compare today's first 30 minutes' volume on the NYSE with total trading for the *prior* session.

Not only does such a comparison—this morning's early results against yesterday's total—supply a crucial *real-time* reading, but it also supplies a type of momentum measure by comparing current against immediate past data. For recent years, the average relationships of first-half-hour trading volume to prior-day aggregates have been as listed in Figure 16–2 (as you will observe, they cluster narrowly around 13 percent).

Once again, I have excluded triple-witching Fridays—both for morning data and as day-before bases—because of their significantly higher volumes. In addition, where holidays occur, my percentages compare

FIGURE 16-2

The Average Relationships of First-Half-Hour Trading Volume to Prior-Day Aggregates

First 30 Minutes	Full Day	Percentage
Monday	Friday	12.0
Tuesday	Monday	13.8
Wednesday	Tuesday	13.1
Thursday	Wednesday	12.8
Friday	Thursday	13.0

the following morning's 30-minute volume with the preholiday session's total. For example, when a Monday holiday occurs, Tuesday morning volume is divided by the prior-Friday session total. In using this comparison technique, one must be especially careful to take the following steps so as not to misinterpret percentages under special circumstances:

- Ignore readings when triple-witching Friday is either the base day or the new morning.
- Ignore readings involving slow-trading days around major holidays (Thanksgiving, Christmas, July 4, New Year's Day).
- Ignore readings involving days before and after Monday holidays (Memorial, Labor Days).
- Ignore readings when severe weather on the East Coast affects trading.
- Discount readings where significant news—general or corporate—is a factor on either day.

Including all trading days (whether or not to be discounted or outright ignored), the distribution of percentages in recent years forms nearly a perfect bell curve, as shown in Figure 16–3. A detailed examination of the top few dozen readings in the period 1999 to 2000 illustrates how significant "high" readings in the first hour seem to be. A 2-year chart of the S&P Spider ETF is provided for reference (Figure 16–4). The 10 highest readings (from 39 percent+ to 20.6 percent) each represent either triple-witching situations or post-holiday returns to normal volume patterns. Following those 10, we see the market events shown in Figure 16–5. As counting will reveal, 6 (40 percent) of these events were reversals, and another (the last listed) briefly preceded a reversal; another 6 (40 percent) occurred at breakdown points or upside breakaway gaps; 1 was a busy window-dressing day; and only 1 of 15 seemed to have no technical or psychological significance. That is quite a record, enough so that one must conclude that unusually high early-morning trading activity is saying something significant in almost every instance.

A SHORT-TERM FERVOR INDICATOR

Abnormal bursts of morning trading volume are the footprints of a crowd whose pent-up overnight thinking is highly opinionated and fervent. People are just waiting for the market to open and cannot abide not taking action in the direction of the prior day's (or days') move. In effect, "everyone" is projecting a continuation of the past move. These unusually high

FIGURE 16-3

The Distribution of Percentages in Recent Years

Half Hour As Percent of Prior-Day Total	Percent of Occurrences	
Under 10%	5%	minimum 6%
10–11%	11%	
11–12%	18%	
12–13%	22%	mean 13%; median 12.8%
13–14%	19%	
14–15%	11%	
15–16%	7%	
Over 16%	7%	maximum 40%

FIGURE 16-4

S&P 500 Spiders: Four Low-Volume Tops (Arrows)

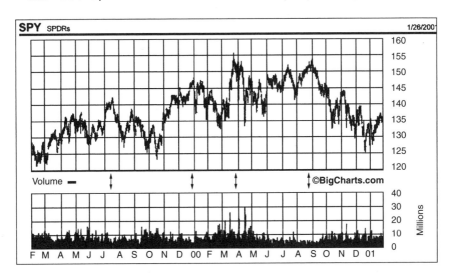

readings of the first-30-minute percentage may be thought of as either volume spikes or the culminations of crescendos, when volume is plotted by the half hour rather than by the full day. Thus, we have the principle of fractals at work: The same, known patterns such as waves and tides repeat in both larger and smaller magnitudes. Here we are seeing it in terms of amounts of volume in shorter time frames.

Not only is a high reading on this indicator worth strongly noting, but on occasion an unexplained low reading may be of help. Such would

FIGURE 16-5

The 15 High Readings in the First Half-Hour, 1999 to 2000

Date	Day	Reading, Percent	Event
01/21/2000	Monday	20.6	Top of a rally
03/31/1999	Wednesday	18.6	Quarter-end window dressing
10/15/1999	Friday	17.4	Major bottom after 3-month decline
03/05/1999	Friday	17.3	Gap up to start run
09/21/1999	Tuesday	17.2	Violation of double bottom
05/12/1999	Wednesday	17.2	High day of 3-month rally
10/28/1999	Thursday	16.9	Upside breakout from downtrend
04/27/99	Thursday	16.8	High of 1-week, 7% rally
06/16/1999	Wednesday	16.7	Penetration of down trendline
03/14/2000	Tuesday	16.7	Upside gap breaking downtrend
04/11/2000	Tuesday	16.6	Breakdown starting 11% drop, taking 1 week
11/09/1999	Tuesday	16.6	No technical reason
08/17/1999	Tuesday	16.6	Temporary reversal high
12/03/1999	Friday	16.5	Island reversal high
08/18/2000	Friday	16.4	2% before high before major decline

be the case if a strong price trend continues but there is an absence of volume confirmation (a fractal of the Chapter 11 scenario) or a price breakout that proves false for not being confirmed by significant volume. Just as you must exclude from consideration extremely high percentage readings observed the mornings after preholiday sessions, you likewise should ignore very low readings that will occur on the mornings of holiday-affected trading days and on Mondays following triple-witching Fridays. Nearly all of the readings below 9.5 percent in recent years have been recorded in such circumstances. Naturally, when a particular trading day generated huge total volume for any reason (including major news), you must consider a fairly low 30-minute percentage on the following morning to be understandable, rather than indicative of a lack of follow-through.

By using this fervor indicator, you may be able to detect, in real time, highly emotional behavior by the overnight crowd. In the Internet age wherein possibly millions of investors are placing orders during the prior night for the next opening, this means of detecting mass opinion can be very useful. It can help you to identify and act upon likely trend reversals in the market and sometimes in the major market-leading sectors. That information can be helpful for taking or closing positions in individual stocks and equally so for exchange-traded funds including sector instruments. You can obtain a currently updated listing of these "basket" products at the NASDAQ Web site, using this URL:

http://quotes.nasdaq.com/asp/ETFsCompare.asp?query=Intraday

As was discussed in Chapter 14, these exchange-traded funds themselves can act as good indicators of crowd activity (whether or not you choose to buy and sell them) if you study their volume patterns.

MORNING VOLUME PATTERNS IN INDIVIDUAL STOCKS

Before beginning this discussion, let me again state that my intention is not specifically to encourage day trading nor convert investors into traders. Rather, my hope is to assist you in obtaining advantageous price executions on normally intended transactions and to help you occasionally spot price-reversal junctures at which you should enter and exit the market rather than remain as a passive, longer-term holder. My approach, of course, is to utilize the information that trading-volume patterns provide as a central guide to making decisions based on a contrarian response to strong crowd activity.

One cannot hope to find such a stable indicator for individual stocks' volume idiosyncrasies as was described earlier for the overall (NYSE) volume totals. There are simply too many unpredictable influences on volume in individual stocks to allow us to expect such a rule of thumb as "13 percent in the first 30 minutes" to apply. Academics would describe this problem as too high a ratio of noise to information. However, this does not mean that sometimes there are not worthwhile patterns of trading volume to watch in individual stocks on an intraday basis. And the morning is often a very important part of the day to observe since it sometimes can guide buying and selling decisions. As in the case of the overall market, early-morning trading can be a valid indicator of pent-up overnight crowd opinion—that is, its size and intensity.

While we discussed earlier in this chapter the need to discount situations in which overall market volume is influenced by major news, in the cases of individual stocks' price and volume patterns, this is generally not advisable. We certainly must know when events are influencing trading volume in a stock, but how the crowd reacts to events is an important consideration in making buy/hold/sell/avoid decisions. Here are some major triggers of significant price/volume action that can occur in an individual stock, often immediately but not always right from the opening of a day's trading:

- Corporate news
- Change of opinion and/or EPS estimates by widely followed analysts
- Inclusion of stock in an industry getting major news-driven attention
- Inclusion of stock in a major market basket such as the S&P 500

Some explanation of the two last points is warranted. Sometimes stocks move significantly without being the subject of any company-specific news. For example, the widely watched monthly book-to-bill indicator has a noticeable effect on virtually all semiconductor stocks on the day of its release, even though no individual company data are revealed. Similarly, a significant change in expectations for oil prices will be reflected in the prices of nearly all airline and oil stocks because of the obvious profit implications of the news. Likewise, at times when it is clear that major amounts of money are entering or exiting the market, stocks included in major market indices will go up or down together as the market feels and/or anticipates transactions in all such stocks. For example, when S&P Index investing was most in vogue (until about March 1999), an indication that investors were pouring money into stock funds had a positive effect on the 500 stocks included in that popular index.

Clearly, however, the most direct and striking event triggers driving price moves on heavy volume in individual stocks are those that are very company specific. Two aspects of news and the market's reaction to it are highly relevant to determining whether an investor or trader should be a buyer or seller. First is the issue of the real importance of a news item. If you could peer back from a time machine that has taken you 5 or 10 years into the future, you would quickly note that quarterly earnings surprises, and especially brokerage analysts' recommendations, are of no lasting true importance in considering the value of a stock. Only rarely does a corporate information release go to the depth of revealing an essential, value-defining turn of events. Examples would be a major shift in industry dynamics caused by a technological or competitive event—or a radical shift in corporate strategy that will better realize shareholder value. Only occasionally will a quarterly report reveal the beginnings of a significant change in corporate fortunes. But stock prices predictably overreact to all earnings and analyst-opinion announcements on a regular basis.

Obviously a stock should be sold or bought when truly important news is revealed that changes the company's fundamental strategic outlook (in more than simply the sense of its likely EPS growth rate). On a tactical basis, however, we often see instances in which news has a considerable short-term impact on price—all out of proportion to any truly lasting significance for corporate value. In these events, the high volume driving that overreaction in price is a strong signal to take buying or selling action contrary to what the excitable but myopic crowd is currently doing. A recent 2-year chart of IBM, Figure 16–6, illustrates this point.

For nearly all of the 24 months shown, IBM had been essentially locked in a trading range between 80 and 135—a wide range to be sure but nevertheless not in a secular up or down trend. Yet during that time window, we observe no fewer than seven instances in which earnings announcements or preannouncements drove price gaps in the stock. These, in chronological order, were in April, July, and October 1999; in June, July, and October 2000; and finally in January 2001. Despite the fact that hundreds of analysts cover the company and many hundreds of institutions own the stock, collectively they were repeatedly in error as to their earnings and growth expectations. When the company revealed new information, the stock price gapped upward or downward on heavy volume. *When the price gap was in the direction of the already-established price*

FIGURE 16–6

High Volume on EPS News Repeatedly Marks Price Reversals

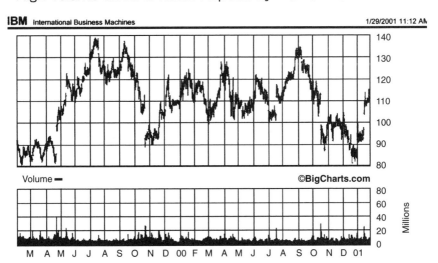

trend, the crowd was overreacting, and the stock quickly began a reversal of price direction. These price reversals occurred in July (top) and October (bottom) 1999, and again in late June and October 2000 (both bottoms). The gap from 97 to 105+ on positive news in January 2001 represented nearly the end of a "trend" upward from 80 in December 2000 as the shares found resistance just above 110.

Generally, when price gaps up or down on very high volume (and the Amgen Inc. chart in Figure 16–7 shows clearly when unusual volume occurred against a background of trading typically in the daily range of 5 to 10 million shares), a practice known as *fading the opening* tends to work profitably. This involves refusing to join the crowd in its frenzied on-balance selling or buying during about the first 45 to 90 minutes of morning trading. Watch carefully to observe when the pace of trading recedes. That is a very reliable clue that the crowd has finished its work on the stock; momentum in price will break, and the price will often actually reverse direction. You can then buy (after a downside gap) or sell (after an upside gap) when using the volume's falling off as your clue. You will have taken advantage of the footprints left by the crowd in two ways: You will refuse to join its numbers and thereby avoid a bad directional decision for the short term, and you will gain a better execution price by waiting until the high volume abates and price begins to reverse.

FIGURE 16–7

10-Day Chart with 3 Morning Reversals to Fade

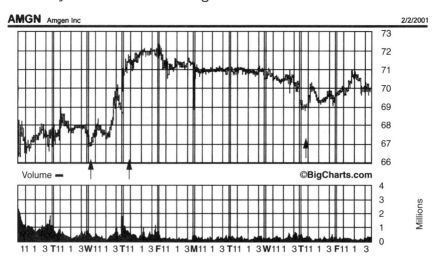

The combination of the previously established price direction, the positive or negative nature of news, the opening price direction, and the abatement of volume creates the set of decision rules given in Figure 16–8. Figures 16–9 and 16–10 are two charts that provide rather vivid contrasts as to preferred tactics, in accordance with Figure 16–8. The key element in determining whether the burst of volume means the price move is over or just starting is the element of surprise—the question is whether the big news *changes* expectations. We know existing expectations by looking at recent price action and by scanning the prevailing tone of news. Our first situation (Figure 16–9) is Atrix Laboratories (ATRX), whose stock benefited from some positive news late in the afternoon of the first of 10 days shown on its chart. The stock quickly ran to and slightly above 23 the following morning on fairly heavy volume. The key deciding point was that in the prior month ATRX had already climbed from 14—a 64 percent move. The new burst of volume represented buyers who had finally become so confident that they could no longer stand being on the sidelines. This circumstance was an upside exhaustion. Fading the opening by selling into strength in the first hour would have worked. With patience, if you considered the news good enough to prompt you to buy, you could have had the stock three points lower within another 5 days—13 percent well earned or saved by sophisticated tactics.

Contrast the situation of PG&E Corp., the huge California electric utility that seemed headed for bankruptcy in the days of early 2001 covered by this chart (a step it eventually took) (Figure 16–10). It had omitted its common and preferred dividends, defaulted on $596 million of debt, and had set February 2 as the date it would run out of cash unless emer-

FIGURE 16–8

A Set of Decision Rules for Morning Gaps

Established Price Direction	Nature of News	Morning Gap Direction	Decision	Tactical Implementation
Down	Bad	Down	Buy	Fade; wait 45–90 minutes.
Down	Good	Up	Buy	Do not wait
Up	Good	Up	Sell	Fade; wait 45–90 minutes.
Up	Bad	Down	Sell	Do not wait.

FIGURE 16-9

Upside Exhaustion: After a High-Volume Opening (Arrow),
Stock Labors

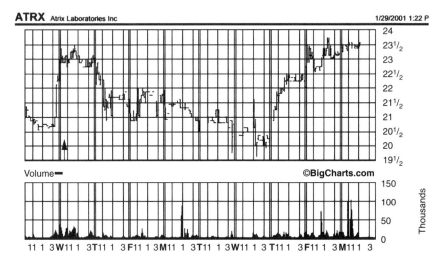

gency relief measures were granted. Its price was down from 25 in early December and 20 in early January to 10 when positive political developments surfaced overnight at the point where the price gaps up from 10 to over 11 (Thursday, January 25). Since the upside price surge on a strong burst of volume represented a reversal of existing opinion and price trend, the proper course was to buy into the strength rather than wait for a pullback—*if* you believed the good news would not later be reversed. In this sort of volatile and highly publicized situation, nervous short sellers in large numbers would predictably add to the ongoing buying pressure. The key element was one of positive surprise, whereas in the Atrix case the good news simply confirmed previous prevailing opinion.

It must be strongly emphasized that what has been discussed here has been short term and tactical in nature. The timing and thus favorable pricing of suggested transaction points was based on interpretation of volume dynamics that represented crowd action in response to news known at the time. Short-term tactical buying and selling run the risk of being wrong on a longer-term fundamental basis. Therefore, a comfortably well priced purchase made on the basis of short-term volume information should not be assumed to be safe as a long-term holding. We have been prescribing tactics here, not strategic investing.

FIGURE 16–10

Sustainable Gaps When High Volume Reflects Opinion-
Reversing News

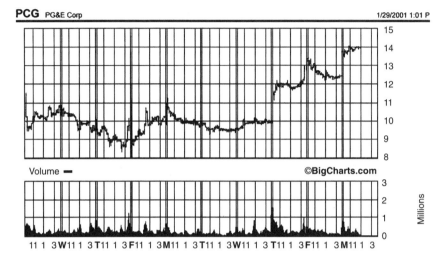

SUMMARY

Fading the opening works if the direction of the price gap on news is a continuation of the prior prevailing price direction and positive or negative opinion climate. When a reversal of opinion has obviously occurred on extremely high volume, attempting to fade the opening more often than not will prove a tactical blunder. If the news climate has truly changed in an important way, the minor tactical advantage to be gained by fading is likely to be swamped by longer-term price change based on the new supply-and-demand balance.

CHAPTER 17

Final Thoughts and an Integration of Themes

I sincerely hope that you have found the material in the preceding chapters enlightening. I well expect that a good deal of it will have been somewhat radical as compared with your prior thinking. My purpose in this chapter is to wrap things together both conceptually and in the form of a brief review.

Our overriding thesis has been that trading volume tells an extremely important tale, so much so that thinking about prices alone is like purposely turning a blind eye to a rich storehouse of technical-analysis information. Extremely high volume is the unmistakable collective footprint of a large crowd. Understanding the psychology of investors and traders, and especially understanding the stages of thinking that drive a crowd to form and act irrationally, leads us to the conclusion that the crowd is usually to be proved wrong in short order. Therefore, you are best to refuse to join it, and if anything to take the opposite action, when the price change driven by mob-size volume extends the previously existing trend. The major exception to using extremely high volume as a signal to act opposite to the prevailing crowd perception and mood occurs when very high trading volume occurs in reaction to new information that causes surprise and therefore the *reversal of prior thinking*.

The above two rules would logically seem to leave in limbo, as a middle case, the question of what to do in the case of a *breakaway, or continuation gap*. In real time, looking at the chart that does not yet plot future prices, you face the dilemma of whether the price gap is a trend-culminating reversal. Several factors should help in making that judgment:

- If the existing trend has prevailed for a long period, chances that the gap is a reversal are higher.
- If the day's volume is clearly above average but not a large multiple of average activity, chances are that the gap will prove one of continuation rather than exhaustion.
- If the high-volume gap takes the stock in the general direction of the overall market and the market itself is not showing exhaustion signs, that prevailing trend has good odds of continuing for the stock.
- If volume is the highest for a single day in 12 to 24 months, expect at least some pullback in the next day or two.
- Carefully observe the price/volume continuation after the first couple of hours: Price continuation on sharply declining volume implies a reversal; a price consolidation on declining volume implies the price probably has further to go once the initial consolidation ends (when volume quiets to more normal levels).

In general, it is wise to watch volume through two lenses. In markets that are not moving especially violently or fast, the price direction that occurs on higher volume is the prevailing one. But when volume becomes extremely high *after* a price trend is already well established, that is evidence of a frothy crowd, and the implication of a price reversal is contained in the extremely high volume. Moderation (in positive price/volume matches) is a good thing, but extremes by definition cannot last.

Let us review the major lessons contained in the chapters that have gone before this, so that they are tied together and so that you can easily return to those you might need to review.

The first section of the book, consisting of three chapters, set out broadly the intellectual case for volume analysis as a valuable way to view the market and on which to make and implement decisions. Chapter 1 presented the very basic and yet undeniable notion that volume records the size and intensity of the crowd and that trading activity is literally the cause of price change. Therefore, attention to price alone is watching the effect without looking behind it to the cause. By implication, volume and price together represent a much more powerful basis for technical analysis than does price alone.

Chapter 2 boldly stated a case against the widely touted theory of efficient markets, which implies that prices move in a random-walk fashion. We defined and explored the world of behavioral finance, a relatively new but very rich intellectual discipline that studies markets in light of what we know about human beings from psychology, anthropology, and sociology: We are not at all times the perfectly calculating and totally rational, logical creatures that economists assume we are. The strong conclusion from this contrast of approaches was, in our view, that markets are inefficient and that those inefficiencies can be taken advantage of if one studies and understands the human emotional swings that drive investors and traders to action in large numbers at the same time (crowd or mob action). Happily, trading volume provides an instant and continuous means of measuring crowd intensity.

Chapter 3 noted a variety of pressures that bias us toward inertia or inaction rather than toward change and action. We introduced and defined the concept of a comfort zone and showed why it is extremely important to take investment and trading action that places us outside that zone at the time. We paid special attention to the problems involved in *selling* positions since that is an area in which so many investors and traders have more difficulty than in buying. The thrust of this chapter was to prepare you for uninhibited action when volume patterns call for it: Today's fast-moving markets make quiet and leisurely contemplation a very expensive habit!

With the groundwork thus laid, the second section of the book, consisting of four chapters, described several established constructs for looking at trading volume. Chapter 4 looked in some detail at the concepts of tick volume and daily net volume. While such approaches are properly based on the foundation that higher volume indicates the predominant thinking of investors caring enough to take action, we noted some mathematical anomalies that can sometimes render these readings neutralized or even misleading.

Chapter 5 focused on up and down price/volume combinations viewed on a daily and trend basis. These are basic to understanding volume dynamics, but occasionally the strong tides of the overall market's direction can cause some misguided readings. Overall, however, this is an important way to look at volume as an indicator of which way price should be heading.

Chapter 6 was the first of two that explained and analyzed the pioneering work of Richard W. Arms, Jr., who has published the majority of all books devoted solely to trading-volume analysis. This chapter described the invention of and rationale for the widely published and followed TRIN index, which measures overall market tone in terms of volume in rising stocks versus volume in declining stocks. While generally positively disposed to its philosophy, we pointed out limited cases in which that measure as computed can be temporarily misleading. Generally these occur on days when the market experiences a significant midday reversal in price direction.

Chapter 7 tackled the somewhat complex but very useful concepts of Equivolume and ease of movement, the follow-on analyses pertaining to individual stocks as developed by Mr. Arms. While cumbersome to follow on actual charts except through the *Metastock* software system, these concepts are very valuable to an understanding of changes in supply and demand that drive price movements to slow down, stall, and reverse. One issue we raised in the context of modern daily reality is that single huge blocks bought or sold by institutions can dominate the chart interpretations and therefore may render them questionable on occasion. Overall, however, we gave the Arms formulations a clear thumbs up.

The third section of our book, in five chapters, moved to break significant and probably radical new ground in the thinking about volume analysis. We began, in Chapter 8, with a realistic look at the huge influence that both institutions and the Internet have in today's market. By representing such a large part of overall trading, and by tending to act as a herd of elephants, institutional investors collectively have the effect of sharply increasing market volatility. This is partly due to their being regrettably but highly short-term oriented in a very intense competitive battle for performance results. Their mere size in the trading marketplace combined with their tendency to independently act alike at critical moments means they destabilize prices frequently. This implies both danger (for the passive, longer-term investor) and opportunity for the nimble and responsive investor able to interpret volume data correctly. We then described the Internet—rather like fire—as simultaneously a wonderful tool (for rapid and deep information gathering) and a terrible force adding to market instability because it makes mob action so easy and so predictable. We urged readers to watch for certain telltale signs of Internet traders at work and to be ready to move contrary to the crowd on short notice, for both capital protection and opportunistic profits.

Chapters 9 and 10, strongly grounded in behavioral finance interpretation of major increases in trading volume, introduced two significant new tools for successful timing of entry and exit. Chapter 9 analyzed multiple-day buildups of volume in a crescendo shape and described the implied thinking of the trading crowd that drives those phenomena. We concluded that very high levels of volume imply an immediate termination of the price move and a likely lengthy of time for the stock to regain its prior equilibrium. Buy/sell/avoid (and even short) action was clearly prescribed for when those formations occur.

Chapter 10 introduced, defined, and explained the volume spike, an even more violent event than the crescendo. Volume spikes also warrant significant and immediate action because of their implied powerful future price influences. There are extremely asymmetrical psychological after-math implications of celebration and fear. Thus the upside price spike on extreme volume has one highly characteristic and immediate followup price pattern (the inverted V), while the downside price disaster on a vol-ume spike is most often followed not by a big bounce but instead by a prolonged period of comatose action (at best) that plays out on a chart in the form of a long, lazy L. We explained what actions should be taken without hesitation by investors and traders because of the extremely pow-erful psychological overhang of both crescendos and especially spikes in volume.

Chapters 11 and 12 picked up on some little-discussed implications of up and down price and volume patterns, focusing on what to do in cases of low trading volume. We explored the serious but not always immediate implications of decreasing volume in price up trends, measured both on a trend basis and at succeeding wavelike price highs. We then took a long look at dull, listless, lower markets marked by continuing low volume. Our conclusion here was that lower price on down volume is not always immediately bullish and that therefore patience is a great virtue.

The final section of the book provided some practical tools for implementing the tactics implied in what went before and in some other special situations. Chapter 13 focused on the information that the various stock exchanges' most-actives lists contain, beyond simply the names and volume printed in these lists. Some second- and third-level implications buried underneath the surface were illuminated and explored.

Chapter 14 turned away from traditional individual stocks and looked, perhaps surprisingly, at the world of mutual funds and the newly exploding universe of exchange-traded funds. We found useful informa-tion in funds' occasional price patterns (even though we cannot see trans-action sizes), and we drew implications for buying and selling sector and theme funds based on the price/volume action in major stocks that they include. Specifically, we explored how the volume/price dynamics of the more actively traded ETFs can not only provide good swing trading opportunities in themselves but can also often have useful implications for overall direction and the prospects for related individual stocks.

Chapter 15 found us looking at the classically described December/January effect entirely from a volume-dynamics perspective. We showed how you can use readily available charts of volume to learn when tax-loss selling is maximizing and then basically ending. This infor-mation of course has highly useful implications for the timing of pur-chases during December. We identified particular groups of stocks (com-mon and preferred) that are especially prone to December/January volume and price patterns. For December, we discussed general rules for applying, or sometimes for overlooking, volume implications in major stocks during the year-end holiday period.

Finally, for those inclined to very short term trading, as well as for those who appreciate the finer points of tactical entry and exit execution for added percentages of profit on a given position, we devoted Chapter 16 to examining intraday volume and its implications. This discussion came in two parts: First we looked at the very interesting implications of total trading (using NYSE data as an example) in the first half hour each morning. Here we identified an indicator that defines extreme crowd action and intensity. Then we turned to intraday volume action in individual stocks, particularly when they exhibit volume and price bursts in the first hour or so of a trading session.

Throughout many of the preceding chapters, we have made references to sources of volume data and to sources of information on events that are likely to cause eruptions in trading volume. Many but not all of these are found on the Internet, where most are free for your inspection and use. We have provided, following this chapter, an appendix containing those references, as well as a brief bibliography of useful books and other reference sources treating volume-related topics.

Go forth now, and multiply...your wealth!

Resources

VOLUME (AND PRICE) HISTORY

The following may be downloaded to spreadsheets:

> http://chart.yahoo.com/t?a=09&b=18&c=00&d=09&e=22&f=00&g=d&s=intc

Choose time period and periodicity. Enter the ticker symbol. Click on "get historical data."

VOLUME AND PRICE CHARTS

> http://www.bigcharts.com

Chart length may be set from 1 day to 10 years or longer (if data exist for that long). The "interactive charts" setting allows various charting techniques focusing on volume. These include a cumulative volume line, plots of positive volume in black and negative volume in red, and "volume by price," which plots shaded horizontal bars indicating the relative amounts of volume traded at various price levels. *Caution:* These bars appear to assign the entire day's volume to the closing price for the day rather than distributing it to the actual price levels on a real-time basis. The "volume by price" function appears to attempt an analysis technique similar in concept to that of Equivolume charting.

VOLUME AND PRICE DATA ON CLOSED-END FUNDS

http://interactive.wsj.com/edition/resources/documents/CEFmain.html

This URL takes a user to just part of the comprehensive and searchable *WSJ Interactive Edition,* available at $29 per year to hard-copy subscribers and at $49 to those who do not buy the paper edition. See Chapter 15 for application of this data.

QUARTERLY EARNINGS: KNOWING EXACTLY WHEN TO EXPECT

http://biz.yahoo.com/research/earncal.e.cgi?s=

The information on this Web site can be used in either of two ways. First, when you enter the symbol of a particular stock, this Web site will immediately tell you the trading day and the time of day (before, during, or after session) when the company is due to report. It also tells you how recently the site's staff has verified that information. A secondary use is the schedule for EPS due for all companies on any given day, such as today or tomorrow. You can obtain this information by entering a date in six-digit format. The reply will alert you to the names of important (opinion-driving) companies' earnings reports that can move the market or a major sector imminently. That can help you avert taking or avoiding action in ignorance of important upcoming events that can move the market substantially. For example, would you want to make a move to buy or sell or short a technology stock without knowing that IBM or Cisco were about to report their quarterly EPS? Talk about being blindsided and having it be your own fault!

How this information relates to volume: It is absolutely true that EPS data are fundamental information. But we know (review Chapters 8 through 10) with high confidence that institutionally held stocks, and those held in large proportion by Internet-enabled traders, are subject to immediate and high-volume buying and selling pressure when predictable news occurs. News does not move prices; large numbers of people trading in reponse to news cause prices to change. Such decisions by large numbers of other investors, particularly the institutions that move large blocks on a moment's notice, represent the formation of a building or immediate crowd, whose volume dynamics will be visible on the tape and in charts and databases. Huge volume moves prices sharply and quickly. You want to know when a predictable event is coming so that you can take appropriate action to buy, sell, hold, avoid, or short in advance—to make profit or avoid losses.

MUTUAL FUNDS' NET MONEY FLOWS

www.trimtabs.com

The four numeric digits represent the latest month and year in MMYY format. See also Chapter 14.

Listing of ETFs including volume traded in current session:

rhttp://quotes.nasdaq.com/asp/ETFsCompare.asp?query5Intraday

SITES RELATED TO EXCHANGE-TRADED FUNDS

www.nasdaq.com

www.iShares.com

www.ml.com

www.amex.com

www.IndexFunds.com

See also Chapter 14.

OTHER INTERNET VOLUME DATA SOURCES

For historical quotes, including volume:

216.33.240.250:80/cgi-
bin/linkrd?_lang=EN&lah=42a611baec5768e950972f8674b83914&lat=
979134063&hm___action=http%3a%2f%2fchart%2eyahoo%2ecom%2fd
%3fs%3dbhy

On Yahoo! (volume is unlabeled as to length, but the average displayed appears to be greater than 6 months but less than 1 year).

216.33.240.250:80/cgi-
bin/linkrd?_lang5EN&lah5b376789f18e8495990f59cec7d9c6993&lat597
9134063&hm___action5http%3a%2f%2ffinance%2eyahoo%2ecom%2fq
%3fs%3dkrem%26d%3d1y"

NON-INTERNET SOFTWARE

Equis' MetaStock
Equis International
3950 S 700 E, Suite 100
Salt Lake City, UT 84107

Via a license agreement, MetaStock allows its users online implementation of Equivolume charting techniques using various time windows. Thus it can be used for longer-term supply-demand volume analysis as well as for short-term trading. If interested, contact Equis International Inc., at 1-800-882-3040 or fax 801-265-3999.

BOOKS

Richard W. Arms, Jr., *Volume Cycles in the Stock Market*, Equis International, Inc., Salt Lake City, Utah, 1994.
Richard W. Arms, Jr., *Profits in Volume*, Larchmont Investors Intelligence, Inc., Larchmont, New York, 1971.
Joseph E. Granville, *A Strategy of Daily Stock Market Timing for Mamimum Profit*, Prentice-Hall, Inc., Englewood Cliffs, NJ, 1970.

INDEX

ABOUT THE AUTHOR

Donald Cassidy is a senior research analyst with the fund-tracking firm of Lipper, Inc., in Denver, Colorado. He has served twice on the faculty of the annual Congress on the Psychology of Investing at Harvard University. He also serves as the current program chair for the Denver chapter of the American Association of Individual Investors (AAII) and has lectured frequently at AAII chapters throughout the country. Cassidy is the author of four previously published books, among them *It's When You Sell That Counts* (1997) and *When the Dow Breaks* (1999). Although cognizant of the highly volatile, sometimes irrational nature of the market and the subtly interacting forces that shape it, he attempts to apply rational analysis to the buying, holding, and selling of stocks by individual investors.